Complexity Theory in Public Administration

This book reframes theoretical, methodological and practical approaches to public administration by drawing on complexity theory concepts.

It aims to provide alternative perspectives on the theory, research and practice of public administration, avoiding assumptions of traditional theory-building. The contributors explain both how ongoing non-linear interactions result in macro patterns becoming established in a complexity-informed world view, and the implications of these dynamics. Complexity theory explains the way in which many repeated non-linear interactions among elements within a whole can result in processes and patterns emerging without design or direction, thus necessitating a reconsideration of the predictability and controllability of many aspects of public administration.

As well as illustrating how complexity theory informs new research methods for studying this field, the book also shines a light on the different practices required of public administrators to cope with the complexity encountered in the public policy and public management fields.

This book was originally published as a special issue of *Public Management Review*.

Elizabeth Anne Eppel is a Senior Research and Teaching Fellow in the School of Government at Victoria University of Wellington, New Zealand. Her research interests are complexity in public policy processes, governance networks, and collaborative governance.

Mary Lee Rhodes is Associate Professor of Public Management at Trinity College Dublin, Ireland. Her research is focused on complex public service systems and the dynamics of performance. Her current research is on the nature and dynamics of social innovation and impact, and she is developing research on social finance, and resilience of urban systems.

Complexity Theory in Public Administration

Edited by
Elizabeth Anne Eppel and Mary Lee Rhodes

LONDON AND NEW YORK

First published 2020
by Routledge
2 Park Square, Milton Park, Abingdon, Oxon, OX14 4RN

and by Routledge
52 Vanderbilt Avenue, New York, NY 10017

Routledge is an imprint of the Taylor & Francis Group, an informa business

First issued in paperback 2021

British Library Cataloguing in Publication Data
A catalogue record for this book is available from the British Library

ISBN 13: 978-0-367-33396-6 (hbk)
ISBN 13: 978-1-03-208867-9 (pbk)

Typeset in Minion Pro
by RefineCatch Limited, Bungay, Suffolk

Publisher's Note
The publisher accepts responsibility for any inconsistencies that may have
arisen during the conversion of this book from journal articles to book chapters,
namely the inclusion of journal terminology.

Disclaimer
Every effort has been made to contact copyright holders for their permission to
reprint material in this book. The publishers would be grateful to hear from any
copyright holder who is not here acknowledged and will undertake to rectify
any errors or omissions in future editions of this book.

Contents

Citation Information

The chapters in this book were originally published in *Public Management Review*, volume 20, issue 7 (July 2018). When citing this material, please use the original page numbering for each article, as follows:

Editorial

Complexity theory and public management: a 'becoming' field
Elizabeth Anne Eppel and Mary Lee Rhodes
Public Management Review, volume 20, issue 7 (July 2018), pp. 949–959

Chapter 1

Association between decisions: experiments with coupled two-person games
Peter Koenraad Marks and Lasse M. Gerrits
Public Management Review, volume 20, issue 7 (July 2018), pp. 960–979

Chapter 2

Understanding the influence of values in complex systems-based approaches to public policy and management
Philip Haynes
Public Management Review, volume 20, issue 7 (July 2018), pp. 980–996

Chapter 3

'What insights do fitness landscape models provide for theory and practice in public administration?'
Mary Lee Rhodes and Conor Dowling
Public Management Review, volume 20, issue 7 (July 2018), pp. 997–1012

Chapter 4

Engaging with complexity in a public programme implementation
Walter Castelnovo and Maddalena Sorrentino
Public Management Review, volume 20, issue 7 (July 2018), pp. 1013–1031

For any permission-related enquiries please visit:
http://www.tandfonline.com/page/help/permissions

Notes on Contributors

Walter Castelnovo is Assistant Professor of Information Systems and Inter-organizational Networks at the University of Insubria, Italy. He is also the e-government advisor of the Association of the Municipalities of the Region Lombardia, Italy, that represents more than 1,000 municipalities.

Daniel Chamberlain is a Research Fellow in Social Network Analysis in Disease Prevention in the School of Psychology and Public Health at La Trobe University, Australia. His research interests include network analysis and analytical methods for examination of social and public policy in government and third-sector organizations.

Conor Dowling is a Doctoral Candidate in Business Administration, Management and Operations at Trinity Business School at Trinity College Dublin, Ireland. His research focuses on the field of systems management, specifically the resilience of systems.

Elizabeth Anne Eppel is a Senior Research and Teaching Fellow in the School of Government at Victoria University of Wellington, New Zealand. Her research interests are complexity in public policy processes, governance networks, and collaborative governance.

Claire Gear is a PhD Candidate and Research Officer in the Centre for Interdisciplinary Trauma Research at Auckland University of Technology, New Zealand. Her research interests lie in understanding the complexity of responding to family violence within health care settings.

Lasse M. Gerrits is Professor of Political Science at the University of Bamberg, Germany, where he holds the Chair of Control of Innovative and Complex Technical Systems. His research focuses on the properties and functioning of complex socio-technological systems.

Philip Haynes is Professor of Public Policy in the School of Applied Social Science at the University of Brighton, UK. He researches and teaches public policy and management, as applied to a variety of contemporary circumstances. His research focuses on the application of complex systems theory and the use of applied statistical methods to model complexity.

Robyn Keast is a Professor in the School of Business and Tourism at Southern Cross University, Australia. Her transdisciplinary research is primarily orientated towards networked arrangements and collaborative practice across a range of arenas and most recently research collaboration, impact, and sustainability.

Jane Koziol-Mclain is Professor of Nursing and Director of the Centre for Interdisciplinary Trauma Research at Auckland University of Technology, New Zealand. Her research interests include understanding, responding, and preventing violence against women and children.

Peter Koenraad Marks is an Associate Professor in the Department of Public Administration and Sociology at Erasmus University Rotterdam, the Netherlands. Having studied economics and philosophy, his research mainly focuses on complex decision-making processes from an evolutionary (economics) perspective.

Kevin S. Marshall is an Academy Professor, Professor of Law, and Dean of the College of Law at the University of La Verne, USA. He teaches quantitative methods, statistics, and economics at the College of Business and Public Management, as well as teaching law and economics at the College of Law. He serves as an Associate Dean and as a Co-Director of the La Verne Experience.

Jack W. Meek is an Academy Professor and Professor of Public Administration at the College of Business and Public Management at the University of La Verne, USA, where he serves as Director of the Center for Research. He offers courses in collaborative public management and managing complex systems.

Mary Lee Rhodes is Associate Professor of Public Management at Trinity College Dublin, Ireland. Her research is focused on complex public service systems and the dynamics of performance. Her current research is on the nature and dynamics of social innovation and impact, and she is developing research on social finance, and resilience of urban systems.

Amanda Scott is a Farmer Groups Projects Team Leader in the Farm Cooperatives and Collaboration Pilot Programme at Southern Cross University, Australia. She is currently engaged in a doctoral programme examining project sustainability.

Maddalena Sorrentino researches Business Organization at the University of Milan, Italy, and is Professor of e-Government. Her articles have been published in international journals and conference proceedings. In 2013, she was appointed Director of ICONA, a research centre for organizational innovation in public administrations.

Tim Tenbensel is Associate Professor of Health Policy at the University of Auckland, New Zealand. His core research areas are health policy, public management, and public policy. His substantive interests include the governance of health systems and policy, and comparative health policy.

Geoff Woolcott is Associate Professor of Mathematics and Science Education in the School of Education at Southern Cross University, Australia. His research interests include undergraduate retention/attrition, impact and sustainability in collaborative networks, and STEM education.

Introduction

Complexity theory and public management: a 'becoming' field

Since the special edition of *Public Management Review* on *'Complexity Theory and Public Management'* in 2008 (Volume 10 (3)), co-edited by Geert Teisman and Erik-Hans Klijn, academic interest in complexity theory, and how it might be used to understand the world and inform design and intervention in the public policy/public management field, has grown and matured. The inspiration for this special issue arose out of intensive interactions among interested scholars in conference panels (at American Society for Public Administration, International Research Society for Public Management, and the Challenges of Making Public Administration and Complexity Theory group) over the past few years and the realization that a 'stock-taking' was required. While many public management scholars knew a little bit about complexity – and some knew a lot – there was still no consensus about the contribution complexity theory could or could not make to theory and practice. While we did not achieve consensus this time around, the papers selected for this edition provide a picture of where we are and where scholars in this field think we should go, and some examples of the most promising routes to get there. Before summarizing these findings, we provide a brief overview of where we have come from and why we are still a 'becoming' field.

Challenging fundamental assumptions

Nineteenth- and twentieth-century sciences which developed beneath the umbra of Newtonian theories, embedded some pervasive assumptions which might be crudely summarized as (1) relationships between individual components of any system can be understood by isolating the interacting parts, (2) there is a predictability to the relationship among the parts, and (3) the result of interactions and the working whole might eventually be understood by simply summing the parts. So in much the same way as the expert clockmaker might be able to design, build, disassemble, and modify a clock, understanding the individual parts and how they fit together leads to understanding the functioning whole and the capability to replicate it precisely as required. This paradigm is dominated by mechanical metaphors and leads to an assumption that the sum of the parts equals the whole.

Dissatisfaction with the limitations of mechanical explanations led to more sophisticated models which were better at explaining the observed behaviour, initially of the physical world, and then increasingly the biological, ecological, and social worlds (e.g. Byrne 1998; Cilliers 1998; Holland 1995; Kauffman 1993; Prigogine 1978; Prigogine and Stengers 1984; Stacey 1993; Waldrop 1992). Such modelling offered new ontological insights about the nature of our world and the way it behaves. This is summed up briefly by saying that there are recursive, ongoing non-linear interactions between the elements that make up the whole and these elements adapt to each other in non-linear ways. Their interactions create contingency and uncertainty about what the future will become. As a result, the whole lacks the predictability of the machine model. Boulton (2010) refers to a complex world view as 'becoming' because individual components in these worlds are interdependent and in processes of ongoing interaction with each other with the result that the world is not static and fixed, but dynamic, ever-changing, and becoming something different from what it was in the past. Recognition of such inherent uncertainty leads to a conclusion that Newtonian-like mechanical models are inadequate for these types of systems because the sum of the parts *does not* equal the whole. Understanding of the whole cannot be based only on an understanding of the disaggregated parts because of the ongoing non-linear change caused by the interactions between the parts. This shift in understanding brings us to a complexity world view: 'sandwiched between a view that the world works like a machine and a view that the world is chaotic, unpredictable and without structure' (Boulton, Allen, and Bowman 2015, 29).

In this complexity-informed world view, ongoing non-linear interactions result in macro patterns becoming established. Complexity theory explains the way many, repeated non-linear interactions among elements within a whole result in macro forms and patterns which emerge without design or direction. Further, an initial pattern might be disrupted by external events or internal processes and reform into some new pattern. Boulton and colleagues sum up what they call the 'central tenet of complexity theory' and its contribution to understanding change as 'the detail and the variation' of each action – the effect of a regulation on various actors for example – 'coupled with the interconnection' of action and environment that 'provide the fuel for innovation, evolution and learning' (Boulton, Allen, and Bowman 2015, 29). That is, the future is a contingent, emergent, systemic, and potentially path-dependent product of reflexive non-linear interactions between existing patterns and events. Its variety, diversity, variation, and fluctuations can give rise to resilience and adaptability; is path dependent, contingent on local context and on the sequence of what happens; subject to episodic changes that can tip into new regimes; has more than one future; can self-organize, self-regulate; and have new features emerge.

Introducing a complexity frame to public management

As an alternative to Newtonian mechanics, this last observation about the contribution of complexity theory for understanding unpredictability and change in human systems leads us to its relevance for the study of public policy and public management. Scholars and practitioners of public policy and public management are concerned with how to create or change particular patterns of interaction between actors to get a particular result: for example, how might governments design a set of institutions to bring about certain behaviours; or given a set of institutions, how might the interactions between actors and the institutions be governed to achieve a particular outcome; and how might unintended negative effects be avoided or positive ones enhanced? Furthermore, complexity theory facilitates a focus on multiple levels of scale simultaneously. Thus the individual actors, and multiple layers of institutions of varying complexity which interact, can all be brought into view through the multi-scalar complexity lens.

We note, within the diverse scientific traditions of public policy and public management theories, attempts to explain dynamism and non-linear contingency in how change takes place have become an increasingly pertinent concern (Eppel 2017). In the last 20 years – and rising sharply from around 2008 (Gerrits and Marks 2015) – we see increasingly explicit use of complexity theory concepts for explaining the way the public policy/management worlds behave and how we might better design and manage change in these worlds. David Byrne has also deepened our understanding of the methodological implications of complexity for the social sciences generally (Byrne, 1011, Byrne and Callaghan 2014).

Scholars such as Sanderson (2009), Room (2011), and Morcol (2012) have all argued for complexity theory for understanding of how the social world of policy processes work. Cairney (2012, 2013; Cairney and Geyer, 2017) caution us that the looseness with which complexity concepts are sometimes applied could be an impediment but they also see a place for complexity theory as a bridge between academic and policymaker perspectives in support of pragmatism and insights about how to influence emergent behaviour. Sanderson (2009) advocates that the ambiguity and uncertainty arising from a complex adaptive world can be mitigated through the use of an epistemology based on pragmatism and complexity theory. Room (2011) suggests a blending of extant theories such as institutionalism with complexity theory for better understanding the micro/macro dynamics of public policy. He suggests that there is a complementarity in which complexity theory supplies the micro mechanisms lacking in institutional theory and institutional theory supplies a macro framing specific to public policy which complexity theory lacks. Morcol (2012) argues further that complexity theory provides mechanisms and concepts for understanding the macro/micro problems at the heart of public policy process. That is, complexity theory provides a micro mechanism for explaining the macro patterns of interest to public policy scholars. Growing interest in complexity and policy is evidenced in the establishment of a new *Journal on Policy and Complex Systems* in 2014.

In a parallel and consistent vein, Teisman and colleagues in the Netherlands (Teisman, van Buuren, and Gerrits 2009), Rhodes and colleagues in Ireland (Rhodes et al. 2011), Koliba and colleagues in the United States (Koliba, Meek, and Zia 2011), and Eppel and colleagues in New Zealand (Eppel, Turner, and Wolf 2011) have each employed complexity theory concepts to better understand the core processes of public management such as agenda setting, policy formation, decision-making, and implementation. These authors have more or less independently come to the conclusion that complexity theory and network theory are required and should be linked together to provide an adequate basis on which to develop governance theory and practice guidelines in modern public management contexts. The extent of complementarity between complexity theory and network governance (Klijn and Koppenjan 2014; Koppenjan and Klijn 2014) and new public management theories is reflected in the establishment of the journal *Complexity, Governance and Networks* in 2014.

Others have taken aim at how public sector change might be better managed generally by enlisting complexity thinking and concepts to inform processes of designing and generating change (Boulton, Allen, and Bowman 2015; Geyer and Rihani 2010; Innes and Booher 2010). These authors identify common themes such as the impossibility of prediction and therefore the need to adopt more experimental approaches to intervention based on the assumption that there will be new phenomena (unknown unknowns) likely to emerge endogenously. What has occurred previously will continue to affect the present (and the future). As a result, any externally applied change will have uncertain effects, some of which will lead to a helpful change and some not so. Doing public policy and public management in such a world requires cognisance of the above characteristics – and particularly the dynamics of self-organization, path-dependency, adaptation, and emergence – in how we approach policy and change (Rhodes et al. 2011). We also need complexity's lens to see the whole while taking into account the relationships between the elements at different levels of scale. Koliba and Zia (2012) talk about the need for complexity friendly methods for modelling the complex governance system. Innes and Booher (2010) built their theory of collaborative rationality for public policy on analysis of the ongoing dialectic interaction between collaboration and praxis as a means for understanding complex change. Cairney and Geyer (2015) have made a substantial contribution to thinking about the contribution of complexity theory to policy studies and how it might add to understanding of particular policy fields, such as health (Tenbensel 2013) or concepts such as power (Room, 2015) as well as complexity friendly methods for research and practice.

Overview of papers in this edition

This plethora of contributions and theoretical explorations cries out for framing and assessment to help guide scholars engaging with complexity in the public management/policy domains. To that end, our call for contributions asked authors to consider how complexity contributes to public management theory and practice using one (or more) of three lenses: (1) complexity theory-informed *alternative perspectives* on the framing of problems and design of processes of public administration to be considered, (2) insights into *alternative institutions* that are shaping public administration and management processes, and (3) *alternative practices* to match the complexity of the environment and the challenges faced by public management scholars administrators.

Furthermore, we note the need for a distinction to be made between the use of complexity theory to create and test concepts and theories to *describe* the world as it is (which is often the domain of the natural sciences), and the use of these concepts and theories to *design* and bring about change (this latter often the domain of social sciences). While these perspectives inform each other, they often rely on different ontological and epistemological foundations, and this is apparent in the papers in this special edition where we see both describe and design features in the way authors have used complexity theory.

Alternative perspectives

Alternative perspectives provided by complexity theory have evolved markedly in the intervening years between this issue and the last special issue of PMR addressing complexity. We have already mentioned the application of complexity concepts to understanding multi-actor decision-making and institutional change for instance. The authors in this issue further explore models which attempt to incorporate the specific use of complexity concepts such as feedback loops, adaptation, attractors, and emergence to reframe understanding of common phenomena experienced in public administration such as policy processes, implementation, natural resources management, and public-sector reform.

In all of the papers in this issue, there is the explicit recognition that a complexity perspective entails the rejection of assumptions of predictability and control in public management, and the adoption of assumptions of multiple, interacting self-organizing entities that learn and change over time. While there are periods of stable behaviour and features of the system that function as constraints on elements of the system, the diversity and adaptation of entities creates the possibility for both evolutionary and unpredictable, sudden change.

An example of two inter-country independent decision-making processes that became coupled over time is used by Marks and Gerrits to illustrate the contribution of *game theoretic* models to understanding complex public administration processes. Their game theory model is tested through an experiment aimed at explaining how representatives of the two governments involved who met each other in two presumed independent decision-making arenas took the history of their interactions from one to the other, thereby influencing the overall outcome. Thus they demonstrate the interdependency and connectedness between systems that otherwise might be assumed independent. Further, the authors provide a testable formalized model that describes the interaction and co-evolution of independent agents over time for future scholars to build upon.

Haynes makes use of complexity theory to focus on multiple levels of public administration systems. He extends the conceptualization of the public administration complex system to include the behaviour disposition of the individual in relation to their public and personal values, to conclude that the multi-level capacity in complexity theory is, in part, bounded by public service values. Further, he uses the complexity concept of *attractors* to explain how public service values at different levels (individual, family/community, professional, and political) can play a role in constraining (or indeed enabling) system change over time. Both Haynes and Marks & Gerrits extend the understanding of complex adaptive systems (CAS) theory and public management by taking their analysis of participating actors below the level of description of the organization and the institutions. They consider the largely unconscious psychological dispositions of individual actors and their history with other actors and its influence on patterns of institutional and organizational decision-making which are relevant to the design.

Rather than develop new models, Rhodes and Dowling assess to what extent *fitness landscape* models (Wright 1932; Kaufmann and Levin 1987) have been used effectively by public management scholars to date through a systematic review. Fitness landscapes are evolutionary models that capture how the behaviour and characteristics of independent agents operating in a shared context result in individual and system-wide outcomes. The authors remark on their frequent use at the level of metaphor and the limited attention paid to mapping the concepts of the model to the features of the empirical phenomenon being described. This conclusion might easily be applied to a number of other complexity concepts (Cairney and Geyer 2017), which, after several decades of scholarly effort, raises concerns about the translation of these concepts into the public management domain. Nevertheless, Rhodes and Dowling conclude that in combination with network theory, fitness landscape models are 'more aligned with the actual features of complex governance systems than game theory models which rely on highly stylized assumptions about how agents behave and equally fuzzy definitions of performance' (Rhodes and Dowling, this issue). We return to these 'fuzzy definitions of performance' in our conclusion.

Alternative institutions

Alternative institutions are those that can influence the actions of interdependent, autonomous agents as they iteratively explore alternative solutions to wicked problems, such as distributed authority arrangements, multi-sector for a for decision-making and multi-channel feedback arising from new communication technologies. For example, in Haynes' contribution, the notions of public service values and public value are explored through the lens of CAS theory. The paper offers a concrete and practical example for understanding the dynamic influence of values on complex policy systems. Haynes argues for recognition of 'soft' patterns of values such as belief systems and their dynamic influence on organizational behaviours as well as 'hard' patterns such as rules and structures and shows how the CAS lens enables this.

Castlenovo and colleagues attend to the issues raised by the federal–state–local governance structures and how these might be re-imagined/understood using complexity theory. For them, their complexity-based lens acts as a heuristic device to understand the misalignment of locally implemented outcomes with the centrally defined objectives of a nationwide public programme in Italy where the 'Napoleonic' administrative traditions dominate – arguing for a rethinking of these traditions.

Tenbensel, rather than arguing for a particular type of institutional change, builds on the approach taken by Room (2011) and advocated by Cairney and Geyer (2017) in bringing institutional theory together with complexity theory using Crouch's concept of recombinant governance. Through an examination of the fitness of various governance hybrids in the health sector in New Zealand he demonstrates the usefulness of being able to distinguish among various versions of hybridity and to argue for a more evolutionary perspective on institutional design and change.

Alternative practices

Complexity offers alternative ways of framing intervention and bringing about successful change that navigates the traps of unexpected changes and opens up different ways of achieving innovation. Gear and colleagues take us into the conceptual framing and research methodology needed to examine the complex problem of intimate partner violence (IPV). They identify the limitations faced in developing healthcare interventions in the absence of a complex adaptive systems view. Existing efforts to understand sustainable approaches in primary healthcare settings have been dominated by the direct cause–effect thinking reflected in randomized control trials and like methodologies that have been so prevalent in health research. Reframing the person entrapped by IPV and their world, and the world of a primary healthcare setting as two interacting complex adaptive systems, shifts the research focus to the reflexive interactions that occur between the person experiencing IPV and the primary healthcare setting. According to CAS theory, we would expect these interactions to lead to mutual adaptations within each of these complex systems, and therefore intervention sustainability will occur when the interaction and mutual adaptation generate outcomes that stimulate ongoing engagement by both systems. Without the CAS perspective, the self-organization, coevolution, and emergence that leads to sustainability cannot be studied. The conceptualization and research design developed to study healthcare responses to IPV might also be more widely applicable to other complex social interventions.

Sustainability of the collaborative governance network is also the focus of Scott and colleagues. Complexity theory concepts are used to both describe how sustainability is linked to the adaptability and flexibility of the collaborative project but also to offer insights into how the collaborative process might be designed to encourage the development of sustainability. Like many other papers in this edition, their use of complexity theory is combined with other theories – collaborative governance, in this instance.

Meek and Marshall use a CAS lens to understand how the multi-actor institutional governance of a complex Southern Californian metropolitan water system contributes to an adaptive resilience able to respond effectively to the external stressors of severe and sustained drought. Ongoing self-organization and adaptation within and among the governance actors and other stakeholders are characteristics of the governance system which lead to emergent features which help maintain resilience.

In the Castelnovo paper referred to already, we encounter the empirical descriptions needed to interpret the complexity factors that shaped an implementation trajectory. They offer self-organization, co-evolution, and emergence as mechanisms for understanding the peculiar implementation path which might otherwise be assumed to be the cumulative effect of a series of legislative interventions not always coherent in and among themselves. In so doing they pave the way for the design of alternative implementation practices.

Finally, scholar-teachers have also begun to incorporate complexity theory into teaching practice. It has proved useful for both integrating theories and for helping students and practitioners to better frame and understand the challenges of public management. In schools of government, planning, and business we are starting to see individual modules, components of programmes, and indeed entire master's degrees being developed to introduce students to a complexity 'perspective' and to be exposed to the tools and techniques to understand and intervene in complex systems. Due to constraints of space, this issue does not include any articles on this topic, but instead the editors are working on a separate special issue in 'Complexity, Governance & Networks' dedicated to the ways complexity is being taught to public management/policy students around the world.

Whither complexity in public management?

The relevance of complexity theory for circumventing the weaknesses of a mechanistic approach to understanding public policy and management has been well-trodden ground for decades. That this continues to be pursued as complexity theory spreads across policy domains suggests that it is this fundamental capacity that is at the core of the attraction for many scholars and practitioners. As highlighted above, the use of complexity theory in public management has developed both in relation to the description of phenomena and design of institutions and interventions to effect change.

From a theoretical perspective, the scholarship of the last decade and the papers in this volume demonstrate that complexity theory sits alongside, and in many cases augments existing theories of public policy and public management. Public policy and public management draw on a variety of parent disciplines such as politics, organization science, economics, management, sociology, and psychology (Raadschelders 2011) and bridging or integrating this plurality continues to be an implicit – and in some cases explicit – objective of scholars applying complexity theory to this domain. A complexity perspective can describe how interdependent agents interact over time – within the constraints of history, institutional forms, and/ or values – to increase or decrease overall (or individual) fitness, sustainability, or resilience. It does this without the need to fall back on predictable cause and effect relationships among agents or contexts while still leaving room for the identification of patterns and likely pathways.

Furthermore, the 'positive role for complexity theory as a way to bridge academic and policy maker discussions' (Cairney and Geyer 2017, 1) – and we would add 'practitioners' – is evident in many of the papers. Complexity acts as a challenge to the quest for certainty in policymaking and also prompts discussion about the role of pragmatism in policymaking. In this issue, authors have argued for linking complexity frameworks with institutional theory, network theory, public value theory, and game theory to better understand the dynamics of processes, outcomes, and change in public policy/management systems over time. Its strengths lie in its facilitation of a focus on multiple levels of scale and its provision of micro-level mechanisms for macro-level theories such as institutional theory and punctuated equilibrium theory (Eppel 2017). The key mechanisms explored in this issue are based on game theoretic interactions, search processes on fitness landscapes, evolution arising from recombinant novelty, and information exchange in networks – building on the core complexity dynamics of self-organization, adaptability, and emergence. In respect of institutions, the conclusion one may draw from these papers is that it is unlikely that current institutional forms – whether they be hierarchical, market, network, or values based – exhaust the range of potential institutional forms that could be designed or evolve in the public policy and administration space. Experimenting with new forms would appear to be an important complexity-friendly policymaking practice that would lead to more sustainable public systems.

The concepts of 'sustainability' and 'resilience' make an appearance in several of the articles in this issue as objectives of research and practice that are facilitated by a complexity approach. However, there is little agreement or indeed clear definition about what either of these outcomes represent in the context of public administration. Survival – or the ongoing existence of agents, institutions, or systems if not of the individual humans that make these up – is, of course, one option, but this is not clarified or challenged either in the papers in this issue or in the wider academic community. It is incumbent upon those scholars working in this area and using these concepts to clearly define and debate what they mean if the policy or practice recommendations arising from their research are to be seriously considered.

In addition to this definitional lacuna around sustainability and resilience, the incorporation of performance management research, theory and practice, has been largely absent in the public administration complexity literature. The fitness landscape literature would appear to provide an obvious link to performance, as evidenced by the use of the phrase 'performance landscapes' to describe this approach in organizational theory (Siggelkow and Levinthal 2003; Rhodes and Donnelly-Cox 2008). This leads us to speculate about the compatibility of complexity theory with our basic understanding of the nature of performance management. The issue may partially be due to the multidimensionality of performance management (Bouckaert and Halligan 2008) and the limitations of how performance management has been conceived and practised in the new public management environment (Moynihan et al. 2011). Moynihan and colleagues (2011) point to the limitations of current research on performance management to take adequate cognisance of governance complexity. So there appears to be some room for each scholarly trajectory to learn from the other.

But perhaps more important is that fact that we are still quite far from developing complexity-based models of agent interactions, behaviour, and change over time that demonstrably produce/predict real-world outcomes of any kind, not just performance. However, the kind of direct cause and effect theories we have come to believe represent the pinnacle of scholarly achievement and the reliance on experiments or random control trials to prove same are unlikely to address the sorts of 'wicked' problems (Rittel and Webber 1973) that lie at the heart of public policy and management. The need to continue to adopt and refine complexity-informed theory, institutions, and practice in a domain of human endeavour as rich and varied as public administration is as vital now as it was a decade ago.

ORCID

Elizabeth Anne Eppel http://orcid.org/0000-0001-5331-2911

References

Bouckaert, G., and J. Halligan. 2008. *Managing Performance: International Comparisons*. Abingdon: Routledge.

Boulton, J. G. 2010. "Complexity Theory and Implications for Policy Development." *Emergence: Complexity and Organisation* 12 (2): 31–40.

Boulton, J. G., P. M. Allen, and C. Bowman. 2015. *Embracing Complexity: Strategic Perspectives for an Age of Turbulence*. Oxford: Oxford University Press.

Byrne, D. S. 1998. *Complexity Theory and the Social Sciences: An Introduction*. London: Routledge.

Byrne, D. S. 2011. *Applying Social Science: The Role of Social Science Research in Politics, Policy and Practice*. Bristol: Policy Press.

Byrne, D. S., and G. Callaghan. 2014. *Complexity Theory and the Social Sciences: The State of the Art*. Abingdon: Routledge.

Cairney, P. 2012. "Complexity Theory in Political Science and Public Policy." *Political Studies Review* 10 (3): 346–358. doi:10.1111/j.1478-9302.2012.00270.x.

Cairney, P. 2013. "Standing on the Shoulders of Giants: How Do We Combine the Insights of Multiple Theories in Public Policy Studies." *Policy Studies Journal* 41 (1): 1–21. doi:10.1111/psj.12000.

Cairney, P., and R. Geyer, eds. 2015. *Handbook on Complexity and Public Policy*. Cheltenham: Edward Elgar.

Cairney, P., and R. Geyer. 2017. "A Critical Discussion of Complexity Theory: How Does 'Complexity Thinking' Improve Our Understanding of Politics and Policy Making?" *Complexity, Governance and Networks* 3 (2): 1–11. doi:10.20377/cgn-56.

Cilliers, P. 1998. *Complexity and Postmodernism: Understanding Complex Systems.* London: Routledge.

Eppel, E. 2017. "Complexity Thinking in Public Administration's Theories-in-Use." *Public Management Review* 19 (6): 845–861. doi:10.1080/14719037.2016.1235721.

Eppel, E., D. Turner, and A. Wolf. 2011. "Complex Policy Implementation: The Role of Experimentation and Learning." In *Future State: Directions for Public Management in New Zealand,* edited by B. Ryan and D. Gill, 182–212. Wellington: Victoria University Press.

Gerrits, L., and P. Marks. 2015. "How the Complexity Sciences Can Inform Public Administration: An Assessment." *Public Administration* 93 (2): 539–546. doi:10.1111/padm.12168.

Geyer, R., and S. Rihani. 2010. *Complexity and Public Policy: A New Approach to 21st Century Politics, Policy and Society.* Abingdon: Routledge.

Holland, J. H. 1995. *Hidden Order: How Adaptation Builds Complexity.* Reading, MA: Addison-Wesley.

Innes, J. E., and D. E. Booher. 2010. *Planning with Complexity.* Abingdon: Routledge.

Kauffman, S. A. 1993. *The Origins of Order. Self Organisation and Selection in Evolution.* New York: Oxford University Press.

Kauffman, S. A., and S. Levin. 1987. "Towards a General Theory of Adaptive Walks on Rugged Landscapes." *Journal of Theoretical Biology* 128 (1): 11–45.

Klijn, E.-H., and J. F. M. Koppenjan. 2014. "Complexity in Governance Network Theory." *Complexity, Governance and Networks* 1: 61–70. doi:10.7564/14-CGN8.

Koliba, C., and A. Zia. 2012. "'Complexity Friendly' Meso-level Frameworks for Modelling Complex Governance Systems." In *COMPACT 1: Public Administration in Complexity,* edited by L. Gerrits and P. Marks, 119–139. Litchfield Park, AZ: Emergent.

Koliba, C., J. W. Meek, and A. Zia. 2011. *Governance Networks in Public Administration and Public Policy.* Boca Raton, FL: CRC Press.

Koppenjan, J. F. M., and E.-H. Klijn. 2014. "What Can Governance Network Theory Learn from Complexity Theory? Mirroring Two Perspectives on Complexity." In *Network Theory in the Public Sector: Building New Theoretical Frameworks,* edited by R. Keast, M. Mandell, and R. Agranoff, 157–173. London: Routledge.

Morcol, G. 2012. *A Complexity Theory for Public Policy.* New York: Routledge.

Moynihan, D. P., S. Fernandez, S. Kim, K. M. LeRoux, S. J. Piotrowski, B. E. Wright, and K. Yang. 2011. "Performance Regimes Amidst Governance Complexity." *Journal of Public Administration Research and Theory* 41 (Supplement 1): i114–i155. doi:10.1093/jopart/muq059.

Prigogine, I. 1978. "Time, Structure and Fluctuations." *Science* 201 (4358): 777–785. doi:10.1126/science.201.4358.777.

Prigogine, I., and I. Stengers. 1984. *Order Out of Chaos: Man's New Dialogue with Nature.* Toronto: Bantam Books.

Raadschelders, J. C. N. 2011. *Public Administration: The Interdisciplinary Study of Government.* New York: Oxford University Press.

Rhodes, M. L., and G. Donnelly-Cox. 2008. "Social Entrepreneurship as a Performance Landscape." *Emergence: Complexity and Organizaton* 10 (3): 35–50.

Rhodes, M. L., J. Murphy, J. Muir, and J. A. Murray. 2011. *Public Management and Complexity Theory: Richer Decision-Making in Public Services.* New York: Routledge.

Rittel, H., and M. Webber. 1973. "Dilemmas in a General Theory of Planning." *Policy Sciences* 4: 155–169. doi:10.1007/BF01405730.

Room, D. G. 2015. "Complexity, Power and Policy." In *Elgar Handbook on Complexity and Public Policy,* edited by R. Geyer and P. Cairney, 19–31. Cheltenham: Edward Elgar.

Room, G. 2011. *Complexity, Institutions and Public Policy.* Cheltenham: Edward Elgar.

Sanderson, I. 2009. "Intelligent Policy Making for a Complex World: Pragmatism, Evidence and Learning." *Political Studies* 57: 699–719. doi:10.1111/j.1467-9248.2009.00791.x.

Siggelkow, N., and D. Levinthal. 2003. "Temporarily Divide to Conquer: Centralized, Decentralized, and Reintegrated Organizational Approaches to Exploration and Adaptation." *Organizational Science* 14 (6): 650–669. doi:10.1287/orsc.14.6.650.24840.

Stacey, R. D. 1993. *Strategic Management and Organisational Dynamics: The Challenge of Complexity.* London: Prentice Hall.

Teisman, G., A. van Buuren, and L. Gerrits, eds. 2009. *Managing Complex Governance Systems: Dynamics, Self-Organization, and Coevolution in Public Investments*. New York: Routledge.

Tenbensel, T. 2013. "Complexity in Health and Health Care Systems." *Social Science and Medicine* 91: 181–184. doi:10.1016/j.socscimed.2013.06.017.

Waldrop, M. M. 1992. *The Emerging Science at the Edge of Order and Chaos*. New York: Simon and Schuster.

Wright, S. 1932. "The Roles of Mutation, Inbreeding, Crossbreeding and Selection in Evolution". *Proceedings of the Sixth International Congress of Genetics* (1): 356-366.

Elizabeth Anne Eppel
Mary Lee Rhodes

Association between decisions: experiments with coupled two-person games

Peter Koenraad Marks ⓘ and Lasse M. Gerrits ⓘ

ABSTRACT

Actors making public decisions about a certain policy issue in one particular arena also meet in other arenas where they will have to make decisions on other issues. By incorporating information from across coevolving arenas, actors make associations between the decisions in the different arenas. To understand the dynamics of associations, we deployed a formal game-theoretic approach and run an experiment. Subjects played two different games, each representing a different decision-making arena. The results show that history builds-up and that subjects made associations between the two games, partly explaining the behaviour of decision-makers interacting in multilevel decision-making settings.

1. Introduction

Inspired by the successes of the Japanese Shinkansen trains in the 1960s and the French and German high-speed trains later, the Dutch government decided that they also wanted high-speed rail (Gerrits and Marks 2014; Gerrits et al. 2014; Marks and Gerrits 2017). In the early 1990s, the plans developed into the HSL-Zuid high-speed project. The planning and construction lasted for about 20 years before becoming operational. One persistent issue in the decision-making was the track alignment across the border between Belgium and the Netherlands. The Dutch preferred a crossing point that would be more cost efficient for them than for the Belgians. Naturally, the Belgians demanded a crossing point that would be cheaper for them but more expensive for the Dutch. The decision-making in this arena concerning the cross-border alignment lasted about a decade.

These two governments were also entangled in long-lasting dispute about an unrelated issue; deepening of the Dutch Westerschelde estuary. The Belgian port of Antwerp cannot be reached by ships because the estuary's shallow depth. Dredging could solve the problem but the Belgians would need permission for this from the Dutch, who are reluctant to give that permission out of fears of environmental damage as well as not being eager to give Antwerp a competitive advantage over

Dutch ports. The decision-making in the arena concerning the Westerschelde lasted for about 15 years (Meijerink 1999; Gerrits 2012).

These two unrelated decision-making processes become coupled because the representatives of both governments met each other in both arenas and took with them the history build-up from one arena to the other. The decision-making was concluded when the Belgian minister Van den Brande agreed about the Dutch preferred crossing point at the Belgian border in exchange for a Dutch permission to deepen the Westerschelde. Both complex decision-making processes become coupled due to actors acting and interacting in one arena, then meeting again in the other one. Naturally, they carry over the dynamics from the one arena to the other one. In other words: actors making collective decisions about a certain issue in one particular arena also meet in other arenas where they have to make collective decisions on other issues. This history and the associations these actors can make when moving between the different arenas helped lifting the deadlock.

We investigate the relationship between the actors' internal models, history build-up and the decision-making in coupled arenas. We develop and test a complexity-informed game-theoretic model that tests the relationship between actors interacting over time in different arenas in an experimental setting as a succinct proxy for collective decision-making in multiple arenas. The research question is: how do interacting actors make associations between their decisions in two coupled arenas and how does that association influence the outcomes?

Following Holland's work (1995, 2012), but also e.g. Knott, Miller, and Verkuilen (2003), Henry, Lubell, and McCoyy (2011), and Lavertu and Moynihan (2013), we first develop a formal game theoretic model, the so-called associative approach (Marks 2002). The associative approach is a mathematical model that structures the ways in which actors interacting in one arena, and the history associated with that interaction, influence the decisions made in other coupled arenas. Second, we carry out an experiment to test the associative approach (cf. e.g. Axelrod 1984, 1997; on the merits of game theoretical models in studying complex systems, and e.g. Molm 1990, Lavertu and Moynihan 2013; for a discussion of the merits of experimental approaches in social sciences and in public administration in particular). Controlled experiments allow comparison of players' decisions in equivalent conditions, holding other factors constant making it possible to disentangle the effects of associations between decisions in coupled arenas (cf. Molm, Takahashi, and Peterson 2000). The use of experimental methods in understanding complex decision-making processes may form 'a useful part of the apparatus for moving from the level of the individual actor to the behaviour of the system, ultimately yielding testable theories to explain the endogenous generation of macro behaviour from the microstructure of human systems.' (Sterman 1989, 228).

We acknowledge that some readers unfamiliar with mathematics and game theory will find the model quite abstract and possibly difficult to understand. We have therefore put a description of the model in the main text with limited references to mathematics. The full mathematical model is presented in the Appendix. The text is structured into five sections: (1) the formal game theoretic model of associations between decisions, (2) the experimental design and laboratory setting, (3) the results of the experiment, (4) a discussion about the implications of the results to collective decision-making, and (5) the main conclusions regarding decision-making in complex coupled arena's.

2. Associations between decisions

The perception of what other actors want to achieve, and how they want to achieve it, influences actor decisions. Naturally, decision-makers such as politicians and administrators want to push through their preferred problem and solution definitions. However, conflicts between the various problem-solution combinations mean that not all wishes can be fulfilled and certain combinations will prevail over others. Decision-makers will seek alignment with some partners, and increase distances with opponents if they think this will help further their particular problem-solution combination for that issue. As Knott, Miller and Verkuilen state in the realm of public policy:

'There has been much literature written on decision-making in decentralized environments with limited information. Decision-makers are limited in both what they can control in the decision domain and what information they can obtain. Under these circumstances, decision-makers adapt to decisions made by others in a decision process, not a singular event. The overall outcome of the decision process is the collective result of the interactions among decision-makers.' (2003, 341)

The above quote is our starting point for expansion on the complexity of decision-making process in multiple arenas. Actors not only have to deal with limited information (Simon 1955), they also have to act in various different decision-making arenas where they encounter people from different public organizations as well as stakeholders (Koppenjan and Klijn 2004; Klijn and Koppenjan 2015). This establishes coupling between arenas.

The coupling can be strong when most of the actors from arena 1 (such as the HSL-Zuid arena) also meet in arena 2 (such as the Westerschelde arena), or weak when there is little overlap between the actors in arena 1 and 2. Due to the connections between actors and the decisions they make, a history of collective decision-making is built up. For example, certain actors may find it easier to cooperate now due to the fact that they have done so successfully in the past; or, conversely, more difficult because they carry negative experiences from the past. These history build-ups influence collective decision-making processes in various arenas. By *incorporating information* from *history build-up* in the collective decision-making process, actors construct *internal models* (Holland 1995; Allen, Strathern, and Varga 2010). As such, they make *associations* between the decisions in the different arenas that have become coupled (Marks 2002).

The internal model forms the basic building block that drives that emergence of complexity (Holland 1995). The continuous interaction between actors on the basis of their internal models within and across arenas builds a complex situation over time, as well as cements their behavioural rules if they return acceptable results. The actions of individuals are guided by an interpretative framework that includes both beliefs about the functioning of system and its components, but also the values or goals that are aimed for (Allen, Strathern, and Varga 2010, 55). As another complexity scholar puts it:

'Our information processing capacity is limited and that humans employ biases and heuristics (e.g. anchoring and adjustment, the representativeness heuristic, and the availability heuristic) in order to reduce mental effort.' (Vennix 1999, 381)

The actors make sense of the world by making associations between different decision settings. This helps them handling the complexity of coupled arenas. At the same time, the same associations and subsequent coupledness appear to increase the complexity of decision-making considerably in comparison to situations were all arenas are fully isolated. As such, associations lower the individual perception of complexity as well as drive the complexity on the macro-level. Naturally, it some-times pays off to pursue a complexity absorptive response to a complex environment (cf. Ashmos, Duchon, and McDaniel 2000) because complexity needs to be mirrored with complexity as per Ashby's law of requisite variety. The counter-argument is that the associations help actors in dealing with the complexity of different settings by providing a focal point, i.e. the associations reduce the complexity of the situations for the actors. This is inevitable when working within complex adaptive systems (e.g. Lefebure and Letiche 1999; Boisot 2000; Cooksey 2000), even if it risks over-simpli-fication (Beahrs 1992; Strand 2002; Morçöl 2002). In short, the complexity of situa-tion leads actors to respond in ways that allow them to deal with that complexity within an arena, while simultaneously contributing to that complexity across arenas. In Holland's own words:

> '[…] agents are defined by an enclosing boundary that accepts some signals and ignores others, a "program" inside the boundary for processing and sending signals, and mechanisms for changing (adapting) this program in response to the agents' accumulating experience. Once the signal/boundary agents have been defined, they must be situated to allow for positioning of the relevant signals and boundaries.' (2012, 24).

2.1. *Decision-making dynamics from a game-theoretic perspective*

One of the main methods of inquiry in the complexity sciences is modelling using behavioural rules derived from game theory. Game theoretical models have been proven to be especially helpful when studying complex systems in terms of interac-tions and emergent properties. For example Axelrod (1984, 1997) and Holland (1995) used the prisoner's dilemma to demonstrate the mechanisms of complex systems, and Kauffman (1993) needed game theory to make his fitness landscape models work. Game theory concerns the formal modelling of strategic interaction between indivi-duals and many social phenomenon can be presented in terms of games (cf. Hargreaves Heap and Varoufakis 1995, 1). As such, it is a tool that helps to clarify issues relating to human behaviour and social institutions.

For the present purpose, game theory gives us a device with which we can investigate how interactions between decision-makers can build complex situations across decision-making arenas. When two decision-makers try to reach a collective decision, they will have to interact. Such a situation can be modelled as a particular two-person game. Games can vary from dominated strategy to coordination games, or from prisoner dilemma to zero-sum games, depending on the payoff structure associated with the possible choices for these decision-makers. However, as we said above, decision-makers don't operate in a vacuum. They may meet again in other arenas where they have to decide on another policy issue. In game-theoretical terms, it may be that the new interaction setting will have the same payoff structure as in the first game, but hardly ever are two games exactly the same (cf. Sugden 1986, 50). When decision-making in one arena is followed by decision-making in another coupled arena, the decision-makers play different kinds of games after each other.

Model building inevitably means reducing some of the complexity associated with the messy character of real-world collective decision-making. However, simplifications in a model help focusing on the core-mechanics of decision-making in coupled arenas (cf. e.g. Friedman 1953; Sober 1994). Our model assumes that only two players will make a decision (cf. Knott, Miller, and Verkuilen 2003). History is introduced by letting these two players play two games in a row, the second game being completely different from the previous one, as if they were making collective decisions in two different but coupled arenas. The essential point is that the history that two players create together through their interaction in the first game or arena provides information for the decision in the second game or arena, i.e. the results from the previous game build an internal model (Holland 1995) and create a focal point for the latter game (see Schelling 1960). Rational players will use the asymmetries created through their interactions to formulate their strategies (Bacharach 1993; Janssen 2001).

2.2. The associative approach

Naturally, players see a resemblance between the former and latter game. By incorporating information from the first game into the second, players make an association between the decisions in the two games, i.e. the games become coupled through this association. There are many different ways players can make associations between multiple games, of which some are more prominent than others (cf. Mehta, Starmer, and Sugden 1994a, 1994b). That is, every player conceives the game being played differently, which then becomes a variable in the two-person decision problem (cf. Bacharach 1993; Bacharach and Bernasconi 1997). Given the limited cognitive capacities of players, a preceding but different game can be more prominent than a repeated (same) game for helping them solve the latter games. The external information of the preceding different game can be more prominent because it is more readily accessible (cf. Young 1996, 1998). This information can break the symmetry of a second game and thus raise the chance of coordination (cf. Bhaskar 1997). The associations between games as made by the players induce asymmetries between strategies. That is, the former game can create a focal point in the latter. Players can make many different associations depending on what external information they process and in which manner they do so. Prominence is 'created' by players having certain associations in their frame, while not having others. In short, when players or actors move from one arena to the other, they can negotiate the complexity of doing so by relying on prominence.

We will present the model here as narrative; see Appendix for the full formal model. Players have a given set of possible actions they can undertake. Based on the connection with a previous different game, players make associations for the decisions they can make in the current game. The association means that the initial set of possible actions becomes partitioned, i.e. the decisions can be categorized using the associations the players make. Not all associations will help a player in categorizing the decision set, or certain associations come to mind easier (cf. bounded rationality, Simon 1955). The different associations may be thought of as the frame through which a player looks at the problem. (Bacharach 1993). This frame F is a subset of the partitioned set of possible actions. Naturally, players believe that they consider all possible associations because they are not capable of thinking of associations existing outside their frame F. In other words, players optimize their behaviour on the actions they think are possible and that are always restricted to their frame F. Of course a player has beliefs about the possible associations the other player can use. Players tend to think that their strategy is more sophisticated than the strategy of the other player (Camerer, Ho, and Chong 2004). As such, a player believes that the other player holds the same associations as himself, or less, i.e. the other player is said to be type G, $G \subseteq F$. Given that the player is of type F, the conditional probability that the other player is of type G is denoted by $V(G \mid F)$. The availability of association β is denoted by v_β, hence an association β that is not available is denoted by $(1\ v_\beta)$. Players will try to maximize their returns by making the decision from the set of possible actions that is partitioned due to the associations the players has and beliefs of associations the other player has. This is the model in a nutshell.

3. Design of the experiment

We carried out an experiment mimicking actors operating in two different arenas. The experiment consists of two different games played after each other, each game being a proxy for a decision-making arena of a *different type* with the *same actors* engaging in collective decision-making. The first game was the hash-mark game, the second a distribution game.

The hash-mark game consists of 17 vertical hash-marks. Starting players are randomly assigned for each play of the game. Each player must on each, turn alternating with the other player, cross out 1, 2, 3, or 4 hash-marks. The game continues until all hash-marks have been crossed out. The person who crosses out the last hash-mark loses the game.

The second game is the distribution game, also called battle-of-the-sexes game (BOS-game). In the BOS-game, participants choose between two alternatives without being able to communicate with each other. If both participants choose mutually consistent alternatives, i.e. distributing the reward in the same way between them, they will get the amount prescribed by their chosen alternative. This amount will then be added up to their individual total earnings for the experiment. The alternatives they can choose differ in the two versions of the experiment. In the first version there is only a financial reward in the last game of the two, while in the second version both games have a financial reward. In both versions, 48 first year students from different faculties of the [university name blanked for review purposes] participated, distributed over four different sessions. Only students with no knowledge about game theory or theories of decision-making could participate to create a level playing field. Student anonymity was guaranteed and it was also promised that all the money they would make by playing the games would be paid in cash right after the experiment in private to prevent the other participants from feeling envious regarding how others played.

Each subject was randomly and anonymously drawn and were of type A_i or type B_i ($i = 1,\dots, 7$). The type A players were put in one room and the type B-players in the other. Each type A player would play another type B player exactly once. As the opponents were in different rooms they have no way of communicating with each other. In total, the participants played the combination five or six times in one session. The randomization is done to break up any groups of friends, and to make sure all the participants know that they are playing a real but unknown opponent. The subjects were informed that the subject pool consists of volunteers from various faculties. They were told that the experiment concerns the study of behaviour in interaction situations. This statement of purpose is necessary because it satisfies their curiosity about why someone is willing to pay them money for playing games. The statement is specific enough, yet, broad enough to avoid any 'demand effects'. The experiment starts with a test to see whether the participants understand the rules of the games, and thus lowering the opportunities for confusion during the experiment.

In both versions of the experiment, the outcome of the first game is common knowledge for both players. However, the subjects do not know whom they are playing. They only know that they are playing an opponent in the other room. Also in both versions, the outcome of the second game in the combination is privately revealed to every player, because the payment of the subjects is based on this outcome.

3.1. *Experiment 1*

No matter whether you are the winner or the loser of the hash-mark game the financial gain is zero. The money that has to be agreed upon for distribution in the second game is 10 euro, specified in two alternatives:

Alt 1. You get € 3.- and your co player gets € 7.-.
Alt 2. You get € 7.- and your co player gets € 3.-.

If players have no extra information available, they have no conclusive reason to choose one alternative over another, because they know their opponent has the same problem and this is then common knowledge. In a large population, the expected outcome by traditional game theory will be that the players mix their strategies: alternative 1 will be played in 30 per cent of the cases, and alternative 2 in 70 per cent of the cases, resulting in matching and mismatching of alternatives as given in Table 1.

The associative approach predicts that players will make different choices due to their framing based on the information from playing the hash-mark game prior to the BOS-game. This extra information may cause players to attribute a dominant position to the winner and a subservient position to the loser of the hash-mark game in the distribution game, based on the so-called Lockean principle of distributive justice (see Locke [1690] 1986; Hoffman and Spitzer 1985). Players frame the winner as more entitled to a larger share. That is, players in such settings think it is 'normal' for the winner to claim the larger share in the distribution game, and that it is 'normal' for the loser to agree with this. If the players see this *convention* as being relevant to the play of the game they make the entitlement association. This means the winner of the hash-mark game will choose alternative 2 much more often than the loser, and vice versa. This results in a much higher matching percentage in the left bottom cell of Table 1 (for a mathematical proof of the calculations see Appendix).

Table 1. Fractions of expected outcomes.

		Player B	
		Alt. 1	Alt. 2
Player A	Alt. 1	0.09	0.21
	Alt. 2	0.21	0.49

3.2. *Experiment 2*

In this version, the winner of the hash-mark game receives 4 euro, the loser still receives nothing, and the money that the players can share in the distribution game is 7 euro in total, instead of 10.

Alt 1. You get € 3.- and your co-player gets € 4.-.

Alt 2. You get € 4.- and your co-player gets € 3.-.

Again, in a large population, the expected outcome by traditional game theory will be that the players mix their strategies: alternative 1 will be played in 43 per cent of the cases, and alternative 2 in 57 per cent of the cases, resulting in Table 2 that shows the fractions for the different possible outcomes in the distribution game.

The possible financial rewards for both games show that the difference in payoff in the second game is smaller than the difference in payoff in the first. In line with the Lockean principle of distributive justice, people think that overall the winner of the hash-mark game should still receive more than the loser. However, in the combination of the hash-mark and the distribution game the total payoff to both players can be more equal (Hobbes 1996). This has also shown up in many experiments (e.g. Fehr and Schmidt 1999; Huck and Oechssler 1999; Levine 1998). According to the associative approach, if players use the labels of winner and loser (of the hash-mark game) the winner will choose alternative 1 much more than the loser, and vice versa, resulting in a much higher matching percentage in the right top cell in the table

4. Experimental results

The a-priori assumed relations that need to be analysed are shown in Figure 1.

To analyse whether players do make associations between games, the focus variables of the experiment should be on the outcome of the hash-mark game and the outcome of the distribution game, without other interfering variables. Data on a range of possible intervening variables (*Sex, Faculty, Cultural background,* and *Risk-averse behaviour*) was collected and none of these had a significant impact on the outcomes recorded in both versions of the experiment (see Appendix). Therefore, two a-priori relations remain:

HM start → HM result: the player that starts the hash-mark game can always win (please try it yourself to find out how), while the second player can only win if the starting player makes a mistake. Given the coding of the variables the expected relation between the two is negative, because if the *hash-mark game start* variable goes up – from the starting to the second player – the *result of the hash-mark* game goes down – from winning to losing.

HM result → distribution alternative: subjects will claim the larger share when they have won the hash-mark game, and settle for the smaller share if they lost in version 1, i.e. a positive relation, and vice versa in version 2, i.e. a negative relation.

We will now discuss the results of the two versions of the experiment.

Table 2. Fractions of expected outcomes.

		Player B	
		Alt. 1	Alt. 2
Player A	Alt. 1	0.184	0.245
	Alt. 2	0.245	0.327

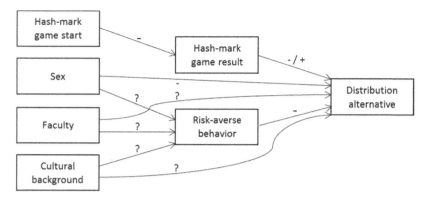

Figure 1. A-priori assumed relations between all variables.

4.1. *Version 1*

The participants did not figure out that they could always win if they started (see Appendix), eliminating the possibility of the random device deciding who will be winner or loser of the game. As such, the winner of the hash-mark game is indeed recognized as having to put in the effort to win. The participants also did not learn how to win the hash-mark game, or did not learn to take advantage of the no-learning situation of the starters (see Appendix). That is, the relation of the starting position in the hash-mark game and the winning position does not influence the possible association that players can make between the hash-mark result and the distribution alternative.

The entitlement association, i.e. the relation between *HM result* and *Distribution alternative*, has a significant positive coefficient (see Appendix). That is, winners of the hash-mark game chose the larger share almost 50 per cent more than losers, or, vice versa, losers chose the smaller share almost 50 per cent more than winners. The remaining significant relation is that the two groups, winners and losers, behave differently when choosing an alternative (see Table 3).

The total percentages of alternatives 1 and 2 are almost the same as traditional game theoretic prediction; i.e. winners (and losers) will choose alternative 1 in 30 per cent of the cases and alternative 2 in 70 per cent of the cases. However, the choices made by the different groups do differ from the total percentages. There is a 45.3 per cent difference in choosing alternatives 1 or 2 for the group of losers compared to the winners (respectively,

Table 3. Alternatives chosen based on losing/winning HM-game.

			Distribution alternative		
			Alternative 1	Alternative 2	Total
HM result	Lose	Count	79	60	139
		% within HM result	56.8%	43.2%	100%
	Win	Count	16	123	139
		% within HM result	11.5%	88.5%	100%
Total		Count	95	183	278
		% within HM result	34.2%	65.8%	100%

56.8–11.5 per cent and 88.5–43.2 per cent). To assess whether the group behaviour deviates from traditional game theory, the following hypotheses will be tested:

H_0: Winners and losers will play according to traditional game-theoretic prediction: $p_{W0} = p_{L0} = 0.7$.

H_1: According to the associative approach winners (losers) will claim the larger share a lot more: $p_{W1} \gg 0.7$ ($p_{L1} \ll 0.7$).

The observed proportion of winners (losers) choosing alternative two is 0.885 (0.432), which is outside the respective boundaries of 0.764 and 0.636. Stronger still: the correlation even holds if the confidence area is extended to 99 per cent (significance level of 1 per cent) making the boundaries 0.79 and 0.61, respectively. In other words, the null hypothesis is rejected and the alternative corroborated. This means that the decisions of the players, divided in losers and winners, in the second game based on the history build-up in the first game as predicted by the associative approach. Comments and remarks of participants in both the post-questionnaire and the comment sheets of the experiment made clear that some participants always claim seven when they win the hash-mark game and three when they lose.

A partial correlation check shows that participants do not use the association more frequently in later rounds ($\rho = -.031$; $p = .303$; $N = 275$). However, the post-questionnaire made clear that after a couple of rounds, or in hindsight, some participants changed (or thought they should have changed) their tactics from always claiming seven or three to basing their alternative on the result of the previous hash-mark game. The substantial amount of associating players helped to create a higher payoff in the subject pool. The result of the first game resonates in the second game creating a payoff that is 0.67 euro higher (32 per cent) than what the players would earn according to the expectations of the traditional game-theoretic perspective.

4.2. Version 2

As in the first version of the experiment, the participants did not figure out how to win the hash-mark game when playing (see Appendix). The winners of the hash-mark game were immediately rewarded with four euro, while the losers did not get anything. Putting in the effort for winning the hash-mark game is thus immediately rewarded, and does not undermine the possible egalitarian or entitlement position in the distribution game, where the players have to agree on distributing seven euro.

The relation between *HM result* and *Distribution alternative* is significant at a 1 per cent level. This means that being a winner or loser has a significant influence on the alternative chosen. The correlation between the two variables confirms that in this version the loser of the hash-mark game is more inclined to demand the larger compared to the winner. Table 4 shows the amount and percentages of participants who lost or won the hash-mark game and their respective alternatives chosen in the distribution game.

The total percentages of the chosen alternatives in this version of the experiment are close to the average outcome expected by traditional game theory, i.e. winners and loser will choose alternative 1 in approximately 43 per cent (3/7) of the cases and alternative 2 in approximately 57 per cent (4/7). However, there is a 20.8 per cent difference in choosing alternatives 1 or 2 for the group of losers compared to the winners, respectively 59.4–38.6 per cent, and 61.4–40.6 per cent. To see whether this

Table 4. Alternatives chosen based on losing/winning HM-game.

			Distribution alternative		
			Alternative 1	Alternative 2	Total
HM result	Lose	Count	39	62	101
		% within HM result	38.6%	61.4%	100%
	Win	Count	60	41	101
		% within HM result	59.4%	40.6%	100%
Total		Count	99	103	202
		%within HM result	49.0%	51.0%	100%

behaviour deviates significantly from traditional game theory for the winners (losers) the following hypotheses will be tested:

H0: Winners and loser will play according to traditional game theoretic prediction: $H_0 = p_{W1} = p_{L1} = 4/7$.

H1: According the associative approach winners (losers) will claim the larger share a lot less: $H_1 = p_{W1} \ll 4/7$ ($p_{L1} \gg 4/7$).

The winners of the hash-mark game chose alternative 2 only 40.6 per cent times compared to the boundary of 49 per cent. In other words, the frequency of winners choosing alternative 2 is outside the confidence area (even at the 1 per cent significance level), which means that the null hypothesis is rejected and the alternative hypothesis corroborated. The percentage of losers that chose alternative 2 is still within the boundary at a significance level of 5 per cent, which means that the 5 per cent difference between what traditional game theory and the associative approach predict about the behaviour of the losers is not large enough, or the experimental data is too small. This variance may be contributed to differences between behaviour of losers and winners as the winners are aware of the 4 euro they receive for winning the hash-mark game while the losers only know this subconsciously. Because the losers do not have this extra information (readily available) in their frame to help them solve the problem at hand, they tend to randomize between the two alternatives rather than opting for alternative two.

Similar to version 1, the individual participants did not start using the possible association more frequently in later combinations during play ($\rho = -0.000$; $p = .498$; $N = 199$). While not all participants make the egalitarian association, the total money amount generated in this version is significantly higher than the outcome expected by traditional game theory. That is, the group of associating players helps make the total financial earnings nearly 2 euro, 30 eurocents higher than when all participants would behave as expected by traditional game theory.

5. Implications and extensions

As example, March (1994) and many others have shown in the realm of organization, management and decision-making: history build-up between public actors is very real but the exact dynamics behind it need to be carefully researched. The experimental results show that players, as proxy for the decision-makers discussed in the introduction, consciously use information of the history build-up in the combination of the two games. That is, in the first version the players clearly couple the first and second game. Here, we see Holland's internal model as presented in Section 2 at work: the history build-up causes players to associate between the games, and provides them beliefs that their opponent has certain associations. These frames of the players, i.e. the possible decisions they can make and that they think the other player can make, helps them resolve the distribution problem much better. In other words: their refined internal models help them cope with the complexity of coupled arenas. Although slightly weaker than in the first version of the experiment, the players in the second version are also better in matching. However, this is mainly due to history build-up over the two games: the winners choose the lower share much more often than the larger share. In other words, the frame through which the winners looked at the second game builds on the association and coupling of the two. This results in an overall higher matching of alternatives, even though the decisions, rooted in a shared history, are not always in full alignment. Overall, the framing of the players and the beliefs of the frames of other players and the possible associations these players can make between the coupled games helps players focusing on particular outcomes in favour of randomization (cf. focal points by Schelling 1960) or it helps break a deadlock (cf. Gerrits and Marks 2017). As such, it demonstrates that players as actors develop internal models that help them to deal with two coupled arenas in which two very different decision-making processes take place.

Even though the formal model and the corresponding experiment seem to be a major reduction of the complexity of decision-making processes in real cases, it does help in understanding the intricacies of actors trying to find clues in order to help them reach (better) results. Let us return to the high-speed rail case from the introduction. The package deal – in the shape of a deeper estuary for the Belgians and track alignment favoured by the Dutch – is quite common in public administration and management literature. We can now understand such a package deal in terms of decision-making in coupled arenas. They have build-up history in the two separate arenas which helps them make associations between the possible problem and solution definitions for the respective issues and as such their framing. This partitions their set of action possibilities that helps them resolve the respective deadlocks. In other words: their refined internal models help them navigating the complexity of the two decision-making processes in the coupled arenas. Decision-making in the first arena shaped the structure in the second arena.

Naturally, the research presented here should be extended. The formal model can be tested in increasingly more realistic situations instead of controlled experimental situations. It is worth incorporating into the model the possibility of prior experience that contributes to the internal model of the actors. For example, there is a long history of bilateral negotiations about cross-boundary issues between the Netherlands and Belgium, so the decision-making in the two arenas didn't come out of the blue. Some (Belgian) civil servants would even refer to the treaty of 1848 between the two countries as a foundation for why they went for certain decision alternatives. This joint history influences the frames with which the respective actors enter the arena and as such predefines possible associations they can make. This, in turn, limits their action space. A shared background means that the decision-makers position themselves differently to other decision-makers, or that their frame is already predefined in comparison to a situation where this background is absent. The frame of reference also means decision-makers are likely to seek alignment with other decision-makers based on history build-up (cf. Henry, Lubell, and McCoyy 2011).

Another addition to the model that could be tested would be to incorporate communication prior to the actual decision-making. Prior communications would find their way in the frames that actors have at their disposal. Players will find out what possible associations others have due to communication, possibly enhancing their frame. After all, it is extremely unlikely that decision-makers would be able to enter the final decision-stage unbiased, uninformed, and uncoordinated. The testing of the model that incorporates prior communications would enhance understanding of the associations and the actions by the actors. Lastly, extending the amount of players, the number of options available and/or the diversity of interaction situations is needed to do justice to the empirical richness of collective decision-making (cf. Malatesta 2012). For example, the number of actors involved in the two arenas discussed here run into the double digits and the space of possible outcomes was also considerable and changeable as new options became available and others disappeared due to external forces.

6. Conclusion

We started this article with the observation that part of the complexity of collective decision-making comes from actors moving back and forth between coupled arenas and the updating of their internal model to become more effective in dealing with that complexity in order to reach their goals. To research this coupledness, we followed the game theoretical approach favoured in the complexity sciences and presented the associative approach. The associative approach was modelled and then tested in an experiment. In the last step, we discussed the implications of the experimental results for understanding complex coupled decision-making processes. The results show that the history build-up in the first setting between the decision-makers creates focal points for the next setting. This helps the actors in the decision-making process to better align choices. In other words: history is key. We have demonstrated that the associative approach in this model can explain at least a fraction of the behaviour of decision-makers interacting in complex situations.

The formal model developed for this article helps conjecturing on what may be necessary, but does not yet provide full answers to all facets of decision-making in coupled arenas. Both theoretical and empirical research is needed in order to extend the initial model of the associative approach.

Disclosure statement

No potential conflict of interest was reported by the authors.

ORCID

Peter Koenraad Marks (iD) http://orcid.org/0000-0003-4644-0434
Lasse M. Gerrits (iD) http://orcid.org/0000-0002-7649-6001

References

Allen, P. M., M. Strathern, and L. Varga 2010. "Complexity: The Evolution of Identity and Diversity." In *Complexity, Difference and Identity, 41 Issues in Business Ethics 26*, edited by P. Cilliers and P. Reiser, 41–60. doi:10.1007/978-90-481-9187-1_3,

Ashmos, D. P., D. Duchon, and R. R. McDaniel. 2000. "Organizational Responses to Complexity: The Effect on Organizational Performance." *Journal of Organizational Change Management* 13 (6): 577–594. doi:10.1108/09534810010378597.

Axelrod, R. M. 1984. *The Evolution of Cooperation*. New York: Basic Books.

Axelrod, R. M. 1997. *The Complexity of Cooperation: Agent-based Models of Competition and Collaboration*. Princeton, NJ: Princeton University Press.

Bacharach, M. 1993. "Variable Universe Games." In *Frontiers of Game Theory*, edited by K. Binmore, A. Kirman, and P. E. Tani, 255–275. Cambridge, MA: MIT Press.

Bacharach, M., and M. Bernasconi. 1997. "The Variable Frame Theory of Focal Points: An Experimental Study." *Games and Economic Behavior* 19 (1): 1-45.

Beahrs, J. O. 1992. "Paradoxical Effects in Political Systems." *Political Psychology* 13 (4): 755–769. doi:10.2307/3791500.

Bhaskar, V. 1997. "Breaking the Symmetry: Optimal Conventions in Repeated Symmetric Games." Paper presented at the 17th Arne Ryde Symposium of Focal Points, Trolleholm castle, August 20–21.

Boisot, M. 2000. "Is There a Complexity beyond the Reach of Strategy?" *Emergence* 2 (1): 114–134. doi:10.1207/S15327000EM0201_08.

Camerer, C., T.-H. Ho, and J.-K. Chong. 2004. "A Cognitive Hierarchy Model of Games." *The Quarterly Journal of Economics* 119 (3): 861–898. doi:10.1162/0033553041502225.

Cooksey, R. W. 2000. "Mapping the Texture of Managerial Decision Making: A Complex Dynamic Decision Perspective." *Emergence* 2 (2): 102–122. doi:10.1207/S15327000EM0202_06.

Fehr, E., and K. M. Schmidt. 1999. "A Theory of Fairness, Competition, and Cooperation." *Quarterly Journal of Economics* 114 (3): 817–868. doi:10.1162/003355399556151.

Friedman, M. 1953. "The Methodology of Positive Economics." *Essays in Positive Economics* 3: 3.

Gerrits, L. M. 2012. *Punching Clouds: An Introduction to the Complexity of Public Decision-Making*. Litchfield, AZ: Emergent.

Gerrits, L. M., and P. K. Marks. 2014. "Vastgeklonken aan de Fyra: Een pad-afhankelijkheidsanalyse van de onvermijdelijke keuze voor de falende flitstrein [Bolted to the Fyra: A Path-dependency Analysis of the Inevitable Choice for a Failing Bullet Train]." *Bestuurskunde* 23 (1): 55–64. doi:10.5553/Bk/092733872014023001008.

Gerrits, L. M., and P. K. Marks. 2017. *Understanding Collective Decision Making: A Fitness Landscape Model Approach*. Cheltenham, UK: Edward Elgar.

Gerrits, L. M., P. K. Marks, S. Ongkittikul, and M. Synnott. 2014. "Assessing High-Speed Railway Projects: A Comparison of the Netherlands and the United Kingdom." *TDRI Quarterly Review* 29 (1): 16–24.

Hargreaves Heap, S., and Y. Varoufakis. 1995. *Game Theory: A Critical Introduction*. London: Routledge.

Henry, A. D., M. Lubell, and M. McCoyy. 2011. "Belief Systems and Social Capital as Drivers of Policy Network Structure: The Case of California Regional Planning." *Journal of Public Administration Research and Theory* 21 (3): 419–444. doi:10.1093/jopart/muq042.

Hobbes, T. 1996. *Leviathan*. Oxford: Oxford University Press.

Hoffman, E., and M. L. Spitzer. 1985. "Entitlements, Rights, and Fairness: An Experimental Examination of Subjects' Concepts of Distributive Justice." *Journal of Legal Studies* XIV: 259–297. doi:10.1086/467773.

Holland, J. 1995. *Hidden Order: How Adaptation Builds Complexity*. Jackson: Perseus Books.

Holland, J. H. 2012. *Signals and Boundaries: Building Blocks for Complex Adaptive Systems*. Cambridge, MA: MIT Press.

Huck, S., and J. Oechssler. 1999. "The Indirect Evolutionary Approach to Explaining Fair Allocations." *Games and Economic Behavior* 28 (1): 13–24. doi:10.1006/game.1998.0691.

Janssen, M. C. W. 2001. "Rationalizing Focal Points." *Theory and Decision* 50 (2): 119–148. doi:10.1023/A:1010349014718.

Kauffman, S. A.. 1993. *The Origins of Order: Self-organization and Selection in Evolution*. Oxford, MA: Oxford University Press.

Klijn, E. H., and J. Koppenjan. 2015. *Governance Networks in the Public Sector*. London: Routledge.

Knott, J. H., G. J. Miller, and J. Verkuilen. 2003. ""Adaptive Incrementalism and Complexity: Experiments with Two-Person Cooperative Signaling Games." *Journal of Public Administration Research and Theory* 13 (3): 341–366. doi:10.1093/jopart/mug023.

Koppenjan, J. F. M., and E. H. Klijn. 2004. *Managing Uncertainties in Networks: A Network Approach to Problem Solving and Decision Making*. London: Routledge.

Lavertu, S., and D. P. Moynihan. 2013. "The Empirical Implications of Theoretical Models: A Description of the Method and an Application to the Study of Performance Management Implementation." *Journal of Public Administration Research and Theory* 23 (2): 333–360. doi:10.1093/jopart/mus049.

Lefebure, E., and H. Letiche. 1999. "Managing Complexity from Chaos: Uncertainty, Knowledge and Skills." *Emergence: Complexity and Organization* 1 (3): 7. doi:10.1207/s15327000em0103_2.

Levine, D. K. 1998. "Modeling Altruism and Spitefulness in Experiments." *Review of Economic Dynamics* 1 (3): 593–622. doi:10.1006/redy.1998.0023.

Locke, J. [1690] 1986. *The Second Treatise On Civil Government*. Amherst, NY: Prometheus Books.

Malatesta, D. 2012. "The Link between Information and Bargaining Efficiency." *Journal of Public Administration Research and Theory* 22 (3): 527–551. doi:10.1093/jopart/mur028.

March, J. G. 1994. *Primer on Decision Making: How Decisions Happen*. New York: Simon and Schuster.

Marks, P. K. 2002. *Association between Games: A Theoretical and Empirical Investigation of A New Explanatory Model in Game Theory*. Amsterdam: Thelathesis.

Marks, P. K., and L. M. Gerrits. 2017. "Evaluating Technological Progress in Public Policies: The Case of the High-Speed Railways in the Netherlands." *Complexity, Governance & Networks* 3 (1): 48–62.

Mehta, J., C. Starmer, and R. Sugden. 1994a. "The Nature of Salience: An Experimental Investigation of Pure Coordination Games." *American Economic Review* 84 (3): 658–673.

Mehta, J., C. Starmer, and R. Sugden. 1994b. "Focal Points in Pure Coordination Games: An Experimental Investigation." *Theory and Decision* 36: 163–185. doi:10.1007/BF01079211.

Meijerink, S. V. 1999. *Conflicts and Cooperation on the Scheldt River Basin: A Case Study of Decision-Making on International Scheldt Issues between 1967 and 1997*. Dordrecht: Kluwer Academic Publishers.

Molm, L. D. 1990. "Structure, Action, and Outcomes: The Dynamics of Power in Social Exchange." *American Sociological Review* 55 (3): 427–447. doi:10.2307/2095767.

Molm, L. D., N. Takahashi, and G. Peterson. 2000. "Risk and Trust in Social Exchange: An Experimental Test of a Classical Proposition." *American Journal of Sociology* 105 (5): 1396–1427. doi:10.1086/210434.

Morçöl, G. 2002. *A New Mind for Policy Analysis: Toward A Postnewtonian and Postpositivist Epistemology and Methodology*. Westport, CT: Praeger Publishers.

Schelling, T. C. 1960. *The Strategy of Conflict*. Cambridge: Harvard University Press.

Simon, H. 1955. "A Behavioral Model of Rational Choice." *The Quarterly Journal of Economics* 69 (1): 99–118. doi:10.2307/1884852.

Sober, E. 1994. "Let's Razor Occam's Razor." In *Explanation and Its Limits*, edited by D. Knowles, 73–973. Cambridge: Cambridge University Press.

Sterman, J. D. 1989. "Modeling Managerial Behaviour: Misperceptions of Feedback in a Dynamic Decision Making Experiment." *Management Science* 35 (3): 321–339. doi:10.1287/mnsc.35.3.321.

Strand, R. 2002. "Complexity, Ideology, and Governance." *Emergence* 4 (1): 164–183. doi:10.1080/15213250.2002.9687743.

Sugden, R. 1986. *The Economics of Rights, Co-operation and Welfare*. Berlin: Springer.

Vennix, J. A. M. 1999. "Group Model-Building: Tackling Messy Problems." *System Dynamics Review* 15 (4): 379–401. doi:10.1002/(SICI)1099-1727(199924)15:4<379::AID-SDR179>3.0.CO;2-E.

Young, H. P. 1996. "The Economics of Convention." *Journal of Economic Perspectives* 10 (2): 105–122. doi:10.1257/jep.10.2.105.

Young, H. P. 1998. *Individual Strategy and Social Structure: An Evolutionary Theory of Institutions*. Princeton, NJ: Princeton University Press.

Appendix

Formal model

Players have a possible set of actions they can undertake, which is finite and given by $\Sigma = \{1, \ldots, m\}$. Based on the connection with a previous different game, players make associations for the decisions they can make in the current game. Each of these associations induces a partition of Σ. A basic partition is a partition of Σ induced by a single association. B denotes the set of basic partitions. A typical element of B will be denoted β. 'Nature' predetermines the probabilities with which players see certain associations. Players may learn from playing previous games and incorporate this into their approach of later games. If players have learned that there is a possible association they can make between the games, this means that in a later combination – not necessarily between the same two players – nature assigns different availabilities to the players. The frame of a player is denoted by F, which is an arbitrary subset of B. The probability of all associations that are possible in F come to mind of player is denoted by $V(F)$: The availability of F. player believes that the other player holds the same associations as himself, or less, i.e. the other player is said to be type G, $G \subseteq F$. Given that the player is of type F, the conditional probability that the other player is of type G is denoted by $V(G \mid F)$. The availability of association β is denoted by v_β, hence an association β that is not available is denoted by $(1 - v_\beta)$. It is assumed that the availabilities of the different associations are not dependent on each other. The probabilities $V(F)$ and $V(G \mid F)$ can be stated if we write v_β for the availability of association β.

$$V(F) = \prod_{\beta \in F} v_\beta \prod_{\beta \in F \setminus G}(1 - v_\beta)$$

$$V(G|F) = \prod_{\beta \in F} v_\beta \prod_{\beta \in F \setminus G}(1 - v_\beta) \; for \; G \subseteq F$$

$$V(G|F) = \text{Undefined} \; for \; G \not\subseteq F$$

"The expected payoff for a type F player is given by

$$\pi_i(p(\cdot)|F) = \sum_{G \subseteq F} V(G|F) \cdot \pi(p_i(F), p_{-i}(G)),$$

where $p_i(F)$ denotes the randomization chosen by type F, $p_{-i}(G)$ denotes the randomization chosen by type G and $\pi(p_i(F), p_{-i}(G))$ denotes the players' expected payoff when these randomizations are chosen." (Janssen 2001, 127).

Do note that: Availabilities are defined between zero and one, which needs some explanation because an association is in the frame of a player, or not. However, the idea of availability can be seen as nature programming the player to 'assign' probabilities to other players having certain associations in their frame. In other words, nature determines the player's beliefs about the cognitive capacities of other players. For instance, nature determines the following thinking for a player: I think that there is a 70 per cent chance that the other player makes and uses this particular association. For this player it would mean that the availability of this particular association would be $v = 0.7$. Another way of looking at the idea of availability is that in a population the average probability of members of this population making a particular association is, for instance, 0.7. Given shared background, players have this particular association available with 0.7, and not available with 0.3. An association can be labelled, or be perceived as, more prominent when it is more available. However, when the availabilities of, for instance, two associations are 0.6 0.7, respectively, one cannot say that the second is more prominent than the first: They are both prominent. Intuitively thinking, when the difference in availability is large, one can say that one of the two is more prominent. But this does not prevent the possibility that players can coordinate/match by using a less available association.

Calculations of associative approach in experiment 1

The strategy a player will adopt depends on the associations in his frame and the conditional probabilities of the other player having (a subset of) his frame, i.e.:

• no association	$\rightarrow$	$(1 - v_1)(1 - v_2)$	$0 \leq v_1, v_2 \leq 1$
• entitlement association	$\rightarrow$	$v_1(1 - v_2)$	
• egalitarian association	$\rightarrow$	$v_2(1 - v_1)$	
• both associations	$\rightarrow$	$v_1 v_2$	

The calculation of the expected payoffs for both players when they claim either the larger or the smaller share of the money can be depicted in the following equations, where π^i is the expected payoff for player i ($i = w, l$), where w is the winner and l is the loser of the hash-mark game.

$$\pi^w(7) = (1 - v_1)(1 - v_2)\tfrac{21}{10} + v_1(1 - v_2)7 + v_2(1 - v_1)0 + v_1 v_2 X$$

$$\pi^w(3) = (1 - v_1)(1 - v_2)\tfrac{21}{10} + v_1(1 - v_2)0 + v_2(1 - v_1)3 + v_1 v_2 X$$

$$\pi^l(7) = (1 - v_1)(1 - v_2)\tfrac{21}{10} + v_1(1 - v_2)0 + v_2(1 - v_1)7 + v_1 v_2 X$$

$$\pi^l(3) = (1 - v_1)(1 - v_2)\tfrac{21}{10} + v_1(1 - v_2)3 + v_2(1 - v_1)0 + v_1 v_2 X$$

The last term denoted by X is unspecified, because one is not able to determine what the outcome will be: The outcome depends on what the player believes the probabilities of the other player having the associations are. To be able to specify the claims, the last term (X) of the equations can be specified by showing the cases in which the minimum of one claim (i.e. $X = 0$) exceeds the maximum of the other (X = claim maximum). In these cases it is always rational to act according to the claim, because the expected payoff of following it is always higher, i.e. it is a dominant strategy. It is rational for the winner to claim seven if the minimum expected payoff of claiming seven is equal to or exceeds the maximum expected payoff of claiming three. In formula: min π^w (7) $\geq$max π^w (3), which is satisfied if:

$$v_2 \leq \frac{7v_1}{3 + 7v_1}.$$

It is rational for the winner of the hash-mark game to claim the smaller share in the distribution game, if max π^w (7) $\leq$min π^w (3), which is satisfied if:

$$v_2 \leq \frac{7v_1}{3 + 7v_1}.$$

For the loser of the hash-mark game, it is rational to claim the smaller share when max π^w (7) $\leq$min π^w (3), and the larger share when min π^w (7) $\geq$max π^w (3), which are satisfied if $v_2 \leq \frac{3v_1}{7+3v_1}$, respectively, $v_2 \geq \frac{3v_1}{7-7v_1}$.

Coding variables

Start hash-mark game	1 =	Start
	2 =	Second
Result hash-mark game	0 =	Lose
	1 =	Win
Distribution alternative	1 =	Alternative 1
	2 =	Alternative 2
Distribution result	0 =	Non-matching offers
	1 =	Matching offers
Sex	0 =	Male
	1 =	Female
Cultural background	0 =	Dutch
	1 =	Non-native Dutch
Risk behaviour alternatives	0 =	€ 3.- for sure
	1 =	Toss of coin 20 vs. 0
Faculty	1 =	Economics
	2 =	Business administration
	3 =	Law
	4 =	History & Arts
	5 =	Economics & Law
	6 =	Philosophy
Possible association version 1	0 =	Lost HM & chose alternative 2
		Won HM & chose alternative 1
	1 =	Lost HM & chose alternative 1
		Won HM & chose alternative 2
Possible association version 2	0 =	Lost HM & chose alternative 1
		Won HM & chose alternative 2
	1 =	Lost HM & chose alternative 2
		Won HM & chose alternative 1

Results analyses variables version 1:
Correlation *HM start* and *HM result*: 278 (*N*) valid entries to test the correlation. Starting players win almost 8 per cent more than players that go second. The one-sided significance (*p*) is 0.094, and thus is the relation not significant in a 95 per cent confidence interval.

Correlation *results game* to each individual players: The relation for each individual player is not significant (ρ = −0.000; *p* = .499; *N* = 275). Starting players did not learn how to win the game (ρ = .089; *p* = .149; *N* = 136). And the players who go second in the hash-mark game did not learn how to take advantage of the no-learning situation of the starters (ρ = .091; *p* = .291; *N* = 136).

Correlation *HM result* and *Distribution alternative*. When the result of the hash-mark game goes up (the variable is coded as 0 = lost HM, and 1 = won HM) the alternative chosen in the distribution game goes up (coding: 1 = alternative 1, and 2 = alternative 2). The corrected coefficient is 0.482 (ρ = .000; *N* = 275).

Correlations

		Risk behaviour	Cultural background	HM start
Sex	Pearson Correlation	−.122	.195	.000
	Sig. (2-tailed)	.408	.183	1.000
	N	48	48	278
Risk behaviour	Pearson Correlation		−.209	.018
	Sig. (2-tailed)	n.a.	.155	.769
	N		48	278
Cultural background	Pearson Correlation			−.026
	Sig. (2-tailed)	n.a.	n.a.	.669
	N			278

One-way ANOVA test of Faculty

	F	Sig.	N
Sex	2.339	.087	46
Cultural background	1.769	.167	46
Risk behaviour	1.776	.166	46
HM start	1.059	.367	272

Correlations distribution alternative

		Distribution alternative
Cultural background	Pearson Correlation	−.045
	Sig. (1-tailed)	.229
	N	278
Risk behaviour	Pearson Correlation	.059
	Sig. (1-tailed)	.162
	N	278

One-way ANOVA test of Faculty

	F	Sig.	N
Distribution alternative	1.189	.314	272

Results analyses variables version 2:

Correlation *HM start* and *HM result*: starting players ($\rho = .022$; $p = .412$; $N = 100$) or the second player ($\rho = .023$; $p = .821$; $N = 100$)

Correlations

		Cultural background	HM start
Sex	Pearson Correlation	.130	−.077
	Sig. (2-tailed)	.379	.199
	N	36	278
Cultural Background	Pearson Correlation		−.042
	Sig. (2-tailed)	n.a.	.489
	N		278

One-way ANOVA test of Faculty

	F	Sig.	N
Sex	2.267	.141	35
Cultural background	0.110	.742	35
HM start	0.117	.733	208

Correlations

		Distribution alternative
Sex	Pearson Correlation	−.055
	Sig. (1-tailed)	.181
	N	274
Cultural background	Pearson Correlation	−.050
	Sig. (1-tailed)	.205
	N	274

Correlation *HM result* and *Distribution alternative*: Corrected correlation for the almost significant ($p = .084$) variable sex is -0.228 ($p = .001$; $N = 199$), which means that when the result of the hash-mark game goes up, from 0 for losing to 1 for winning, the other variable goes down from alternative 2 to alternative 1 by almost 23%.

One-way ANOVA test of Faculty

	F	Sig.	N
Distribution alternative	.077	.781	207

Understanding the influence of values in complex systems-based approaches to public policy and management

Philip Haynes ⓘ

ABSTRACT

Attempts to apply complexity theory to public management have focused on the dynamic systems environment. This accepts that in public systems there are many externalities, unstable processes, and indeterminate outcomes. Resulting practices have focused on system resilience, patterns of practice, and adaptability. This article revisits complex systems and theorizes public organizations as dynamic systems of public values. The rigour of such an original approach requires a juxtaposition of values with complexity theory. Theorizing value systems in public policy implies they are a key element of complexity and provides a significant development for understanding stable and unstable dynamics in public organizations.

Introduction

A considerable volume of literature and research has been published in the last 25 years about the application of complexity science to the social sciences (Byrne 1998; Cilliers 1998; Allen, et al, 2011; Byrne and Callaghan 2013; Boulton, Allen, and Bowman 2015). This literature has influenced the application of theory to management and practice both in the general business environment and more specifically in the public services. Complexity theory has provided a rich range of descriptions of public organizations as complex adaptive systems that exposes the indeterminate nature of these systems and the limitations and challenges this creates for public managers (Allen, et al, 2011; Eppel, Matheson, and Walton 2011; Boulton, Allen, and Bowman 2015). Beyond this rich description, some researchers have promoted alternative perspectives about management practice that assist managers to deal with the complexity of their operating environments (Rhodes et al. 2011; Stacey 2011; Haynes 2015).

It is, therefore, important to distinguish between essentially descriptive approaches that seek to evaluate the degree and nature of complexity within the systems where public managers operate, from the research that moves to propose alternative practices that may enable managers to cope and perform better. The latter tend to be conceptual and rarely offer empirical evidence to justify new practices as measurably 'better' in their resulting influences and outcomes. In part, the lack of empirical evidence about the usefulness of practices designed to cope with complexity relates to the ontology of complexity that sees a complex systems environment as being very difficult to subject to a controlled, experimental-based research environment where one can be confident of measuring outcomes. Pollitt (2009) has criticized this lack of evidence. The use of complexity theory cannot remain in abstract discussions of grand meta theory but must be applied to practical examples of policy management.

The aim of this paper is to consider how the growing body of literature and research published about public service values and their influence on public services can be juxtaposed with the complexity perspective. This is of relevance to the contemporary practice environment where there are examples of management science being applied that result in moral failure (Francis 2013). This is due to an inability to incorporate values as an element of practice. The paper integrates the turn to public service value and values with the knowledge accumulated through the application of complexity theory to public management. It does this by exploring the concept of value plurality and value hierarchies and theorizing multiple value influences on public management decision-making, including value conflicts. It examines the relevance of complexity theory concepts (Cilliers 1998) to understanding the dynamic influence of values on complex policy systems.

Public value and values

The New Public Managerialism (NPM) of the last 40 years has had a seminal influence on the study and practice of public management and public administration (Lane 2000). It has moved the subject of public administration in a managerial direction where part of the shift in emphasis is the de-politicization of an administrator (who serves a political or politically appointed master) as a locally empowered manager (Hughes 2012). These reforms are influenced by management practice in business and the private sector and founded on concepts and values linked to marketization and privatization. All this has taken place in an age where there is a growing dominance of market values (Sandel 2013).

Part of the revision of NPM in the last twenty years has been linked to a rediscovery and re-identification of 'public value' (Moore 1995) and similarly the influence on managers of 'public values' (Box 2015). These are the two different but compatible approaches to public value. First is an approach that asserts a need for public managers to realize the public value of their policy activities. This is the 'public good' and collective benefit of public policy. This public value, it is argued, should be at the core of public management practice and evidenced in the strategies and operations of public policy (Moore 1995; Benington and Moore 2011). Second, another group of studies has examined what personal, social, and political values influence public managers (Box 2015). Alongside the major contribution of public value/s scholarship to public management is another revision of NPM, and this is the influence of complex systems approaches (Teisman and Klijn 2008; Teisman, Van Buuren, and Gerrits 2009; Rhodes et al. 2011; Haynes 2015).

Complexity theory and public management

In a seminal issue of *Public Management Review*, published a decade ago, Teisman and Klijn (2008) outlined the key concepts and issues resulting from the juxtaposition of complexity theory with public management. They drew attention to the multiple contexts influencing public managers, the dynamic pace of change in the policy environment, and the radical implications for our understanding of the public manager's role and task. Complex system approaches criticize the classical control ethos of NPM. This is the idea that managers can be made fully responsible for the performance of their services through the economic mantra of managing economy of input, efficiency of inputs to outputs, and the effectiveness of those outputs to generate good outcomes. These classical management methods assume a high degree of system predictability and control, something that complex systems approaches argue does not exist. Complex systems approaches assert that public managers work in unpredictable systems where individual practitioners have limited influence (Snowden and Boone 2007). These organizational systems are contingent on the external environment, they overlap in complex ways with other public and private systems, and they are full of multiple levels and networks of human relationships and communications. These communications and resulting behaviours often – but not always – get copied and reproduced as interactive feedback. The myriad of people who experience these inter-actions are also capable of innovating and self-organization and can contribute bottom up creativity and/or resistance. As Klijn (2008) concluded in his seminal piece for the first complexity theory special edition of *Public Management Review* (PMR), complex public policy systems rather defy being manageable, and if public managers are to have any chance at all of success, they must be highly adaptable and facilitators of what opportunities for change do emerge.

The engineer turned philosopher, the late Cilliers (1998, 3–4), provides us with one of the most formative definitions of social complex systems. What follows is a paraphrase and summary of his definition, a conceptual model that is returned to for a concluding analysis at the end of the paper.

A complex system has many cases (like people and organizations) and elements (like places and processes). There are many dynamic interactions between these cases and elements, but their separate ability to know and respond to all the information in these interactions is limited. The interactions that occur in the system take two primary forms: reinforcing feedback and checking feedback. Reinforcing feedback is a positive acknowledgement of communication received and can result in a copy-ing and further communication of the information. It is amplified and scaled up in the system and has greater influence. Conversely, checking feedback is a negative feedback and curtails previous responses. The possibility that interactions result in a scaling up of behaviour in a complex system illustrates the importance of different levels within the system. In public policy, we typically think of three such levels to system operation: macro (the national or continental level), the meso (the local or organizational level), and the micro (the life and cognitions of the individual citizen). While complex systems are in general acknowledged as open, without permanent boundaries (and overlapping with other systems and sub-systems), they are never-theless restricted in their openness. Much of this limitation is due to their inability to share and communicate all information equally. Dynamic flows of energy influence systems. These flows are episodic and nonlinear. Finally, all systems have a history and are, to some extent, path dependent on that history and the previous events that have shaped the system.

Values as attractors to order

For the matter of defining complex systems, we will add one other concept previously used by others, but not present in Cilliers's (1998) overarching account. This is the concept of the attractor. It is important for assisting in understanding the process of system patterns over time. In complex systems theory the attractor is a mechanism that defines periods of relative stability in what otherwise will be long periods of instability and chaos (Urry 2003). In mathematics, an attractor defines the boundaries of system change and creates the definition of the patterns and shape of system order (Stewart 1995). In social and organizational systems, stability and order in systems can be provided by rules of operation, but also by values.

> The very large number of elements makes such systems unpredictable and lacking any finalised "order"...They are irreversibly drawn towards various attractors that exercise a kind of gravity effect. (Urry 2003, 123)

Attractors in systems work in plurality. Therefore, the different pattern effects may work in both collaboration and competition. Some attractors come to dominate and have more influence than others (Haynes 2012). Values in their plurality can have multiple and contradictory influences on policy systems.

Complexity science and values

While the application of concepts from complexity science methodology to public administration has yielded some innovative approaches to understanding the challenges of public policy design and implementation, one of the epistemological problems, however, with taking scientific methods and exporting them into the applied world of social science, is the resulting value base (or apparent lack of an explicit value base).

> the key to managing post normal challenges – where scale and complexity make for a myriad of uncertainties and knowledge gaps – is to develop a more nuanced understanding of science's limits and its unavoidable linkages with values and interests. (Heazle 2010, 37)

Critical approaches to scientific methods in the social sciences posit the historical inevitability and importance of identifying normative influences given the subject focus of social science when compared to natural science. The 'turn to postmodernism' (Seidman 2004) identified applied social science as subjective at its core, because the science is engaged in by humans about humans and therefore requiring values of humanity. Many cultural and postmodern sociological approaches to scientific enquiry in the post-millennium make the same point about society's use of natural science: with reference to information technology, biotech, and similar 'advances' (see Fuller 2007; Fuller 2009). Scientific method and achievement should not dehumanize and worsen the human condition. David Byrne (2011, 38), one of the best known international scholars to promote the methodology of complexity theory in the social sciences, has stated that a structural approach to scientific knowledge must be combined with a call to action on the basis of that knowledge.

Despite this call to realism inherent in complex-based approaches to public management, the fact remains that complexity theory is founded on scientific thinking that is linked to dynamic physical systems in nature like the weather system (Kauffman 1995; Stewart 1995), and therefore complexity-based management practice may ignore normative and value-based aspects of public systems. So how might the application of complexity science be linked to a normative theory that is aware of the different value given to different techniques and outcomes and able to understand value conflicts in the management of public policy? Can a complexity theory-driven approach to public management practice be combined with an academic debate about what values should drive policy and practice?

A normative application of complex adaptive systems methods is possible. The work of Donella H. Meadows (2009), building on her seminal work about the *Limits of Growth* (Meadows et al. 1972) project, with its holistic systems analysis of global economics and issues of sustainability, offers an example of such a workable and applicable method for combining complex systems analysis with an articulation of what optimal public service values could look like. For example, reinforcing market feedback and rapid repetitive behavioural reinforcement, like the repeated and unregulated selling of mortgage securities before the Financial Crisis of 2007, can be argued to be of a negative normative value for society. Such behaviour and interactions undermined economic stability and generated widespread spirals of debt that have had proportionately worse consequences for the poor (Haynes 2012). The more recent account of scientific uncertainty in complex and open policy systems proposed by Heazle (2010) places values, and value-based conflict and debate, at the core of understanding the relevance of science to complex human systems. For Meadows, transformative system paradigm change was most likely when social and political values were changing. At the core of human complex systems is the relationship between values and behaviour.

Values in public policy and management

Values are beliefs and ideas that we hold in our cognitions about what is important in social and cultural life and they directly affect our behaviour and decision-making processes.

> A value is a complex and broad based assessment of an object...characterised by both cognitive and emotive elements...and because a value is part of an individual's definition of self, it is not easily changed and it has the potential to elicit action. (Bozeman 2007, 117)

International social science research has attempted to define priority core global social values and value contradictions across many cultures (see, e.g., World Values Survey, 2012, Stockholm www.worldvalues.org/).

When researching the influence of values on public managers, Molina (2015, 50) defines value as:

> a complex cognitive-emotional preference for some object, quality, or characteristic that serves as either a means to an end (instrumental value) or an end in itself (terminal value).

The pervasiveness of marketization and privatization in public policy and management since the 1980s has been a key value controversy. Indeed, it is at the core of the concept of NPM and its resulting influence on policy and practice (Hughes 2012).

One of the seminal responses to NPM in academia has been the public value thesis (Benington and Moore 2011). At the policy level, this response to NPM argues for more prominence to be given to how public policy and management activities benefit the collective public good (Moore 1995). This approach has been criticized for being too dependent on a managerial rather than an interdisciplinary 'normativity' approach to values (Beck Jorgensen and Rutgers 2015, 9). Moore's more recent work in 2013 further developed his theory to include a more normative approach as it argues for the creation of public value. The public value approach has been developed into an operational process for mapping the complex nature of public value (Alford and Yates 2014). This should include the influence of the diversity of actors involved in policy systems (Bryson et al. 2016).

In addition, a volume of work has been established that looks specifically at the range of values that influence the behaviour of public managers (Stone 2002; Beck Jorgensen and Bozeman 2007; Van Der Wal, De Graaf, and Lawton 2011; Anderson et al. 2012; Box 2015; Molina 2015). This literature is diverse but includes some common themes. There is an analysis of the 'plurality' of public values (Van Der Wal, De Graaf, and Lawton 2011), where many different values are shown to influence public managers, but some are argued to influence policy and practice more than others in any one time and place (Stone 2002). The scale of influence and importance of some values over others is discussed in an influential paper by Beck Jorgensen and Bozeman (2007). Patterns of which values influence 'where' and 'when' is linked to the situational context. Context can be a mix of policy and professional typologies (Molina 2015). The complex mix of which values influence over time means that values have a dynamic interaction with policy and public management (Beck Jorgensen and Vrangbeck 2011; Beck Jorgensen and Rutgers 2015). While the remit of Beck Jorgensen and Bozeman's (2007) categorization is very broad, they are looking for the influence of values on public life across society. Anderson et al. (2012) quantitative project is more focused on the policy process, including a range of political, professional, and administrative respondents. Stone (2002) focused on the influence of value sub-systems on policy implementation while Molina's (2015) recent focus was on value conflict experiences for specific groups of managers and professionals in the public policy arena.

In combination, this literature places values at the core of public management practice and firmly locates management in a collaborative and contested arena of public governance. The dominant focus of NPM after 1980 influenced a preference for values like economy and efficiency over other traditional public values (Bozeman 2007). As Box (2015, 6) comments:

> At the level of daily organisational management, economic efficiency has become especially important, sometimes eclipsing values such as fairness and equity, social justice, constitutionalism and law, and citizen involvement in governance.

Value conflicts

The research of Beck Jorgensen and Bozeman (2007) and Anderson et al. (2012) to classify public values was ambitious in their broad remit to include the full possible range of values. It is important to acknowledge that in comparison to the post-structuralist conclusions of Beck Jorgensen and Bozeman's (2007) discourse, the numerous values identified cannot be assigned to a proposed framework of influence on public managers. Anderson et al. argue that their classification is deliberately more focused. It nevertheless includes elements that while influential on public management are outside the scope of the role of public management. For this reason, and for the purpose of beginning to conceptualize the complex interaction of public values with systems concepts, the conceptual examples for public management proposed by Stone's (2002) and Molina (2015) are used in this paper as a vehicle for understanding value conflicts at the operational level. There are both similarities and differences in their respective approaches. Stone's (2002) model is of four overarching value components that influence the implementation of public policy while Molina's (2015) four sub-categories of values are broader reference points for the behaviour of both public professionals and managers. Molina deals with the day-to-day issues of policy practice. Both these studies employ clusters of values in hierarchical agglomerations to understand the resulting impact on public managers.

Molina (2015) focused on the relationship of values with public management and professional roles and tasks. He used a mixed method with a framework of thirty different values derived from previous related research and literature. These were grouped into four sub-value categories: ethical, professional, democratic, and human. This was on the basis of previous research classifications, such as that used by the United States National Association of Schools of Public Affairs and Administration accreditation standards. The sub-groupings were not mutually exclusive, and some specific values were argued to be present and influential in more than one group. For example, accountability was argued to be an important value in both the ethical and democractic groupings. Using a simple quantitative ranking scale, where each respondent (n = 100) rated an individual value regardless of its sub-grouping, they found different conceptual results occurred for different public employee role types. Role types were classified as 'stewards, magistrates, and advocates.' Ethical values scored highest for magistrates and advocates, but second highest for the professionals (where professional values scored higher). Ethical values were listed as honesty, integrity, social justice, impartiality, incorruptability, courage, and accountability. Qualitative interviews were used to understand the fine grain conceptualization of values in specific work situations for forty-one respondents.

These types of clustered value systems can come into direct conflict in policy systems and cause considerable ethical and practice dilemmas for public managers. Molina (2015, 49–50) explores the value conflicts that public managers experience in practice and proposes that one key definition in the fault line of these conflicts is when 'values of bureaucracy' conflict with 'values of democracy.' Molina associates 'values of democracy' with individual rights, citizenship and participation, and the 'values of bureaucracy' with the requirement for efficiency and effectiveness. These conflicts translate into numerous policy examples and management decisions. For example, a public medical committee examining the efficiency and effectiveness of a drug decides that the cost benefit is not proven for a given population size. But in contrast an individual argues to their professional practitioner, who agrees, that such a prescription is warranted on the basis of their unique individual circumstances and their lack of realistic and available options with other treatments.

Similar to Molina, but with a different emphasis, Stone (2002) proposes four overarching cluster components of public management values. These are derived from her framework of public policy goals which she argues are compatible with other approaches to classification in the literature. Stone's approach is located in the realm of policy implementation studies. She is expounding a technical model whereby political policy is passed to public managers for implementation, but value conflicts cannot be avoided. Stone's model is therefore used in this paper as another vehicle for understanding specific aspects of value conflict as manifestations of complexity within the system that public managers operate. Stone's model has four clusters of values that are agglomerated into dominant practice approaches. First, there is the collective public ethos of public protection. This is the preservation of the public good. It acknowledges public and welfare benefits of the collective endeavour as organized through government and state interventions in society. At the level of detail, this can include rationale for providing services such as community safety, justice, education, health, and more.

Second, there is a requirement to value the efficient use of resources. Resources are finite in time and place. Public managers are at the heart of systems that have to make collaborative decisions about what should be planned as priority action. Some actions have to be prioritized over others. When resources are committed to programmes and operations, managers are responsible for ensuring they are effective. Resources must be used in the public interest. Often this involves maintaining a strong culture of public service and commitment to public citizens. Managers need to review and evaluate services to ensure they continue to deliver appropriate public benefits.

Third, public managers are expected to deliver services that are equitable. This means treating people fairly and similarly while taking into account their individuality and the diversity of individuals in society. This needs to be considered alongside the goal of equality. While equity focuses on whether people are treated the same by policy mechanisms and allocations, equality deals more with the outcomes of policy, in terms of income, wealth, and health. Conflicts can arise in the focus on equality over equity. It might, for example, lead to a debate about building positive discrimination into a mechanism of allocation, so that those who are systematically and institutionally structurally disadvantaged are prioritized in the policy process over others. Some will attempt to argue this is inequitable.

Fourth, public managers need to balance the public good with the liberty and dignity of the individual. For example, in situations where there is no discernible or immediate collective public benefit, high-quality services may still be important and public benefits can still be articulated and argued precisely because the dignity of the individual is retained, thus preserving the overall value of humanity. Examples are, end of life care, where there is no cure, or the rehabilitation of an offender (preferencing rehabilitation over punishment) after a serious crime has been committed. Again there may be considerable conflicts in policy processes when managers are faced with strong arguments based on the liberty and dignity of one citizen. It is the complexity of these value frameworks in complex policy systems that lead to conflicts that effect the practice of managers.

Value hierarchies

An additional component of the complexity of the interaction of values in policy systems is their hierarchical nature. As stated earlier in the paper, a feature of complex policy systems is they operate across levels, typically macro, meso, and micro.

In organizations, dominant value attractor patterns that do influence both individual and group behaviour result over time (Kontopoulos 1998), but these resulting patterns of influence are not always logical, optimal, or desirable from a public service user perspective. Molina (2015) notes the influence of role on how specific value-based decisions are made. For example, whether the primary role is as manager, professional, or advocate. This results in different value hierarchies being applied in a given situation. Similarly, if a person has a generic public employment with aspects of all these roles, they will often experience role conflict within themselves and their own cognitions (Festinger, Riecken, and Schachter 1956). The application of public values is both a personal and interconnected organizational activity. Hierarchies of public values can be defined as composed of an interconnected and dynamic range of individual, professional, organizational, and legal principles about public interests (Van Wart 1998).

Public managers may experience conflicts as individuals or within a team environment. Vink et al. (2015) describe these value conflicts as 'moral conflicts' that influence decision-making on the front line of public policy. The experience of these conflicts may result in a later change in values hierarchies and how they are applied by managers. The whole application of values is dynamic not static. Over time, some values rise in the hierarchy, being considered as more important than others, while others fall and are considered less important, but still have some influence. For example, should recognition of individual liberty in situations, where religious culture has a strong influence on neighbourhoods, overrule gender discrimination, as in the case of patriarchy in religious neighbourhoods? In the main, policy is deciding in Western societies that in the hierarchy of public values, gender equality, and reducing gender discrimination is more important than preserving ideas of patriarchy in religious culture, this when these values come into direct conflict in the public sphere through manifestations of gender oppressive behaviour. But these value-based tensions can take many years to evolve and be challenging to work out in operational policy areas.

The concept of value hierarchies shows the conflicting nature of values, in that they are founded on different logics and beliefs. Some values exert more influence than others in relation to the context of a specific situation and the resulting operational decision. Value hierarchies are not singular but multiple, for example, they may be defined and imposed by organizations, professional groups, and individuals and not necessarily in the same hierarchical order, or relating to the same patterning of comparable situations. The similarity of situations for managers, as they try to match circumstances to a value reference framework, is likely to be informed by 'patterning,' an important concept in complex systems analysis (Snowden and Boone 2007). Here the manager tries to systematically compare the similarity and difference of past and present cases.

At the micro level, managers refer to cognitive hierarchies of values in their own work. This includes cognitive reference to their own personal history, as well as training and professional experience. An example of such a hierarchy is presented in Table 1. Managers will reference in their decision-making the values that they consider to be important in the context of organizational hierarchies of priorities as defined in their organization strategies and performance policies (Haynes 2015). It is

Table 1. Organization and personal values that influence the public manager.

Public manager – professional employment		Personal – individual life choices	
Value	Behavioural example	Value	Behavioural example
Public protection	Protection of vulnerable from harm, abuse, and exploitation	Duty of care in family and close relationships as a reciprocal obligation	Frequent communications Financial support
Individual liberty	Importance of dignity and choice for service user, including rights to diversity of culture and religion	Relationship interdependence	Respect for partner's and household members personal space
Efficient use of resources	Deploy resources to give the maximum collective benefit	Best use of resources in partner relationships	Plan and prioritize household expenditures, in collaboration
Effectiveness of interventions	Conceptualize longer term outcomes such as quality of life and how these relate to outputs like health treatments	Cooperation and sharing in lifestyle planning	Forward planning in close relationships, such as investments for housing, education, and retirement

often in these organizational practices that they find implicit values to drive their operations. They will also be affected by their personal history and current personal situations, as demonstrated in Table 1. For example, the value of public protection will manifest itself as behaviour to protect the most vulnerable in society. Or in a personal situation, will be reflected in reciprocal obligations as a duty of care to close family members.

The application of values is a cognitive process. The manager uses their limited cognitive ability to process complex information. The cognitive is itself a complex system. Kahneman (2012) has proposed that the cognitive has two main sub-systems. System one is fast and reactive, drawing on personal and historical feelings and emotions, while system two is slow and more rational, as it reflects on available similar past patterns and all available reference points of information.

Here there is an important link between personal identity, personal values, and how they find cognitive affirmation, or not, in a workplace organization (Herriot and Scott-Jackson 2002).

This has some similarities with Paarlberg and Perry (2007) research findings about the primacy of personal values in organizational settings, and the dynamic feedback between personal and employment values and identities. Paarlberg and Perry (2007) found that employees' personal values were more significant an influence on their behaviour than any subsequent influences by an organization to enforce its own corporate values. If employers wanted to change the values of their work force, the best management method appeared to be through the mediation of middle managers, and in the main looking to make explicit connections between employees' existing social and cultural values and the workplace.

Individual values and beliefs from time to time will come into conflict with organizational values. Similar to Maslow's (1943) 'hierarchy of needs,' we can identify an individual's hierarchy of values, and at the root of this is physical survival. People will quickly defer collective aspirations in order to ensure their physical survival and that of their immediate family. An employee with a short temporary contact, experiencing low pay or facing redundancy, will be more preoccupied with their own and family's survival than that of their employer. Even a long-term serving public professional will defer the care and commitment they put into a public organization when their own or family health and care is fundamentally challenged. They will inevitably be less able to demonstrate an explicit and behavioural level of commitment to the values of the organization and its strategies, at that point in time.

It cannot be assumed that values will influence behaviour via a singular process of rational consideration of alternative courses of action (Arthur 2015). A 'value action' gap may be evident where the expectation of what behaviour will result from a given value does not happen (Blake 1999). One reason for this is the difficulty in clarifying a simple expression of values. When people try to assess complexity of circumstances, they have a tendency to fragment the detail into stages and sections of decision-making that they feel are easier to judge, but this does not necessarily make them any better at assessing the whole situation before them. The reason for this is that they are likely to weigh one part of the situation wrongly, when compared with the others. This is the so-called subadditivity problem (Fox and Tversky 2000).

Similarly, the application of values to cognitive decision-making is in part determined by personal historical influences and biases that are not immediately obvious or conscious when decisions are being made. It is important therefore that the education and training of public managers does what it can to address this: 'using behavioural science to direct people towards better choices' (Lunn 2014, 9). It is also important to place these individual cognitive complexities in the wider arena of a complex systems approach to public policy and management. What is needed for public policy is a systems model of management practice that incorporates an understanding of the values influencing policy developments. This allows public managers to make sense of change alongside their own professional values, training, and personal values perspective. In diverse, modern societies that are evolving towards increasing complexity, values and beliefs are similarly complex and mirror these social evolutions.

Figure 1 proposes a hierarchical value reference point for public managers for understanding how values begin to combine dynamically in complex policy systems. The first influence on a manager is their own personal history much of which gives a quick and emotional response to the circumstances they face. This is what Kahneman (2012) refers to as 'system one.' The next influence on the manager is family and community values. Again, much of the influence here is historical and influenced by community, neighbourhood, and perhaps religious stories and sub-cultures. Also influential are the managerial and professional values assimilated during study, training, and supervision. Finally, managers are subjected to the short-term arguments, and ideas of their seniors and politicians often made explicit in political manifestos and organizational mission statements. Like the seminal 'hierarchy of needs' (Maslow 1943), situational context has much to do with where a manager focuses on in this hierarchy during a particular public policy decision.

Although the source of immediate policy values is external to the individual, personal history has sown seeds within the individual's cognitive system that will inform future system interaction and feedback. The manager's cognitive process

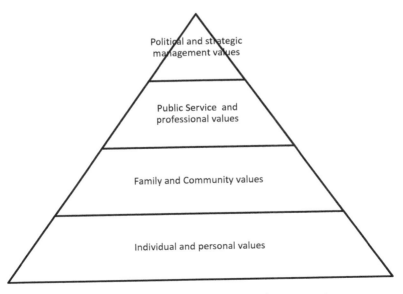

Figure 1. Hierarchical and multiple value influences: public policy and management.

becomes an interactive part of the feedback system. Having the insight to understand how this operates becomes a major element in the manager's portfolio of skills. In the context of complex public organizations, public managers need awareness of their own biases. They also need reflective space and peer support in the organization to make more informed 'system two' decisions (Kahneman 2012). This requires support for the right forms of cooperative practice, such as mentoring and coaching.

Applying complexity theory concepts to understand the matrix of value influences

How can we make sense of the overall matrix and minutiae of multiple values influencing the public policy process and the managers working within it? For the purpose of summarizing the contribution that complexity theory offers to this explanation of the influence of public values, we return to the definition of a complex system based on Cilliers (1998), as summarized earlier in this paper.

A policy system has many cases; these include policy actors and organizations. The public value frame of reference of each of these cases is different. Each individual public manager has their own personal history, and (despite a shared professional training and experience) each will have a unique influence in their value frame of reference. Different aspects of these values will be shared across the social and policy world with others, and some patterns of similarity will result. Given the importance of these value components as the minutiae, we can think of values as elements of the system as one key building block that contributes to defining the overall system itself. Several of the studies mentioned in this paper are important in identifying the minutiae and diversity of these value elements as plentiful components in the system (Beck Jorgensen and Bozeman, 2007; Anderson et al. 2012). Values are important building blocks in a complex policy system.

These values get expressed by cases in their communications and behaviours. Therefore, cases share in their own unique combined ways complex dynamic inter-actions that take place across the policy system. No pattern of these complex inter-actions will ever be identically repeated, but similar patterns can be observed by research and summarized as typologies at higher levels in the system (Stone 2002; Molina 2015). The influence of values is never predictable in detail, but at the higher organizational and national levels, models of forecasts are possible. In complexity theory, such pattern-based forecasts are probabilistic in that, like weather forecasting, there is always possibilities of them being wrong. The inherent weakness in these models of value patterns is that they are based on partial and limited information. Similarly, the managers' own process of working with values is always based on a restricted viewpoint as they have limited information to guide their own reference to values.

Individuals will be prone to the reinforcing and checking feedback received from those in their immediate local system. That is their peers, own managers, and political influences. In this way, the system that policy managers inhabit is only partially open to the influence of other values in any one time and place and never equally open to all influences. The relative degree of openness of policy systems to political democracy and political influence is without question one key 'structural coupling' between sub-systems of influence (Luhmann 1996). One article, for example, argues the positive contribution that open deliberative democracy can make to resolving value conflicts in some policy system environments (Dryzek and Braithwaite 2000).

The dynamic flow of energy in human systems is generated by physical life itself and the propensity of actors to feel and act. In this sense, although beyond the scope of this particular paper, we cannot rule out the energy of emotional affect and subjective feeling and its interaction with public values. This is an area for future research.

Cilliers (1998) also mentions the importance of historical influence on the system. One of the partial determinants of the dynamic influence of values on public policy is through the history of actors, organizations, and states. The total value influence in any one time and space is always subject to some historical influence from the values that have come to influence policy before, and there is no 'year zero' for any policy creation. Much of the public values scholarship discussed in this paper identifies aspects of these histories (Bozeman 2007; Beck Jorgensen and Bozeman, 2007; Beck Jorgensen and Vrangbeck 2011; Anderson et al. 2012).

Finally, we return to the concept of attractors. The marketization of society and public policy has seen an increasing influence of economic values and rules of operation that relate to monetary value (Sandel 2013). These monetary attractors are by no means exclusive in their ability to control and determine the future patterns of public policy, but they have in recent years dominated policy systems and risen to the top of the value hierarchy and therefore influenced specific policy decisions (Kontopoulos 1998). Alternatively, the complex interaction of different values has the potential to create unstable systems where the primary values are unclear. Indeed, in the words of Eppel, Matheson, and Walton (2011, 49), 'When there are a lot of attractor patterns operating, the system appears more chaotic.' This leads to the potential for value conflicts, where there is explicit or implicit disagreement about what the social hierarchy of operational values should be.

Conclusion

Values and their interaction with public policy are an important topic for the application of complexity theory to public management. It has long been argued that reflection, understanding, and development of organizational culture, in terms of facilitating constructive organizational values and communication, is a key skill for managers in any organization, especially within complex organizations (Stacey 2011). There are ethical issues about developing organizational culture but it is inevitably part of the general management sphere of operation. In private organizations, employees need to be able to feel an affinity with the service and products on offer, so they really do believe in the value of what they are selling and delivering. There are problems for all organizations if their employees feel a cognitive dissonance (Festinger, Riecken, and Schachter 1956) about what the organization is doing, and it will affect their motivation and performance at work. What drives public service quality is the macro public value of the contribution that service makes. This has a complex relationship with the plurality of public values.

If an organization reinforces collective values and makes explicit the link between core service values and successful outcomes and the ethical benefits, employees will arguable be less likely to retreat to forms of individualism and seek individual rewards, especially where they can explicitly share in the rewards of the organization and the public good. For this reason, public management education needs to enable managers to locate their own values alongside those of their organization and society and to begin to determine how these value hierarchies influence their own management behaviour and decision-making.

There are dangers if the scientific objectification of complexity theory preferences hard material patterns and mechanisms while ignoring the values of actors and the culture of public organizations. This can undermine the further use and development of complexity approaches to management in public services. Value influences add a layer of dynamic complexity, in addition to the complexity of communications, rules, processes, and resource flows.

Failure to include this values framework in the debate about how best to manage complex systems will leave managers prone to moral failure, such as that identified in the Staffordshire Hospital Inquiry in England (Francis 2013). This inquiry concluded that the value of care was forgotten due to a mechanical focus on performance management. Being clearer about the impact of values, and working through debates about complex hierarchies of values and their influence on organizational behaviour, is a constructive development in contemporary management practice.

Disclosure statement

No potential conflict of interest was reported by the author.

ORCID

Philip Haynes ⓘ http://orcid.org/0000-0002-9880-356X

References

Alford, J., and S. Yates. 2014. "Mapping Public Value Processes." *International Journal of Public Sector Management* 27 (4): 334–352. doi:10.1108/IJPSM-04-2013-0054.
Allen, P., S. Maguire, and B. McKelvey. 2011. *The Sage Handbook of Complexity and Management.* London: Sage.
Anderson, L. B., T. B. Jørgensen, A. M. Kjeldsen, L. H. Pedersen, and K. Vrangbæk. 2012. "Public Value Dimensions: Developing and Testing a Multi-Dimensional Classification." *International Journal of Public Administration* 35 (11): 715–728. doi:10.1080/01900692.2012.670843.
Arthur, B. 2015. "Cognition: The Black Box of Economics." In *Complexity and the Economy*, edited by B. Arthur, 158–170. Oxford: Oxford University Press.
Beck Jorgensen, T., and B. Bozeman. 2007. "Public Values: An Inventory." *Administration and Society* 39 (3): 354–381. doi:10.1177/0095399707300703.
Beck Jorgensen, T., and M. Rutgers. 2015. "Public Values: Core or Confusion? Introduction to the Centrality and Puzzlement of Public Values Research." *American Review of Public Administration* 45 (1): 3–12. doi:10.1177/0275074014545781.

Beck Jorgensen, T., and K. Vrangbeck. 2011. "Value Dynamics: Towards a Framework for Analyzing Public Value Changes." *International Journal of Public Administration* 34: 486–496. doi:10.1080/01900692.2011.583776.

Benington, J., and M. H. Moore. 2011. *Public Value: Theory and Practice*. London: Palgrave.

Blake, J. 1999. "Overcoming the 'Value-Action Gap' in Environmental Policy: Tensions between National Policy and Local Experience." *Local Environment: the International Journal of Justice and Sustainability* 4 (3): 257–278. doi:10.1080/13549839908725599.

Boulton, J., P. Allen, and C. Bowman. 2015. *Embracing Complexity: Strategy Perspectives for an Age of Turbulence*. Oxford: Oxford University Press.

Box, R. 2015. *Public Service Values*. London: Routledge.

Bozeman, B. 2007. *Public Values and Public Interest: Counterbalancing Economic Individualism*. Washington, DC: Georgetown University Press.

Bryson, J., S. Alessandro, J. Bennington, and E. Sorensen. 2016. "Towards a Multi-Actor Theory of Public Value Co-Creation." *Public Management Review* 19 (5): 640–654. doi:10.1080/14719037.2016.1192164.

Byrne, D. 1998. *Complexity Theory and the Social Sciences*. London: Routledge.

Byrne, D. 2011. *Applying Social Science: The Role of Social Research in Politics, Policy and Practice*. Bristol: Policy Press.

Byrne, D., and G. Callaghan. 2013. *Complexity Theory and the Social Sciences: The State of the Art*. Abingdon: Routledge.

Cilliers, P. 1998. *Complexity and Postmodernism*. London: Sage.

Dryzek, J., and V. Braithwaite. 2000. "On the Prospects for Democratic Deliberation: Values Analysis Applied to Australian Politics." *Political Psychology* 21 (2): 241–266. doi:10.1111/pops.2000.21.issue-2.

Eppel, E., A. Matheson, and M. Walton. 2011. "Applying Complexity Theory to New Zealand Public Policy: Principles for Practice." *Policy Quarterly* 7 (1): 48–55.

Festinger, L., H. Riecken, and S. Schachter. 1956. *When Prophecy Fails*. New York: Harper and Row.

Fox, C., and A. Tversky. 2000. "A Belief-Based Account of Decision under Uncertainty." In *Choices, Values and Frames*, edited by D. K. A. A. Tversky, 118–142. Cambridge: Cambridge University Press.

Francis, R. 2013. *Report of the Mid Staffordshire NHS Foundation Trust Public Enquiry*. London: House of Commons.

Fuller, S. 2007. *New Frontiers in Science and Technology Studies*. London: Polity Press.

Fuller, S. 2009. "Humanity: The Always Already, or Never to Be, Object of the Social Sciences?" In *The Social Sciences and Democracy*, edited by J. V. Brouwel, 240–264. Basingstoke: Palgrave Macmillan.

Haynes, P. 2012. *Public Policy beyond the Financial Crisis; An International Comparative Study*. Abingdon: Routledge.

Haynes, P. 2015. *Managing Complexity in the Public Services*. 2nd ed. Abingdon: Routledge.

Heazle, M. 2010. *Uncertainty in Policy Making: Values and Evidence in Complex Decisions*. London: Earthscan.

Herriot, P., and W. Scott-Jackson. 2002. "Globalization, Social Identities and Employment." *British Journal of Management* 13 (3): 249–257. doi:10.1111/bjom.2002.13.issue-3.

Hughes, O. 2012. *Public Management and Administration*. 4th ed. London: Palgrave.

Kahneman, D. 2012. *Thinking, Fast and Slow*. London: Penguin.

Kauffman, S. A. 1995. *At Home in the Universe: The Search for Laws of Self Organisation and Complexity*. Harmondsworth: Penguin.

Klijn, E.-H. 2008. "Complexity Theory and Public Administration: What's New?" *Public Management Review* 10 (3): 299–318. doi:10.1080/14719030802002675.

Kontopoulos, K. 1998. *The Logics of Social Structure*. Cambridge: Cambridge University Press.

Lane, J. 2000. *The New Public Management*. London: Routledge.

Luhmann, N. 1996. *Social Systems*. Stanford: Stanford University Press.

Lunn, P. 2014. *Regulatory Policy and Behavioural Economics*. Paris: OECD Publishing.

Maslow, A. 1943. "A Theory of Human Motivation." *Psychological Review* 50 (4): 370–396. doi:10.1037/h0054346.

Meadows, D. 2009. *Thinking in Systems: A Primer*. London: Earthscan.

Meadows, D. H., D. L. Meadows, J. Randers, and W. W. Behrens. 1972. *The Limits to Growth*. London: Signet.

Molina, A. D. 2015. "The Virtues of Administration: Values and the Practice of Public Service." *Administrative Theory & Praxis* 37 (1): 49–69. doi:10.1080/10841806.2015.999636.

Moore, M. 1995. *Creating Public Value: Strategic Management in Government*. Cambridge, MA: Harvard University Press.

Moore, M. 2013. *Recognising Public Value*. Harvard: Harvard University Press.

Paarlberg, L., and J. Perry. 2007. "Values Management: Aligning Employee Values and Organization Goals." *The American Review of Public Administration* 37 (4): 387–408. doi:10.1177/0275074006297238.

Pollitt, C. 2009. "Complexity Theory and Evolutionary Public Administration: A Sceptical Afterword." In *Managing Complex Governance Systems*, edited by G. Teisman, A. Van Buuren, and L. Gerrits, 213–230. London: Routledge.

Rhodes, M., J. Murphy, J. Muir, and J. Murray. 2011. *Public Management and Complexity Theory: Richer Decision Making in the Public Services*. London: Routledge.

Sandel, M. 2013. *What Money Can't Buy: The Moral Limits of Markets*. London: Penguin.

Seidman, S. 2004. *Social Theory: Contested Knowledge*. Oxford: Blackwell.

Snowden, D., and M. Boone. 2007. "A Leader's Framework for Decision Making." *Harvard Business Review*, Nov.: 69–77.

Stacey, R. 2011. *Strategic Management and Organisational Dynamics: The Challenge of Complexity*. 6th ed. London: FT Press.

Stewart, I. 1995. *Nature's Numbers: Discovering Order and Pattern in the Universe*. London: Weidenfield and Nicolson.

Stone, D. A. 2002. *Policy Paradox: The Art of Political Decision Making*. New York: W.W. Norton and Company.

Teisman, G., and E.-H. Klijn. 2008. "Complexity Theory and Public Management: An Introduction." *Public Management Review* 10 (3): 287–298. doi:10.1080/14719030802002451.

Teisman, G., A. Van Buuren, and L. Gerrits. 2009. *Managing Complex Government Systems: Dynamics, Self Organisation and Coevolution in Public Investments*. London: Routledge.

Urry, J. 2003. *Global Complexity*. Cambridge: Polity.

van der Wal, Z., G. De Graaf, and A. Lawton. 2011. "Competing Values in Public Management." *Public Management Review* 13 (3): 331–341. doi:10.1080/14719037.2011.554098.

Van Wart, M. 1998. *Changing Public Values*. New York: Garland.

Vink, E., L. Tummers, V. Bekkers, and M. Musheno. 2015. "Decision Making at the Front Line: Exploring Coping with Moral Conflicts during Public Service Delivery." In *Making Public Policy Decisions: Expertise, Skills and Experience*, edited by D. Alexander and J. Lewis, 112–128. London: Routledge.

'What insights do fitness landscape models provide for theory and practice in public administration?'

Mary Lee Rhodes and Conor Dowling

ABSTRACT

This paper assesses the extent to which a fitness landscape (FL) perspective on complex social systems offers useful insights for both theory and practice in public administration. It has been claimed that FL models have strong potential for integrating existing theory and facilitating the development of models for theory development and testing as well as offering the prospect of a better understanding of the adaptive moves of agents in search of a better 'fit' with their environment. In this paper, we examine these claims through a thematic synthesis of recent literature purporting to adopt this perspective in public management. Through a systematic review of the literature, we identify the key themes in the application of FLs to theory and practice and the extent to which authors are reaching any conclusions on the precise use of each of the elements of FL models in public management contexts. We conclude that the use of FL models is underdeveloped and that further development would be particularly useful in the context of governance network theory. We close with four specific recommendations for further research and development.

Introduction

The state of public administration (PA) research makes it difficult to grasp a comprehensive understanding of its current state of development. This is further complicated as specialization spawns research communities that often do not, and sometimes cannot, talk with each other. Furthermore, 'government officials and other decision makers increasingly encounter a daunting class of problems that involve systems ... that are prone to surprising, large-scale, seemingly uncontrollable behaviours' (OECD 2009, 2). For many, the traditional tools and strategies of public management seem ill-equipped to deal with contemporary challenges and complexities (Chapman 2002; Weber 2005; OECD 2009).

As a result of the fragmentation of theory and the complexity of practice, scholars and practitioners have been turning to complexity theory (Haynes 2003; Teisman, Van Buuren, and Gerrits 2009; Rhodes et al. 2011). Over the last 20 years, there has been an accelerating development and application of complexity-based theories to integrate the existing PA research and theory-building, and to a lesser extent to address the complexity of the practitioner's world. This paper seeks to understand how one type of complexity theory – namely fitness landscape (FL) models – is being developed both as an integrative theory of PA and a guide for practice.

In the next section, we summarize the FL model and how it has been translated from biology to a range of social science disciplines, drawing principally on Gerrits & Marks (2014b) and Rhodes (2012). We then outline our methodology for systematically reviewing the literature linking FLs to PA and drawing out the main themes that arise from this review. The main body of the paper is a discussion of the literature review and the extent to which the various themes identified appear and are – or are not – converging. We conclude with an assessment of the use of FL models in PA and suggest how the application of these must develop, in order to achieve the potential for contribution to theory and/or practice identified by those (and other) authors.

Origins and translation of the FL model

As noted in Gerrits and Marks (2014b), Wright (1932) based his original ideas for fitness on a conference presentation with little room for mathematic explanation; he wrote his theory in words using the metaphor of the adaptive landscape to explain its main properties. Originally in biology, the Darwinian 'fitness' of biological trait describes how successfully an organism with that trait can pass on its genes. The more likely that an organism is able to survive and reproduce, the higher the fitness of that organism is. In FLs, each 'location' on the landscape has a different fitness value, which is determined by the combination of traits that define that location (see Figure 1). There may be any number of trait combinations that have similar levels of fitness, but the nature of reproduction means that organisms cannot randomly move around the landscape, but rather are limited as the number of changes that can be made in any one period (this is defined as the reproduction cycle of the organism). The distance between locations on the landscape represents the degree to which the combination of traits are similar or different – with short distances representing small differences between organisms and long distances representing quite different combinations of traits for the organism under study. The degree to which changing one or more traits results in a

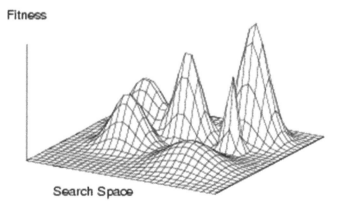

Figure 1. Graphic representation of a fitness landscape.

change in fitness will define the structure of the landscape – with peaks in the FL representing the payoff for optimized adaptation over time. In biological systems, organisms occupying fitness peaks thrive, while those in the 'valleys' die off. Those on the slopes move towards extinction or survival depending up the direction of the changes made through recombination's of traits via reproduction. Wright's mathematical formulation of the landscape model was designed to examine how the frequency of genotypes could change over time based on their movement over the landscape and location (or not) on fitness peaks.

Kauffman and Levin (1987) developed and modified Wright's work on a general FL model that then included a feature in which the fitness contribution of each N gene in a genotype depends on the interaction with K other genes. In other words, the fitness value of a particular allele for a gene is affected by whether or not another allele is present in a different gene.[1] The average number of gene/allele interactions in an organism is represented by K. This is the so called NK-model. Gerrits and Marks (2014b) identify a number of other authors that contributed to the development of this model over time and observed that, 'the model's alluring nature is that it "allows for a very general description of *any* system consisting of N components with K interactions between components and in which there can be any number of states for each N" (Weber 1998, 135 as quoted in Gerrits and Marks 2014b, 3 – italics in the original).'

Gerrits and Marks (2014b) go on to analyse the translation of the NK model from the natural science origins of Wright and Kauffman into the social sciences through a citation frequency study, and in so doing identify that Levinthal's (1997) article 'Adaptation on rugged landscapes' was a seminal one in this translation process. In this article, Levinthal equated 'N' to the different attributes of a firm and created a model that randomly assigned different combinations of Ns with different levels of fitness. In addition, he proposed that K represented the interdependency between attributes in achieving these levels of fitness. Levinthal supported his translation of the NK model to the business world by referring to the well-developed theories of 'strategic fit' in management literature going back to Chandler (1962). In the strategy literature, it is well accepted that firms are constantly having to adapt to changes in the environment and have a number of key strategic choices that they can make which will affect profitability, and that these choices are interdependent. The movement of organizations on the landscape is driven by the selection of different values for each attribute – with some constraints on the number of changes that can be made in any one 'turn.' In the management/economics disciplines, most authors define 'fitness' as profitability or similar financial return measures. However, this consensus on what constitutes fitness is not the case in most other social sciences.

Extending the basic organizational model outlined in Levinthal and Warglein (1999) and Rhodes (2012) proposed a general framework for translating NK models into a theory of governance in PA. The framework consisted of three basic components: (1) independent, heterogeneous organizational agents, that seek to maximize individual outcomes by moving around a landscape; (2) a landscape made up of the range of decisions and environmental factors (N) that are interdependent to some degree (K) and which affect the level to which agent outcomes may be achieved; and (3) measures of outcomes that have both individual and systemic relevance. Drawing on forty-eight cases of organizational agents in the housing system in Ireland, she mapped these components to the observed and reported behaviour of agents and the system overall and concluded that while a number of insights for theory and practice arose from this analysis, there were an even greater number of problems to be solved before it could be claimed that FL models represented the essential features of PA theory or practice. In particular, she identified three gaps: (1) specifying the nature of 'fitness'; (2) accounting for relationships among agents and their effect on the choices made and the level of fitness achieved; and (3) addressing the dynamics of information creation and dissemination among agents.

Gerrits and Marks (2014a) directly address the second of the gaps identified by Rhodes (2012) when they return to Kauffman (1993) to explain that FLs offer the prospect of a framework that could help understand how the adaptive moves of agents in search of a better 'fit' have a *reciprocal* influence on other agents (emphasis ours). Following the typical interpretation of the NK model, the structure of the landscape – made up of the relevant 'N's and a defined level of 'K' – is static, while the movement of agents across the landscape is dynamic. However, the fitness values assigned to each combination of 'N's along the dimensions of variation can vary depending upon the adaptive moves of agent which deform the landscape of its partners. Essentially, the adaptation of one agent will influence the success of strategies adopted by other organisms. Gerrits (2012) explored this reciprocal relationship in more detail in what he called 'co-evolutionary public decision-making.'

The elements of FL models described above provide the bases for the themes that we looked for in the systematic literature review (SLR). In particular, we analysed the extent to which authors specified 'N,' 'K,' 'Agents,' 'Fitness,' the driver, and/or rules of movement across the landscape – often referred to as 'search processes,' relationships among agents and/or the dynamics of information exchange.

We also wanted to understand the basic use of FLs in the PA literature – applying the categories of 'modes of inquiry' identified in Gerrits and Marks (2014a) review of FLs in the social sciences. They identify five 'modes of inquiry': metaphors, sense-making, modelling, theorizing, and mapping cases. In their conclusion, they state that the use of FLs is 'underdeveloped in PA, especially if compared to how it is maturing in economics and organization and management studies (12).' Our paper seeks to go deeper into the PA literature and assess the current prevalence of each mode and then to extend this analysis to identify the key components of FLs embraced and applied as described in the previous paragraph.

Systematic review methodology

As outlined by Tranfield, Denyer, and Smart (2003), a systematic review of literature should aim to be replicable, exclusive, aggregative, and algorithmic. This review accomplishes the first three of these characteristics through a structured and clearly defined set of search and exclusion/inclusion criteria as described below. However, the identification of themes by its nature is more qualitative, though we do 'seed' this process with categories defined by other authors. Nevertheless, at this stage we must concede that our classification of themes in the publications selected may benefit from further refinement through further analysis.

Our approach to selecting articles that represented the use of the FL concept in PA was built on the previous work by Gerrits and Marks (2014b) in which they undertook a broad sweep of literature sources to identify publications in the social sciences that dealt with the FL models. In their search, they identified 230 relevant publications and selected 162 for analysis. The authors also kindly provided their working database of articles which contained 333 articles. Our starting point was this database and we identified eighteen articles that were dealing with applications of the FL concept to PA. We took a fairly tightly constrained approach to defining PA, excluding articles that dealt with organizations in general, public policy-making, democracy, or law. We did, however, consider 'public management' to be a synonym for PA and included any articles dealing with public management in this analysis. The specific inclusion/exclusion criteria used are summarized below.

Inclusion criteria

- Peer reviewed journal articles
- SLRs, i.e. literature surveys with defined research questions, search process, data extraction, and data presentation
- Meta-analyses (MA)
- Full-article publication (not abstract alone)
- English-language publications
- PDF file format

Exclusion criteria

- Informal literature surveys (no defined research questions, no search process, no defined data extraction or data analysis process)
- Academic papers not subject to peer review
- Duplicate publications unless duplicate studies contain unique outcome data.

The first step in data collection was to review previous MA and reviews of the subject. Two prominent articles were used: the review by Gerrits and Marks (2014a) and the exploration of complex adaptive system dynamics by Rhodes (2012). Both of these papers comprehensively reviewed the literature examining the use of FLs in PA. The authors conducted broad searches of major academic journals and the resulting papers represent the most current synthesis of the use of FLs and PA. The most relevant articles from these papers were automatically included in our review, producing seventeen articles, two of these were common to both Gerrits & Marks (2014) and Rhodes (2012). These articles were selected by identifying key uses of fitness landscapes, including mapping, theorizing, and modelling cases. An additional article, Zvoleff and Li (2013), was taken from the extended list of sources used by Gerrits & Marks (2014) in their review; again this was subject to the same assessment process based on the article's key use of FLs.

To ensure our review was as current as possible, we conducted our own search of business and social science databases. We did not restrict this search by date. The keywords used for the title and subject fields were FLs, NK model, PA, performance landscapes, social science, complexity theory, and public policy. The articles found were subject to the same inclusion criteria of their core use of FLs. This process produced many duplicate papers which had already been identified as well as an additional two articles: 'Teisman, Van Buuren, and Gerrits (2009),' and 'Weber (2005).' We also searched in a range of PA journals just using the key phrase 'fitness landscape' and in complexity journals just using the keyword, 'public administration.' This resulted in an additional five articles. We supplemented our search process by examining the reference lists of the studies collected to identify any further articles, but this did not produce any additional material. Note that we did not include articles that simply mentioned FLs as one of several different complexity approaches that could be adopted.

With the completion of our search process, we had collected twenty-seven articles for our review. Within this number, there are a range of papers including pure research, pure practice, and a combination of both. We initially segmented articles into the five common modes of use as suggested by Gerrits & Mark (2012). The general applications for FLs fit into metaphor and sense-making use categories. Articles which had more specific FL uses were segmented into modelling, theorizing, and mapping cases. We then took this division of modes a step further and analysed how agents, landscape, and fitness were being used or defined in the articles, if at all. An example of an exemplary article in the review is a study by Lazer and Friedman (2007). This article references a large amount of supporting literature to make an argument for using a FL as a modelling approach along with social network analysis to represent relationships among agents. It is methodologically rigorous and the reader is given clear meaning for agents, landscape, and fitness.

Thematic analysis of the use of FLs in public management

Table 1 shows the results of the 'modes of inquiry' analysis of the twenty-seven articles selected for this review. The first two columns show our assessment of whether the article is focused on theory or practice or a combination of both. The next five columns indicate the mode of inquiry present in the publication based on the definitions in Gerrits and Marks (2014a). Note that we have grouped 'metaphors' and sense-making under the heading 'General use' to reflect the original authors' observation that these are similar modes. The remaining three modes – modelling, theorizing, and Mapping – were grouped under the category of 'Specific use,' to reflect our own assessment that these were associated with greater efforts at specifica-tion of the various components of the FL model.

The first observation that we can make from Table 1 is that theoretical contributions are more prevalent than practice-oriented contributions. In fact, of the twenty-seven articles analysed, only three of these were focused solely on the implications for practice. While this may be an artefact of our selection criteria for the search, it is not a surprising finding given the challenge of interpreting and applying FL models to practise and the lack of clear advantage in outcomes or process for doing so. Until such time as there are clear and easily understood advantages for managers in PA to adopt an FL perspective, it is unlikely that consultants, professional associations, trade journals, or agencies will incorporate this into their publications to any significant extent.

In terms of the five modes of inquiry, the two that appear most often are 'modelling' and 'sense-making' – which was somewhat unexpected given the state-ment by Gerrits and Marks (2014b) that the use of FLs in PA was 'underdeveloped.' Given this assessment, we anticipated that there would be little in the way of 'specific use' modes and that the more 'general use' modes would dominate the PA applica-tions. The fact that attempts at 'modelling' predominate suggests a more developed use of FLs; however, this categorization needs to be unpicked a bit to understand how the efforts at FL modelling in PA are not what might usually be deemed 'modelling' in other social sciences. In fact, most of the modelling in this literature is confined to

Table 1. Modes of inquiry analysis.

Article	Type		General use			Specific use	
	Theory	Practice	Metaphors	Sense-making	Modelling	Theorizing	Mapping cases
Aagaard (2012) PMR	x	x	x	x			x
Astbury, Huddart, and Théoret (2009)	x	x	x				x
Axelrod & Bennett (1993)	x				x		
Gavrilets (2004)	x				x		x
Gerrits and Marks (2014a)	x	x	x	x	x	x	
Gerrits and Marks (2014b)	x			x	x		
Gerrits (2012)	x		x		x		
Geyer and Pickering (2011)	x	x			x		x
Kiel (2005) PAQ	x			x	x		
Klijn (2008)	x	x	x		x		
Lazer and Friedman (2007)	x			x			
Michael (2004)	x	x		x		x	
Mischen and Jackson (2008)	x	x		x	x	x	
Morcol (2005)PAQ	x	x		x		x	x
Rhodes and Donnelly-Cox (2008)	x	x			x	x	x
Rhodes (2008)	x				x	x	x
Rhodes (2012)	x				x		
Room (2011)	x	x		x	x	x	
Rosaria Alfana (2009)	x			x	x	x	
Schneider and Bauer (2007)	x		x	x			
Sword (2007)	x				x		
Teisman and Klijn (2008)	x						
Teisman, Van Buuren, and Gerrits (2009)	x	x	x				
Toh and So (2011)				x			
Weber (2005)	x				x		
Whitt (2009)	x				x		
Zvoleff and Li (2013)	x				x		

definitions of some or – in very few cases – all of the elements of the NK model in the target PA phenomenon and theorizing about how the outcomes of FL models in other disciplines might transfer into the PA domain. For example, Siggelkow and Levinthal's (2003) model of decentralized and centralized organizational forms and the nature of search processes is referred to in several of the articles as providing the basis for theorizing around similar processes in PA. Rhodes (2012) and Rosaria Alfana (2009) progress this transfer to a significant degree, but neither actually construct a working model in the PA/policy contexts.

In spite of the significant presence of what we might more accurately call 'model-mapping' in the articles selected, it is not our view that this represents a contradiction of Gerrits and Marks (2014a) conclusion that the use of FL models in PA is under-developed. Rather, we suggest that authors are engaged in rather detailed sense-making of their chosen PA phenomena of study and using the specificity of the NK model to help in the transfer of theory from one discipline to another. The fact that this is resulting in minimal PA theory development or mapping to empirical phenomenon is consistent with our conclusion and with Gerrits and Marks' observation.

The results of the analysis of modes of inquiry led us to undertake a further analysis of the specific FL model elements that were defined in the articles selected. As described previously, we expanded the elements to include those identified by Rhodes (2012) and Gerrits and Marks (2014a) as being relevant to the theory and practice of PA. We looked for definitions of six types of elements: (1) agents; (2) 'N'; (3) 'K'; (4) movement or search processes; (5) relationships among agents, include exchange of information; and (6) fitness. The result of this analysis is presented in Table 2.

Table 2. Presence of fitness landscape model elements analysis.

Article	Agents	N	K	Mvmt/Srch	Info/Rltns	Fitness
Aagaard (2012) *PMR*				x	x	
Astbury, Huddart, and Théoret (2009)	x				x	
Axelrod & Bennett (1993)	x					
Gavrilets (2004)	x			x		
Gerrits and Marks (2014a)	x	x	x		x	
Gerrits and Marks (2014b)	x	x	x		x	
Gerrits (2012)	x				x	
Geyer and Pickering (2011)	x	x	x	x		x
Kiel (2005) *PAQ*	x			x		
Klijn (2008)	x			x	x	
Lazer and Friedman (2007)	x	x	x	x	x	x
Michael (2004)					x	
Mischen and Jackson (2008)					x	
Morcol (2005) *PAQ*						
Rhodes and Donnelly-Cox (2008)	x	x				x
Rhodes (2008)	x	x		x	x	
Rhodes (2012)	x	x	x	x	x	x
Room (2011)					x	
Rosaria Alfana (2009)	x	x	x	x	x	x
Schneider and Bauer (2007)				x	x	
Sword (2007)					x	
Teisman and Klijn (2008)	x				x	
Teisman, Van Buuren, and Gerrits (2009)	x				x	
Toh and So (2011)	x				x	
Weber (2005)	x					
Whitt (2009)				x		
Zvoleff and Li (2013)	x				x	

The first observation we can make from the table is that two of the six types of elements are most likely to be defined: agents and relationships/information exchange. It is worth noting that the definition of agents spans a broad range of social actors, including individuals, organizations, states, jurisdictions, etc. while the category of relationships and information exchange has almost as many different definitions as there are occurrences in the table. Thus the frequency of the presence of a definition does not imply that a common definition is being developed.

This observation is even more interesting when one considers the fact that relationships among agents, including information exchange, does not feature in the original biological model and is not part of Kauffman's general NK model either. The frequency of this element suggests that PA scholars are interpreting the dynamic of 'co-evolution' present in the original NK model as arising from some kind of interaction between the agents themselves – not the interaction between 'N's what-ever they may be. Lazer and Friedman (2007),[2] one of the few that present a simulation based on operationalized NK model, build this explicitly into their analysis by modelling links between agents in the form of network ties and using a small number of well-constructed variables to represent different aspects of information diffusion among agents. They find that the connectedness of agents does have a (theoretical) effect on performance of the overall system (as measured by the average performance over time by all agents) and conclude that an efficient network positively affects information diffusion but negatively affects information diversity – therefore having conflicting impact on performance, depending on the timescales.

The second observation is that the main elements of the NK FL model, i.e. N, K, and fitness, appear to be the least well specified in the articles found. N is defined only eight times in the twenty-seven articles, K six times and fitness only five times. There is greater consistency among the definitions of 'N' than is found in any of the other elements, with most authors defining 'N' as a range of choices faced that can be combined in pursuit of higher fitness (which is often referred to as 'performance'). K, where it is defined, is often quite vague, but due to the definition of N can often be construed to mean the degree to which different choices are interdependent. For example, Rhodes (2012) identifies sixteen different strategic choice options and suggests that certain types of agents are more likely to choose particular options; this implies that the interdependency among choices may be sector specific. However, even when it is defined, K is not mapped to any empirical or measurable phenomenon.

Somewhat surprisingly, fitness is the least well specified element in the articles analysed and there is no consistency among those authors that do define it. Geyer and Pickering (2011) have the clearest definition(s) but are actually just giving examples of different applications of FL theory in different theoretical contexts. In theories of economic growth, they propose gross domestic product growth as the measure of fitness, while in theories of conflict they propose the presence or absence of conflict as a measure of fitness. Rhodes (2012) attempts to define the full range of types of fitness measures that could be used in a 'fitness function' for PA and identifies six different 'value objectives' that could be weighted in different ways in such a function. These value objectives arose from the goals of the agents themselves and the pursuit of different objectives resulted in profound differences in agent behaviour and the structure of the performance landscape itself. This suggests that any application of the FL model to PA phenomena that does not clarify the nature of fitness is likely to miss important structural and dynamic features that are specific to the fitness measure chosen.

Finally, the analysis shows that there are a number of articles that define the movement or search dynamic in their PA context. The nature of movement tends to be described using the phrases 'exploration' and 'exploitation' which harkens back to March's (1991) seminal article on exploration and exploitation in organizational learning. It is also a feature of the industry simulation models in Levinthal (1997) and Siggelkow and Levinthal (2003) in which the structure of an organization allows it to make more or less strategic choice changes in a given 'turn' of the simulation. Similarly, albeit without the precision of the simulations, in the PA literature authors tend to equate movement with the degree to which an agent can jump to a new combination of choices. In these instances, exploration implies long 'jumps' to very different combinations and exploitation implies limited changes or movement on the landscape. In the practice literature, in which case studies prevail, the movement of agents represents changes in the direction or strategy of one or more agents and the extent to which this did or did not change the structure of the landscape (made up of choices, environmental factors, and/or other agents). As a whole, however, the precise definition of movement on the landscape eludes most authors and they revert mostly to metaphorical use of agents traversing a physical landscape.

In relation to insights into theory and practice identified in the selected articles, these tend to be clustered around the metaphorical and sense-making use of FLs. The main use of FL is in explaining how a given phenomenon of theory may be understood differently by an often loose translation and application of the FL model. Gerrits and Marks (2014b) give the examples of Toh and So (2011) explaining why the introduction of Information and Communication Technologies (ICT) in public education failed, how Michael (2004) used FL as a narrative device for understanding the expansion of anti-corruption programmes and Sword (2007) suggesting that FL provides an insight into how seemingly powerless actors may not be as powerless as they seem. In our search, we found a similar pattern in Aagaard's (2012) study of the 'fragmentation, differentiation, and integration' processes in the Danish Crime Prevention Council and Astbury, Huddart, and Théoret (2009) study of the 'adaptive' walk' in an environmental education programme in Canada. We would also consider Geyer and Pickering (2011) use of the FL model in international relations less about modelling and more about building a case for a multifactor, multi-optima perspective on existing theories.

Some authors have used FLs in order to expand an argument, for example the argument that planning theories are sometimes misguided (Neuman 2000). FLs are used as metaphors in order to identify similarities between ecologies and market mechanisms, where fitness can be found to be provided by market selection. In an unusually precise approach to case study analysis, an operationalized FL for public decision-making was developed by Gerrits (2012), which accounted for both the process and the content of the decision-making. Fitness is defined as (temporal) goal alignment, i.e. where actors achieve solutions for policy issues by successfully aligning their aims with other actors whose intent is to get their issues solved. The case study of urban renewal in the Netherlands illustrates the workings of the model.

Of the specific insights that authors draw from the application of FL theory, the main ones seem to be in relation to the search for fitness – or the 'adaptive walk' on the landscape. Mischen and Jackson (2008), Lazer and Friedman (2007), Rhodes and Donnelly-Cox (2008), and Gerrits (2012) all make the case for understanding PA phenomena as the search by agents for better outcomes on a 'rugged' landscape – defined as the set of all possible outcomes arising from the combination of choices made by agents. These authors and others comment on the relevance of the 'local optima' aspect in which agents get stuck in one location on the landscape in spite of the fact that it is not the best outcome possible overall. Rhodes and Donnelly-Cox (2008) and Geyer and Pickering (2011) are examples of how authors represent a rugged landscape in social entrepreneurship and international relations respectively. Rhodes (2008) reported that stakeholders in urban regeneration in Ireland felt that the mapping of fitness to locations on the landscape needed to be more dynamic than was accounted for in the model since in reality agents can work to change the 'fitness' of their own locations through lobbying or other competitive/cooperative strategies.

Mischen and Jackson (2008), Lazer and Friedman (2007), and Rhodes (2012) all engage with the issue of relationships or networks among actors and how these might influence the search processes on the landscape. Lazar and Friedman are by far the most developed in their application of network theory and they demonstrate (in theory) how network configuration, information velocity, and copying errors ('transmission fidelity') can change the overall performance of the system. The insight here is that too many or too few connections between agents can negatively impact performance, and the characteristics of information transfer between agents can also have important effects. In this, the authors provide much needed guidance on how to formally characterize 'boundary-spanners' in PA.

In relation to theory development more generally, a number of the early articles focused on how the conceptual elements of FLs appear to be a good fit with a range of theories in PA and the social sciences in general. Authors undertook to map FL theory to selected institutional and behavioural theories to demonstrate how FL models could have the potential for enhancing and integrating theory in PA. Morcol (2005), Kiel (2005), Weber (2005), Schneider and Bauer (2007), Klijn (2008), Teisman and Klijn (2008), Rhodes (2008), Rhodes and Donnelly-Cox (2008), and Geyer and Pickering (2011) are all examples of this sort of article. It is worth noting that six of the nine articles are found in two special issues devoted to complexity in PA: one in *Public Administration Quarterly* (*PAQ* 2005 vol. 29, 3) and one in *Public Management Review* (*PMR* 2008 vol. 10, 3). In a subsequent special issue on the same topic in *PAQ* (2008), there was only one article that used FLs as the underlying framework – and the author combined FL with social network analysis to understand policy implementation processes (Mischen and Jackson 2008). There have been no further special issues on this topic in *PMR* or *PAQ*. Indeed, in spite of the appearance of two new journals specifically targeting the use of complexity theory in PA and policy in 2014,[3] there has been little to show in terms of PA theorizing arising from the engagement with FL theory in the past 10 years.

Conclusion

Our systematic review has confirmed that the uses and interpretations of FLs in PA are underdeveloped in comparison to how they are used in more established fields such as economics and the management sciences (Gerrits and Marks 2014b). The main evidence for this conclusion is the relative lack of attention paid to defining the key elements of the FL model, i.e. N, K, and fitness, compared to other social sciences. Furthermore, apart from one exception (Rhodes 2012), the mapping of model elements to empirical data is generally in the form of a case narrative within which the definition of the main elements of the model are underspecified. Rhodes's (2012) attempt at grounding the model in empirical observation (using forty-eight cases of housing production agents in Ireland) still does not provide us with much comfort as she identifies a large number of gaps and uncertainties arising from her detailed efforts. The interest in FLs in PA also appears to have peaked in 2005–2008 along with the three special issues in leading PA journals.

This does not mean that scholars have not offered insights into the dynamics of PA through the use of FL models. As noted in the body of this paper, these include insights into the nature of change arising from the exploitation/exploration dynamics, how network connections among agents affect overall system performance, how the process of goal alignment between agents can be understood, and – as a general observation – how the metaphor of an 'adaptive walk' over a 'rugged landscape' can provide a new perspective on change and non-linear outcomes.

The more advanced use of FL models in the cognate disciplines of management and economics does suggest that there may yet be fruitful applications in PA domains. In particular, FLs may be important to the further development of governance network theory, specifically in relation to modelling 'strategic complexity' as described in Klijn and Koppenjan (2014):

> Strategic complexity is a result of the strategic choices actors make when they articulate complex problems (Allison, 1971; Kingdon, 1984). Because actors are autonomous and networks lack clear hierarchical control forms, each actor chooses his/her own strategy. As a result, various or even conflicting, strategies may develop around a complex issue (Koppenjan & Klijn, 2004). Furthermore, actors anticipate each other's strategic moves and respond to them (Scharpf, 1997). Because of these interactions, it is difficult to predict what strategies actors will choose, how strategies will evolve during the process, and how the interactions of these strategies will influence the process of problem-solving. (63)

It is exactly this sort of complexity for which the models developed by Levinthal and Siggelkow were developed. Furthermore, the work by Lazar and Friedman provides a clear direction for integrating network theory and complex systems theory through FLs. Network theory in PA is well established (Klijn and Koppenjan 2012; Isett et al. 2011), with significant progress on all three of the practice and research agendas described by O'Toole (1997), and yet there are limits to how well network models on their own can address the purposeful and interdependent actions of agents over time. For this, scholars of public management could draw on the information exchanging multi-agent evolutionary FL models developed in other disciplines. Indeed, we would propose that FLs are prima facie more aligned with the actual features of complex governance systems than game theory models which rely on highly stylized assumptions about how agents behave and equally fuzzy definitions of performance. Nevertheless, issues remain with the translation of the original model of gene interactions to human organisational interactions, as McKelvey et al. (2013) have shown.

In order for FLs models to contribute meaningfully, however, four key areas of development are required. Firstly, greater clarity on the concept of fitness as it applies to public management domains is necessary. Rhodes (2012) provides a comprehensive list of 'value objectives' arising from empirical research in the Irish housing system, but admits that there are challenges in developing measures for these. In addition to limiting the extent to which theory can be developed, a lack of specificity around fitness and performance severely limits the extent to which public managers will perceive the benefits of these models. Furthermore, the dynamics of changing performance landscapes and how agent behaviour affects the relative fitness of locations on the landscape needs more attention (Lazer and Friedman 2007; Gerrits 2012).

Secondly, 'Agents,' 'N,' and 'K' need to be more clearly specified for the various domains in which the FL models are being applied. While the definitions in biology have clear connections to ecosystems, thus far there is little evidence to support that genes and alleles translate across to PA at the level of organizations and public service systems. Work in the area of innovation and markets (Koen 2005) appears to have cracked the translation of 'NK' into economic systems in so far as 'Agents' represent new innovations, 'N' represents ideas/artefacts that can be combined in different ways, and 'K' represents the degree of interdependence among these ideas/artefacts, i.e. to what extent does the effectiveness of one artefact depend on the presence of another. This does not mean that 'Agents,' 'N,' and 'K' have to mean the same thing in international relations, policy systems, and systems of governance. However, the greater the consensus among academics about how these variables map to specific and relevant elements of particular domains, the greater the likelihood of integration into theory and practice.

Thirdly, the work on defining the role and dynamics of relationships among agents should continue. This was never a feature of the original biological FL model and did not appear in the early translation of the model into the social sciences. However, the successful translation of FL models into social sciences rests on incorporating relationships and information-sharing among (human) agents. It is worth noting that a recent scoping review in the healthcare domain (Thompson et al. 2016) found that 'a common theme across descriptions of complexity theory is that authors incorporate aspects of the theory related to how diverse relationships and communication between individuals in a system can influence change' (1). With the advances in modelling networks in PA and other social sciences, relationships, and information-sharing among agents, this has made its way into the FL literature and has helped to tease out how agents gather information in order to make choices on the landscape. In so doing, authors have not only drawn on network configuration theory but also on institutional and information theories, achieving an integration across disciplines that is worthy of considerable praise and ongoing efforts.

Fourthly, specification of movement by agents across the landscape should also be further developed, with continued focus on the use of exploration and exploitation mechanisms. Linking this with the network analysis and information sharing among agents as demonstrated in Lazer and Friedman (2007) has significant potential and addressing the impact of uncertainty in this dynamic would add an important dimension for theoretical and practical application (Rhodes 2012).

With the above in place, scholars would be able to more credibly apply FL models to their domain(s) of study and assess the extent to which the models offer more than simply sense-making and metaphorical insights for PA theory and practice development.

Notes

1. A *gene* is a stretch of DNA or RNA that determines a certain trait. Genes mutate and can take two or more alternative forms; an *allele* is one of these forms of a gene. For example, the gene for eye colour has several variations (alleles) such as an allele for blue eye colour or an allele for brown eyes. (http://www.diffen.com/difference/Allele_vs_Gene – accessed 4 March 2015).

2. This article is not precisely aimed at PA, but the authors do point out that their findings have a broad range of applications in organizational theory, including PA.
3. *Complexity Governance & Networks* and *Journal on Policy and Complex Systems.*

Disclosure statement

No potential conflict of interest was reported by the authors.

References

Aagaard, P. 2012. "The Challenge of Adaptive Capability in Public Organizations." *Public Management Review* 14 (6): 731–746. doi:10.1080/14719037.2011.642626.
Astbury, J., S. Huddart, and P. Théoret. 2009. "Making the Path as We Walk It: Changing Context and Strategy on Green Street." *Canadian Journal of Environmental Education* 14: 158.
Axelrod, R., and D. S. Bennett. 1993. "A Landscape Theory of Aggregation." *British Journal of Political Science* 23 (02): 211. doi:10.1017/S000712340000973X.
Chandler, A. D. 1962. *Strategy and Structure: Chapters in the History of Industrial Enterprise.* Cambridge, MA: MIT Press.
Chapman, J. 2002. *System Failure: Why Governments Must Learn to Think Differently.* London: Demos.
Gavrilets, S. 2004. *Fitness Landscapes and the Origin of Species (Monographs in Population Biology 41 Ed).* Princeton, NJ: Princeton University Press.
Gerrits, L. 2012. *Punching Clouds: An Introduction to the Complexity of Public Decision-Making.* Litchfield Park: Emergent Publications.
Gerrits, L., and P. K. Marks. 2014a. "How Fitness Landscapes Help Further the Social and Behavioural Sciences." *Emergence: Complexity and Organisation* 16 (3): 1–17.
Gerrits, L., and P. Marks. 2014b. "The Evolution of Wright's (1932) Adaptive Field of Contemporary Interpretations and Uses of Fitness Landscapes in the Social Sciences." *Biology and Philosophy* 30 (4): 459–479. doi:10.1007/s10539-014-9450-2.
Geyer, R., and S., Pickering. 2011. "Applying the Tools of Complexity to the International Realm: From Fitness Landscapes to Complexity Cascades." *Cambridge Review of International Affairs* 24 (1): 5–26. doi:10.1080/09557571.2011.558053.
Haynes, P. 2003. *Managing Complexity in the Public Services.* Berkshire: Open University Press.
Isett, K. R., I. A. Mergel, K. LeRoux, I. A. Mischen, and R. K. Rethemeyer. 2011. "Networks in Public Administration Scholarship: Understanding Where We are and Where We Need to Go." *Journal of Public Administration Research and Theory* 21 (Suppl 1): i157–i173. doi:10.1093/jopart/muq061.
Kauffman, S. A. 1993. *The Origins of Order: Self-Organisation and Selection in Evolution.* New York, NY: Oxford University Press.
Kauffman, S. A., and S. Levin. 1987. "Towards A General Theory of Adaptive Walks on Rugged Landscapes." *Journal of Theoretical Biology* 128.1: 11–45. doi:10.1016/S0022-5193(87)80029-2.
Kiel, L. D. 2005. "A Primer for Agent-Based Modeling in Public Administration: Exploring Complexity in 'Would Be' Administrative Worlds." *Public Administration Quarterly* 29 (3/4): 268–296.
Klijn, E. 2008. "Complexity Theory and Public Administration: What's New?" *Public Management Review* 10 (3): 299–317. doi:10.1080/14719030802002675.

Klijn, E. H., and J. F. M. Koppenjan. 2012. "Governance Network Theory: Past, Present and Future." *Policy & Politics* 40 (4): 187–206. doi:10.1332/030557312X655431.

Klijn, E. H., and J. F. M. Koppenjan. 2014. "Complexity in Governance Network Theory." *Complexity, Governance & Networks* 1 (1): 61–70.

Koen, F. 2005. *Innovation, Evolution and Complexity Theory*. Cheltenham: Edward Elgar Publishing.

Lazer, and Friedman. 2007. "The Network of Exploration and Exploitation." *Administrative Science Quarterly* 52 (4): 667–694. doi:10.2189/asqu.52.4.667.

Levinthal, D. 1997. "Adaptation on Rugged Landscapes." *Management Science* 43 (7): 934–950. doi:10.1287/mnsc.43.7.934.

Levinthal, D., and M. Warglein. 1999. "Landscape Design: Designing for Local Action in Complex Worlds." *Organization Science* 10 (3): 342–357. doi:10.1287/orsc.10.3.342.

March, J. G. 1991. "Exploration and Exploitation in Organizational Learning." *Organization Science* 2 (1): 71–87. doi:10.1287/orsc.2.1.71.

Mckelvey, B., M. Li, H. Xu, and R. Vidgen. 2013. "Re-Thinking Kauffman's NK Fitness Landscape: From Artefact & Groupthink to Weak-Tie Effects." *Human Systems Management* 32: 17–42.

Michael, B. 2004. "Explaining Organisational Change in International Development: The Role of Complexity in Anti-Corruption Work." *Journal of International Development* 16 (8): 1067–1088. doi:10.1002/jid.1126.

Mischen, P. A., and S. K. Jackson. 2008. "Connecting the Dots: Applying Complexity Theory, Knowledge Management and Social Network Analysis to Policy Implementation." *Public Administration Quarterly* 32 (3): 314.

Morcol, G. 2005. "A New Systems Thinking: Implications of The Sciences of Complexity for Public Policy and Administration." *Public Administration Quarterly* 29 (3/4): 297–320.

Neuman, M. 2000. "Communicate This! Does Consensus Lead to Advocacy and Pluralism?" *Journal of Planning Education and Research* 19: 343. doi:10.1177/0739456X0001900403.

OECD. (2009). *Applications of Complexity Science for Public Policy: New Tools for Finding Unanticipated Consequences and Unrealized Opportunities*. Global Science Forum. Accessed July 15, 2010. http://www.oecd.org/dataoecd/44/41/43891980.pdf

O'Toole, L. 1997. "Treating Networks Seriously: Practical and Research-based Agendas in Public Administration." *Public Administration Review* 57 (1): 45–52. doi:10.2307/976691.

Rhodes, M. L. 2008. "Complexity and Emergence in Public Management: The Case of Urban Regeneration in Ireland." *Public Management Review* 10 (3): 361–379. doi:10.1080/14719030802002717.

Rhodes, M. L., and G. Donnelly-Cox. 2008. "Social Entrepreneurship as a Performance Landscape: The Case of 'Front Line'." *Emergence: Complexity & Organization* 10 (3): 35–50. doi:10.emerg/10.17357.0c8c14d7991802dbdbdcab0294a0bc9c

Rhodes, M. L., J. Murphy, J. Muir, and J. A. Murray. 2011. *Public Management and Complexity Theory: Richer Decision-making in Public Services*. New York: Routledge.

Rhodes, M. L. 2012. "Advancing Public Service Governance Theory." In *COMPACT I: Public Administration in Complexity*, edited by P. K. Marks, F. Boon, and L. Gerrits, 251–275. Arizona, NM: Emergent Publications.

Room, G. 2011. *Complexity, Institutions and Public Policy: Agile Decision-Making in a Turbulent World*. Cheltenham: Edward Elgar Publishing.

Rosaria Alfano, M. 2009. "Centralization and Decentralization of Public Policy in a Complex Framework." *Eurasian Journal of Business and Economics* 2 (3): 15–34. ISSN: 1694-5972.

Schneider, V., and J. M. Bauer (2007) Governance: Prospects of Complexity Theory in Revisiting System Theory. Paper presented at the annual meeting of the Midwest Political Science Association, Palmer House Hotel, Chicago, IL, April 14.

Siggelkow, N., and D. Levinthal. 2003. "Temporarily Divide to Conquer: Centralized, Decentralized, and Reintegrated Organizational Approaches to Exploration and Adaptation." *Organization Science* 14 (6): 650–669. doi:10.1287/orsc.14.6.650.24840.

Sword, L. 2007. "Complexity Science Conflict Analysis of Power and Protest." *Emergence: Complexity and Organization* 9 (3): 47.

Teisman, G., A. Van Buuren, and L. Gerrits. 2009. *Managing Complex Governance Systems*. New York: Routledge.

Teisman, G. R., and E. Klijn. 2008. "Complexity Theory and Public Management." *Public Management Review* 10 (3): 287–297. doi:10.1080/14719030802002451.

Thomas, J., and A. Harden. 2008. "Methods for the Thematic Synthesis of Qualitative Research in Systematic Reviews." *BMC Medical Research Methodology* 8: 45. doi:10.1186/1471-2288-8-45.

Thompson, D. S., X. Fazio, E. Kustra, L. Patrick, and D. Stanley. 2016. "Scoping Review of Complexity Theory in Health Services Research." *BMC Health Services Research* 16: 87. doi:10.1186/s12913-016-1343-4.

Toh, Y., and H. So. 2011. "ICT Reform Initiatives in Singapore Schools: A Complexity Theory Perspective." *Asia Pacific Education Review* 12 (3): 349–357. doi:10.1007/s12564-010-9130-0.

Tranfield, D., D. Denyer, and P. Smart. 2003. "Towards a Methodology for Developing Evidence-Informed Management Knowledge by Means of Systematic Review." *British Journal of Management* 14.3: 207–222. doi:10.1111/1467-8551.00375.

Weber, B. H. 1998. " "Origins of Order in Dynamical Models." *Biology and Philosophy* 13: 133–144. doi:10.1023/A:1006546407118

Weber, J. 2005. "Introduction to Chaos, Complexity, Uncertainty and Public Administration: A Symposium." *Public Administration Quarterly* 29 (3/4): 262–267.

Whitt, R. S. 2009. "Adaptive Policymaking: Evolving and Applying Emergent Solutions for U.S. Communications Policy." *Federal Communications Law Journal* 61 (3): 483–589.

Wright, S. 1932. "The Roles of Mutation, Inbreeding, Crossbreeding and Selection in Evolution." *Proceedings of the Sixth International Congress of Genetics* 1: 356–366.

Zvoleff, A., and A. Li. 2013. "Analyzing Human–Landscape Interactions: Tools That Integrate." *Environmental Management* 53.1: 94–111. doi:10.1007/s00267-012-0009-1.

Engaging with complexity in a public programme implementation

Walter Castelnovo ⑩ and Maddalena Sorrentino

ABSTRACT
The heuristic device of a complexity-based lens is applied to the local implementation of a public programme to understand the possible misalignment of its outcomes with the central planners' goals. The authors supersede the dominant use in complexity theory of simplifying or ambiguous metaphors to focus, instead, on the core concepts of emergence, co-evolution, and self-organization. The paper reinterprets extant literature and analyses an exemplary case, concluding that policy implementation must be approached pragmatically as a self-organizing system and that the public managers need to strategically *engage* with complexity in a manner that is consistent with such a pragmatic understanding.

Introduction

Complexity is the science of organization – especially its origin and evolution – and is therefore the natural framework for considering organization and connected entities (Haynes 2015; Langley 1999; Maguire, Allen, and McKelvey 2011). The complexity approach is of particular interest to the organizational research because it offers a fundamentally new way to conceptualize and reframe the understanding of many of the phenomena common to the study of organizations (Mathews, White, and Long 1999, 439). However, while the use of complexity theory in contemporary studies is increasing, complexity principles are still mostly used as a metaphorical device for creating new insights rather than as a means to understanding and managing organizations (Burnes 2005), also in the political studies domain. This situation led Cairney (2012, 347) to argue that 'the language of "complexity" is used too loosely' to give meaningful advice to policymakers.

The study applies a complexity-based lens as the heuristic device to understand how the local implementation of a public programme in a country of 'Napoleonic' administrative tradition led to outcomes that failed to mesh with the centrally defined objectives. The authors illustrate and analyse the interaction between multiple tiers of government and the hurdles and challenges to implementation and take-up. In the words of Peters, reforming the public machinery is always a challenging endeavour and is particularly 'difficult, if perhaps not impossible in some instances' (Peters 2008, 129). In southern Europe, as well as through the French colonial empire, the emphasis on codified law, on formality, and on a centralized administrative organization with a weak local self-government level has a pervasive influence in public reform trajectories (Kuhlmann and Wollmann 2014; Peters 2008). While the dynamics and outcomes of change can be positive or negative in any context, the historical roots of the Napoleonic administrative system amplify the overall degree of organizational complexity and therefore require careful analysis to better grasp the public machinery's response to external perturbations. Hence, to avoid 'inappropriate simplification' (Haynes 2015, xv), a holistic understanding is needed where a complexity-based interpretive lens must factor in these enduring legacies.

To illustrate why the local implementation of public policies varies from place to place, the paper adopts the position of Butler and Allen (2008), who link complexity thinking to organizational change. Following the original idea proposed in their study to discard a pure metaphorical use of complexity principles in favour of a conceptual clarification, the focus of this article is on emergence, co-evolution, and self-organization, three of the more common concepts of complexity that can be expected to kick in during programme implementation. These interrelated concepts and the way in which they interact are used to develop a framework for subsequent application and discussion. The paper seeks to (a) identify the key concepts of a complexity-based analytical approach and (b) break new ground by quasi-operationalizing those concepts in the local implementation of a public programme.

Specifically, the paper analyses the policy domain of administrative reform in Italy; in particular, the local government implementation of the Sportello Unico per le Attività Produttive ('SUAP') Law introduced in 1998. The reform had the aim of reducing the daunting administrative burdens on businesses, making it mandatory for each of the country's 8,000+ municipalities to set up a one-stop business shop as a single point of contact (SPC) for firms to expedite the procedures to open, change, or close a business activity (Forti 2000; Capano 2003; Ongaro 2004; OECD 2009; Castelnovo, Sorrentino, and De Marco 2016). The SUAP therefore was tasked with streamlining the full business authorization/licensing/permit process, including the coordination of all the public agencies involved (e.g. local healthcare authorities, fire brigade, provincial and regional governments, and regional environment authorities).

Devised as a highly complex, legalistic, and laborious process, Italy's one-stop business shop reform programme met with a hostile reception from the local authorities, forcing the central government to impose increasingly harsher regulations, which, however, still failed to 'get the job done.' Indeed, Italy's administrative machinery remains highly fragmented, the SUAP public players continue to be poorly coordinated, and incompatible techno-organizational solutions continue to multiply. Applying the complexity-based interpretive lens to the Italian SUAP reform trajectory offers new insights into the forces that set it on such a zigzag implementation path and hence shaped the outcomes.

The qualitative paper proposes a twofold contribution to the extant literature that applies complexity thinking to the public sector. First, following Cairney, it sets out to reduce the looseness of the language of 'complexity' used in the dominant metaphoric discourse by defining a 'quasi-operationalization' of emergence, co-evolution, and self-organization. Factoring these complexity concepts into the analysis of the implementation of the SUAP programme sheds new light on some of the phenomena common to public services experience (starting with the problematic interaction between the different tiers of government) and to evidence the mechanisms of policy change and the focal points for analysis of success or failure (Eppel 2016).

Second, the paper advances the knowledge of organizational change in Napoleonic administrative systems given that, as noted by Cairney and Geyer (2015b), the studies on complexity thinking applied to the public sector address predominantly the Anglo-Saxon countries. Indeed, the fragmentation and heterogeneity of the administrative system and the often obsessively detailed law-making of the Napoleonic tradition make the Italian local government context a good case for critical study.

The authors therefore take a conceptual approach to respond to the paper's two key research questions:

Q1. How can the concepts of emergence, co-evolution, and self-organization be operationalized starting with the analysis of the implementation of a nationwide policy programme?

Q2. To what extent does the complexity of the implementation process shape the direction and development of a public programme, in particular, in a country of the Napoleonic administrative tradition?

The multi-tiered, legalistically bound Italian administrative system makes reform highly challenging for the recipient public organizations, which, to increase the programme's chances of success, are forced to prioritize the management of complexity. The authors therefore argue that, instead of adopting a strategy to *reduce* complexity, the policymakers and implementers should *engage* with complexity to more effectively align the public service response and to better understand the policy implementation process and dynamics (Butler and Allen 2008; Rhodes et al. 2011; Cairney and Geyer 2015a).

Methodologically, the paper adopts a qualitative approach to make sense of the different implementation outcomes of one specific reform, using the narrative strategy of process research (Langley 1999) in which careful attention is given to how events develop over time. The qualitative process data used here are sourced from earlier studies conducted by the authors of this article, their personal experience in various implementation projects, and documentary evidence.

Drawing on the various theoretical contributions which emphasize the need to push beyond the merely metaphorical concepts of complexity theory, the paper defines a complexity-based interpretive lens that enables a deeper exploration of the operational terrain on which public programmes are thrust. The exemplary case of Italy's one-stop business shop (SUAP) is discussed and mined extensively to inform answers to the two research questions and to draw some reflections on the implications of complexity thinking for the public management practice. A main implication is to engage with complexity. To do this, it is necessary to accept the changing nature of the environments in which public organizations operate and to adopt managerial strategies flexible enough to address complexity and the contextual dependencies typical of social systems. This is contrary to the prevailing notion that complexity can have a potentially negative impact on the implementation of a national policy programme and therefore is a critical factor that must perforce and always be reduced. The evidence delivered by the analysis of the Italian SUAP case suggests that to engage with complexity, a public manager must (1) think holistically rather than linearly to grasp the big picture, including the multiple causal factors and policy objectives; (2) break with the logic of best practices that still percolates in the public sector mindset; (3) supersede the traditional dichotomy between evaluation and implementation to focus, instead, on the feedback process and how performance is constructed.

Finally, the paper closes with the limitations of the present study and future research development paths.

Issues in complexity thinking

Despite the growing number of studies that focus explicitly on complexity theories in the organizational domain, important questions still remain about the conditions that enable the effective applicability of those theories to the social domain (Stacey 1995; Plowman et al. 2007; Byrne 1998; Anderson 1999; Duit and Galaz 2008). In the strictly organizational sense, Levy (2000, 82) has already pointed out how complexity cannot simply be imported from the natural sciences and applied 'off-the-shelf' to industries and firms. Such an approach could generate translation errors mainly due to a lack in analytic clarity in conceptualization (Gerrits and Meek 2011), and lead different people to understand complexity, and seek to apply its insights, in very different ways (Cairney and Geyer 2017). As von Ghyczy (2003, 87) observes, 'it's tempting to draw business lessons from other disciplines – warfare, biology, music. But most managers do it badly.' To which Richardson (2008) adds that many academics also 'do it badly.'

Cairney and Geyer (2015b) say that we should be careful about comparing the natural, physical, and social worlds, unless we are content with the use of complex systems simply as metaphors. The use of metaphors within organizations is quite common and Lissack (1997) argues that the use of metaphor from complexity theory can change the way managers think about the problems they face, recast organizational processes in ways that inspire novel representations, and guide managerial action. Maguire, Allen, and McKelvey (2011) point out that the metaphors derived from the complexity theories are also an interpretive tool that promises real value for managers (Marks and Gerrits 2013) to help elucidate some of the non-mechanistic, non-linear dynamics of organizations. Similarly, Lichtenstein (2011) says that complexity metaphors can be useful for helping us to picture the world in a more holistic, dynamic, and unpredictable way. However, by critically discussing the use of complexity metaphors in the organizational domain, Burnes (2005) concludes that it is difficult to claim that complexity theories have the potential to bring about a fundamental re-evaluation of the nature, purpose, and operation of organizations, unless it can be shown that a complexity-based approach 'is able to resolve the problems of managing and changing organizations more effectively than other approaches that are on offer' (87).

Using complexity simply as a metaphor risks reducing it to just shorthand for complicated, instead of using complexity concepts as tools to elucidate 'the mechanisms through which micro-level events and interactions can give rise to macro-level system structures, properties and behaviours' (Maguire, Allen and McKelvey 2011, 9). To be really useful, metaphorically derived assertions about organizations have to be exposed to empirical scrutiny in order to lay the foundations of an alternative conception of organization and management.

Applying complexity theory in an empirical study led Houchin and MacLean (2005) to observe that complexity theory is only partially successful as a device for describing organizational development and change. The limitations that have surfaced in the complexity thinking applied to empirical cases have been known for some time (Cairney 2012; Krolczyk, Senf, and Cordes 2010; Klijn 2008; Maguire, Allen and McKelvey 2011). Cherry (2014, 42), for example, notes that these 'remain abstract and have rarely been operationalized in ways that make a difference to practice.' In fact, the meaning and implications of complexity have been less commonly elucidated and rarely tested through empirical study. According to these scholars, the application of the complexity theories in the organizational domain remains abstract and informed by universal principles, which makes them applicable to a wide range of phenomenon areas with the drawback of being not very 'practical' (Krolczyk, Senf, and Cordes 2010).

Klijn (2008) highlights the need for an empirical operationalization of the complexity concepts to make them applicable in the study of empirical phenomena. The 2008 special issue of the Public Management Review on 'Complexity Theory and Public Management' was a first move in this direction but empirical analysis using complexity theory concepts in public administration is still relatively scarce (Maguire, Allen and McKelvey 2011), leaving much work still to be done.

Cairney and Geyer (2015a, 2015b) observe that the application of complexity theory in the organizational domain will only be valuable if it can produce some results, which involves more the application of 'complexity thinking' to the study of real-world problems than the use of rigid theoretical frameworks. The authors argue for a pragmatic approach that 'involves a recognition and acceptance of the limits of our knowledge and understanding, and ability to gather evidence, developing models when we know that they only tell us part of the story' (459).

In order to 'facilitate organizational academics and practitioners in "seeing" the complexity inherent in socio-technical organizations' (Richardson 2008, 20), a complexity-based interpretive lens is one way to apply a complexity thinking approach to look at real-world problems. Developing a complexity-informed lens for public policy analysis means identifying which existing complexity concepts can ensure the most coherent design (Eppel, 2012). Fortunately, the leading scholars to apply complexity thinking to the public domain have narrowed down the literature's many variations on the theme to a manageable number of underpinning concepts. For example, Richardson (2008, 14) observes that the existence of non-linear feedback in complex systems that allow for emergence, self-organization, adaptation, and learning has become synonymous with complexity thinking. Cairney and Geyer (2015a) assume interdependency, co-evolution, positive and negative feedback, path-dependency, emergence, and punctuated equilibrium as the complexity theory's main features. Eppel, who has worked the hardest to apply complexity thinking to the empirical analysis of real cases of nationwide public sector reform programmes, develops a complexity-based analytical lens that includes the concepts of components interaction, co-evolution and adaptation, feedback, emergence and self-organization, far from equilibrium, and path-dependency (Eppel 2012, 2016).

Following an approach similar to the one advocated by Eppel and Rhodes et al. (2011), the authors of this paper apply a 'complexity thinking' approach to analyse the on-the-ground implementation of a specific public reform programme in a country of Napoleonic administrative tradition. The aim is not to formalize a theory but, rather, to develop and test the analytical potential of a complexity-based interpretive lens in a real-world case. Accordingly, the paper provides the empirical descriptions needed to interpret the complexity factors at work and the main forces that shaped the Italian SUAP trajectory. More specifically, it demonstrates how the concepts of emergence, co-evolution, and self-organization enable a deeper understanding of the peculiar path trodden, which otherwise risks looking like the cumulative effect of a series of legislative interventions not always coherent in and among themselves (Castelnovo, Sorrentino, and De Marco 2016). The paper will exemplify how these fundamental complexity concepts take concrete form in the reality, surpassing their simple metaphorical use in the next, logical step towards their quasi-operationalization.

Conceptual model of a generic implementation process

This section describes a conceptual model of a generic public policy implementation process based on the complexity concepts identified immediately above. Space limitations mean that the authors are unable to conduct a systematic, comprehensive review of the relevant literature on public policy implementation here. Instead, the most critical forces at work are cited as a preliminary clarification of the ways in which a complexity-based interpretive lens can inform the two research questions. This pragmatic approach focuses exclusively on mapping the route taken by a generic programme implementation process, from its starting point (the initial conditions) through to the desired outcomes, which led different agents to interact in unpredictable ways, generating possible deviations from the initial expectations (Teisman 2008).

Rhodes (2008) and Klijn (2008) see agent interaction as a fundamental aspect of the implementation process, concluding that the combined actions of individual agents in the system lead to the emergence of new features that solidify and form the structures of the social system (308). From a complexity perspective, the context-specific and socially constructed behaviour of the agents and their relations is what leads to uncertainty in the implementation of a public programme (Morçöl 2012, 22). During the interaction, the agents adapt to each other, self-organize and co-evolve over time; these processes of self-organization can lead to the emergence of entirely new and unpredictable results (Eppel, Matheson, and Walton 2011).

As highlighted by Klijn (2008), dynamics in systems often show signs of unstable or at least temporarily stable situations that can be suddenly disrupted, what complexity theorists call 'punctuated equilibrium' (Teisman 2008; True, Jones and Baumgartner 2007; Bryan and Baumgartner 2012). Activating a central government policy programme can create significant organizational and financial costs for the local implementers. As observed by Jacobs and Weaver (2010, 12), 'where policy imposes costs on actors, those actors may adjust their behavior and invest in patterns of activity in ways that minimize the burdens that they face.' The need to adapt to the new legislative and regulatory requirements creates conditions of disequilibrium to which the organization's implementers respond by activating processes of adjustment, co-evolution, and self-organization, which, in turn, can generate new configurations, new behaviours, and new practices, even though these do not fully correspond to those originally envisaged.

Houchin and MacLean (2005) observe that the 'natural' tendency of a complex social system is the creation of equilibrium rather than novelty, which seems particularly true in the case of highly regulated administrative systems, such as those of the risk-averse Napoleonic tradition. Therefore, if the interaction among the implementation process agents produces a new situation of equilibrium, the organization will tend to maintain that state, at least until other conditions materialize that force it back to its previous state of disequilibrium.

The dynamic between temporary states of equilibrium and disequilibrium can be described as feedback loops. In fact, Bryan and Baumgartner (2012, 3) note that 'policymaking is a continual struggle between the forces of balance and equilibrium, dominated by negative feedback processes, and the forces of destabilization and contagion, governed by positive feedback processes.'

When the local implementers work towards achieving the desired new state defined by the policy, a *positive feedback loop* is generated that reinforces and amplifies the intervention's potential to transform the organization (Houchin and MacLean 2005). Vice versa, when the action of the local actors is opposed to achieving the desired new state, a *negative feedback loop* is generated, which tends to reduce if not annul the policy's potential to transform the organization. When this latter condition materializes, it may be necessary to rethink programme implementation and search for new alternatives (Jacobs and Weaver 2010). Typically, to keep the programme on its proper course, the government intervenes to adjust and/or reinforce the relevant norms, or to reduce the number and influence of the implementers. Consequently, in real-life systems, both negative and positive feedback loops operate together (Morçöl 2012, 100). In particular, if negative feedback loops predominate, a system will be more stable. Conversely, the positive feedback loop prevails when 'the exponential growth or decline in a system' induces the implementer organizations to embark on adaptation and transformation processes designed to restore a new situation of (temporary) equilibrium.

Figure 1 offers a rough guideline to the relational dynamics engaged in by the major forces on the ground that both reinforce and constrain change in the functioning of a generic programme implementation cycle, considering both positive feedback loops (left) and negative feedback loops (right). In Morçöl's words (2012), the two kinds of loops are the 'engines' of self-organization, co-evolution, and emergence.

Having identified the major ground forces at work and the key assumptions that underpin the adoption of a complexity-based view, the following section applies the conceptual model proposed here to a real-life case. Basically, the analytical approach used is similar to the examples applied by some authoritative contributions, such as

- the implementation of local government reform programmes (Haveri 2006),
- the implementation of housing policies in the United Kingdom (Butler and Allen 2008),
- the implementation of infrastructure programmes in the United Kingdom (Teisman 2008),
- the implementation of policies for tertiary education in New Zealand (Eppel 2016; Eppel, Turner, and Wolf 2011),
- the study of leadership (Lichtenstein and McKelvey 2011),

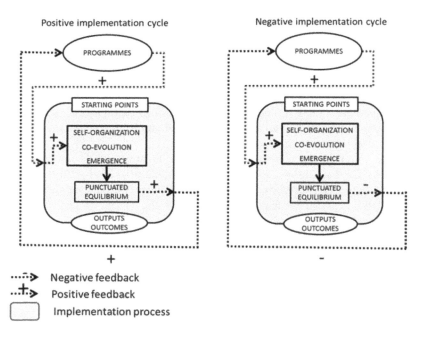

Figure 1. Conceptual model of a generic implementation process. Source: The authors.

- the study of urban regeneration projects and healthcare information systems in Ireland (Rhodes 2008; Rhodes et al. 2011), and
- the implementation of healthcare reform in the United States (Jacobs and Weaver 2015).

The aim of the paper is to pursue the path taken by these notable antecedents with a contribution that sheds light on how, in the context of an administrative tradition heavily weighted to a legalistic approach such as Italy, emergence, co-evolution, and self-organization are key concepts that can help to better explain the dynamics that influence the extent and direction of policy implementation.

An exemplary case: analysis of a nationwide reform programme

Research has pointed out the relative scarcity of complexity theories (or complexity perspective) applied to real-life empirical cases, especially in studies of the implementation of broad-scope public policies (see, for instance, Klijn 2008; Cairney 2012; Maguire, Allen and McKelvey 2011). This section uses the case of Italy's one-stop business shop to show how a theoretical account of the three interrelated complexity factors of self-organization, co-evolution, and emergence can make sense of many of the facts at hand. The discussion of the case as a narrative strategy of qualitative process research (Langley 1999) elucidates the reform's timeline.

The Italian one-stop business shop: overview

The purpose of Italian Law 447/1998, otherwise known as the SUAP or one-stop business shop programme, was to streamline the country's highly fragmented and complex scenario of lengthy business authorization, licensing, and permit procedures whereby each Italian council was free to apply the protocols, forms, and tariffs deemed the best fit for their constituency (Forti 2000). Specifically, the SUAP called for each Italian municipality to establish a SPC (the one-stop business shop) for firms to expedite all the official requirements for opening, changing, or closing a business activity (Ongaro 2004; OECD 2009). In particular, the single organizational unit of the one-stop business shop had to both coordinate all the relative local public bodies (e.g. healthcare service, fire brigade, provincial and regional governments, regional environmental department) and manage the relevant administrative procedures through either (1) in-house or (2) joint-management via inter-municipal coopera-tion. At the time, Italy was gripped by a devolutionary trend that aimed to strengthen local organizational autonomy and enable the transfer of competences; hence, the legislator left it to the councils decide which form was the most appropriate (Capano 2003).

To comply with Law 447/98, the councils therefore had to put together the pieces of a complex organizational puzzle that often demanded capabilities and resources they did not have. So, it is hardly surprising that law-making alone failed to either deliver the goods or the expected outcomes of simplifying the authorization proce-dures and easing the bureaucratic load on businesses (Castelnovo, Sorrentino, and De Marco 2016). Continuous SUAP adjustments were then written into law by succes-sive governments, with two goals: (1) to force all the municipalities to activate a one-stop shop, and (ii) to leverage technology to transform the SUAP into a more simplified virtual service centre. Figure 2 snapshots the SUAP's legislative timeline.

The stream of legislation outlined in Figure 2 was driven by the central govern-ment's need to 'neutralize' local resistance and to clear the way for a fully operational SUAP. The 1998–2010 period can be described as a negative implementation cycle (see Figure 1, right-hand column), given that most of the local governments either just ignored the laws (there being no penalties for non-compliance) or merely paid lip service by going through the formalities of setting up a SUAP without effectively

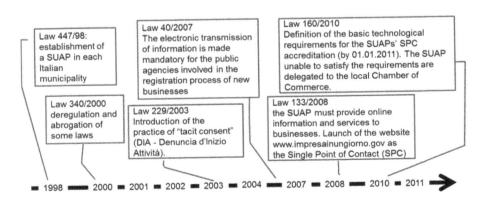

Figure 2. SUAP programme legislative timeline. Source: The authors.

operationalizing it. Both factors indicate a negative feedback loop stemming from the local governments' resistance to change, or even their very real inability to manage the change. Only a few local governments pro-actively stepped up to the SUAP plate, launching organizational transformation strategies that delivered an operationally effective SUAP (positive feedback loop).

In fact, it took the not-so-gentle nudge of Law 160/2010 to get the desired effects of the SUAP programme to finally kick in – 16 years after its 1998 launch date – with 8,014 of Italy's total 8,092 councils reporting a fully on-stream SUAP in 2014. Even then, Law 160/2010 did not come without a price, given that it forced those councils already running an effective, full-scope one-stop business shop to delegate management to the local Chamber of Commerce if their technological and organizational solutions failed to meet the central government's new requirements.

Complexity factors at work

Italy's SUAP programme, the flagbearer of the policies to simplify the state's administrative machinery through ICT, was the central government's response to the EU's prodding to implement digital government. The scale and scope of the SUAP reform and the fact that its success was entirely dependent on whether the councils had the resources/funds to ensure the system could operate and fulfil its mission makes it a particularly interesting case study. In fact, the central government's law-makers not only failed to conduct the due diligence needed to learn whether the local implementers possessed the necessary technological, organizational, and administrative governance capabilities but also neglected to ensure any form of governmental control. This 'hands-off' approach effectively dumped the job of implementation squarely onto the councils, leaving them to deal with it alone as best they could, and led the feedback mechanisms to shape the pre-2010 implementation phases of the SUAP programme (→ self-organization – A1). (The reason for codifying the 'complexity factors at work' identified in this section (A1, B2, C3, etc.) is to clarify the quasi-operationalization of the complexity concepts in Table 1 of the 'Discussion and implications' section.)

The multi-actor, inter-sector, and inter-institutional SUAP reform was hoisted onto a highly fragmented, heterogeneous administrative stage where the actors (especially the smaller townships, about 75 per cent of Italian municipalities) are rarely endowed with the means to manage complex processes of system innovation. Indeed, not only did few of Italy's local governments have the capabilities to manage the changes required by the SUAP law but also many of those that embarked on organizational change to comply with it adapted the national norms to their specific local contexts (→ self-organization – A2). Thus, in open defiance of the government's interventions to create a fully standardized one-stop business shop network, the variegated mix of small and large townships that makes up Italy's municipal landscape led to the adoption of highly different approaches to the development and operationalization of the SUAP.

In fact, the implementation of the one-stop business shop has led to the practice of those behaviours defined by Butler and Allen (2008) as self-organizing since 'national policy is reinterpreted at the local level, with each local organization uniquely mixing elements of national policy with their own requirements' (421). Created as organizational structures, many SUAPs emerged spontaneously from the interaction of agents

Table 1. Quasi-operationalization of the complexity concepts (Source: the authors).

Key Complexity Concepts	SUAP-specific Complexity Factors	Example of conditions that shaped the implementation of the SUAP
Self-organization	A1–A4	• A local agent (or group of agents) introduces implementation methods not envisaged by the original programme design (e.g. delegating management to the *Comunità Montane* or public services companies) • An agent (or group of agents) identifies and involves other agents in the implementation process not envisaged by the original programme design (e.g. the provincial governments, the *Comunità Montane*, or public services companies) • An agent (or group of agents) identifies and makes improvements to the implementation process not envisaged by the original programme design (e.g. involving the local stakeholders in the governance of the implementation process)
Emergence	B1–B5	• Organizational structures/units not envisaged by the original programme design (e.g. the formation of local committees of coordination) • Organizational roles not envisaged by the original programme design (e.g. delegation to the local Chambers of Commerce as per Law 160/2010) • Reorganization of the workflows according to methods not envisaged by the original programme design (e.g. the redesign of the many intra-organizational workflows and the domino effect on the different inter-organizational workflows of the SUAP-related public agencies)
Co-evolution	C1–C3	• An agent changes its structure and/or behaviour in response to the behaviour of another agent during the implementation process (e.g. all the actors involved launch internal reorganization processes to better support the SUAP activities) • The implementer agents, or some of them, agree to adopt joint operational methods that require changes not needed when each works in isolation (e.g. the mutually acceptable definition of local operational rules and standards) • An agent (or group of agents) sets in motion actions to reduce heterogeneous factors as a condition to improve the implementation process (e.g. the joint issuance of training courses by different public agencies affected by the implementation process)

following their local rules and responding to feedback from other agents and their environment (→ self-organization – A3; emergence – B1), without central direction, manipulation or control, central government policies or rules notwithstanding (→ emergence – B2). This explains why, to comply with the SUAP law, some small councils delegated management to a nearby, similarly sized counterpart or to their *Comunità Montana* (or the Provincial government) or chose to use voluntary aggregations of municipalities or public services companies.

The high degree of variation in the Italian SUAP system (macro-level) as a result of the interaction of the local agents (micro-level) is diametrically opposed to the goal of maximum standardization set by Law 447/1998, highlighting two aspects of SUAP implementation typical of emerging phenomena: 'micro–macro effect' and decentralized control (→ emergence – B3).

Italy's legalistic administrative tradition (typical of the Napoleonic model) causes the central government to use rigid regulatory frameworks to design and plan system innovation/reform processes. This compliance-driven route forced the local SUAP implementers to interact to define the intra- and inter-organizational workflows and, where possible, to consolidate common practices into uniform, standardized online procedures (→ co-evolution – C1); some agents even had to review their internal operational procedures or reconfigure their organizational units. Hence, those councils and local agents who successfully implemented a SUAP embarked on a mutual adaptation process that produced organizational solutions which also met the needs of the context, even though these sometimes strayed from the legislator's implicitly defined model (→ co-evolution – C2; self-organization – A4).

The process of co-evolution/adaptation was promoted by specially appointed local 'Coordination Committees' that, in bringing together the SUAP agents and other local stakeholders, introduced new players and new roles to the one-stop business shop scenario (→ emergence – B4). These local 'taskforces,' which were not part and parcel of the SUAP law but the spontaneous result of emergent processes, actively participated in both the development of staff training courses (→ co-evolution – C3) and the standardization of inter-organizational procedures and workflows to align them with the organizational solution adopted (→ emergence – B5).

The different methods used by the local implementers to adapt the SUAP to the context of jurisdiction resulted in a proliferation of organizational models and solutions of every kind. To correct this drift, Italy's central government wrote new laws (see timeline, Figure 2) to restrict the organizational autonomy of the local governments, which it ruled a source of complexity and an impediment to the realization of the one-stop business shop. In particular, the new laws:

- weakened the power of the councils to manage the SUAP procedures at their own discretion (e.g. by introducing the practice of tacit consent);
- centralized specific, mainly front-office activities (for instance, through the setting up of a national SPC as per the EU directives);
- defined the technological and organizational requirements that either qualified the SUAP as fully operational or disqualified the non-compliant municipalities from its independent management;
- allowed the councils to voluntarily delegate the SUAP's operations to the local Chamber of Commerce, making it mandatory for the disqualified non-compliant.

The hard line taken by the government completely disregarded the proven efficiency and efficacy of certain local organizational models, signalling the demise of, for example, the associated SUAPs managed by public services companies, the SUAPs set up by the *Comunità Montane* on behalf of their municipal members, and the associated SUAPs managed by aggregations of municipalities, dismantled merely for not complying with the new regulations. The two critical factors that fuelled the continual rollout of the new laws, rules, and regulations which ended up crushing the existing SUAP system were (1) the poor coordination of the SUAP with other sector laws and council regulations (in particular those of inter-municipal cooperation), and (2) the government's attempt to impose tighter, more direct controls on the implementation process, possibly contradicting certain mainstays of the national one-stop business shop policies embedded in the original 1998 SUAP act.

However, despite the government's attempts to use the power of the law and ongoing regulatory adjustments to get the local implementers to adopt uniform solutions, at the time of writing, 18 years later, the Italian SUAP network is still fraught with complications. The implementation process has turned into a drawn-out narrative in which a wide range of organizational solutions have become doable, one example being the option introduced by Law 160/2010 to delegate the SUAP to the local Chamber of Commerce. Interestingly, this 'emerging' solution was not on the cards when the reform first took flight and is in stark contrast to the goals of Law 447/1998 to strengthen the role and autonomy of the councils and to reduce the levels of intermediation between business and the PA. The fact that Law 160/2010 turned the tide is attested by the fact that 40 per cent of the SUAPs were in the hands of the local Chamber of Commerce in 2014, which is a clear sign of self-organization and emergence, although that indicator is subject to major variations of 0–89 per cent at the regional level.

Discussion and implications

The sharp twists and turns of the SUAP reform path illustrate many of the analytical points made in this article, including 'the indeterminacy of organizational systems and the difficulty with isolating cause and effect' (Haynes 2015, 19) and non-linearity effects that make it hard to predict trends, particularly in the longer term. A combination of these factors and the intrinsic limitations of complexity thinking, because complexity theory is not a fully articulated theory (Morçöl 2012, 262), helps explain the strong tendency of scholars to use metaphors to describe complexity principles.

This study tries to break through the metaphorical boundaries on the premise that the inherent complexity of public programmes is linked to their state of constant flux, which, in turn, is driven by conditions of feasibility and the actions and interactions of the agents. It therefore stands to reason that a programme can have many potential outcomes which often diverge from the initial expectations and that rigid theories and simple legalistic conceptions of implementation are inadequate for understanding what happens on the ground (Peters 2015, 90).

In the exemplified case of Italy's one-stop business shop reform, the mix of co-evolution, self-organization, and emergence emphasizes the non-linearity of the paths taken by the local implementers to comply with a centrally designed programme, highlighting, without getting lost in the too-specific details, how these major ground forces interact in an empirical setting. To achieve the aims set out at the beginning of the paper, the insights gleaned from the analysis can help piece together the answers to the two research questions.

Q1. How can the concepts of emergence, co-evolution and self-organization be operationalized starting with the analysis of the implementation of a nationwide policy programme?

Table 1 summarizes the conditions that led to self-organization, co-evolution, and emergence during the implementation of the SUAP reform and lays the foundations for a quasi-operationalization of these concepts.

Q2. To what extent does the complexity of the implementation process shape the direction and development of a public programme, in particular, in a country of the Napoleonic administrative tradition?

The implementation and outcomes of the SUAP programme were the results of the dynamic tension between two opposing visions: that of the central government's 'planned' and intrinsically rationalist 'innovation by law' method, consisting of continual interventionist adjustments to increase its control and direction of the results throughout, and that of the local government implementer's more contingent approach, oriented to the real-life (contextually defined) constraints and opportunities of complying with the law. The SUAP case sheds much light on the interaction between these two conflicting fixed views, which, due to Italy's strong legalistic tradition of governance, has led to pervasive co-evolution and self-organization and, via the relative feedback loops, shaped the material implementation of the reform. Interestingly, the co-evolutionary relations occurred at two levels: between the actors and between the policies. This medley of dynamic interactions has foiled the central government's repeated attempts to force the councils to adopt a single business model designed to reduce the complexity of the system. The current SUAP network continues to deploy multiple organizational solutions, including directly operated, associated management and delegation to the Chamber of Commerce, therefore confirming the view of Christensen and Lægreid (2012, 5) that complexity is 'a systemic feature of public sector organizations that needs to be taken into consideration when reorganizing the administrative apparatus, rather than regarding it as a disease that must be eliminated.' In other words, to implement public reforms, it is necessary to rewrite the rules to *engage* with complexity rather than trying to reduce it (Rhodes et al. 2011, our italics).

Engagement is interpreted here as being realistic and taking on the challenge of problem solving. Haynes (2015, 48) advice to 'embrace complexity and grasp opportunities' is also an invitation to the policymakers and the public managers to chart a realistic course and to accept the changing nature of the systems in which they operate. Addressing wicked problems calls for public officials to forge new ways of thinking, leading, managing, and organizing which recognize the complexity of the issues and processes (Head and Alford 2015, 12); public officials also need to acknowledge that there are limits to their capacity to determine the outcomes and to control the direction that the emergence of new forms of order takes (Haynes

2015, 31). To this end, a holistic rather than linear thinking is capable of grasping the big picture, including the multiple causal factors and policy objectives.

To engage with complexity, the policy makers must, above all, break with the logic of best practices that still percolates in the public sector mindset. The complexity and heterogeneity of public organizations debunk the notion that a universal organizational Best Practice Plan (Butler and Allen 2008) exists. As the SUAP case clearly shows, identifying a specific solution as the best practice to adopt (implicitly or explicitly) for defining the legal and regulatory norms of a reference model is no guarantee that its on-the-ground application will eliminate different and often unpredictable results.

To the public manager, engaging with complexity means retiring the governance and accountability model 'based on assumptions of predictability, the elimination of uncertainty by planning and analysis methodologies and control by compliance' (Rhodes et al. 2011, 206) to bring on board a model that consents 'frequent adaptation and a real time approach to navigating emergent reality – at all levels'. Consequently, managers must 'rethink the nature of hierarchy and control, learn the art of managing and changing contexts, promote self-organizing processes, and learn how to use small changes to create large effects' (Burnes 2005, 82). Moreover, complexity thinking negates the traditional (and misleading) separation between evaluation and implementation: 'it is the feedback process itself that offers ... the best understanding of how performance is constructed' (Haynes 2015, 86). Therefore, in order to identify critical issues and adjust the organizational processes, for instance, to reinforce feedback, it is necessary to first understand this two-way relationship.

Clearly, central government intervention alone will not solve the problem of translating the implementation strategies into concrete actions. So what is the deal here? What is the point of providing the implementers working in a complex operational environment with guidelines whose 'best answers' or 'golden rules' are, at most, only wishful thinking? One practical solution suggested by Haynes (2015) is to invite the managers at various levels to use the public values as a compass: 'Values are at the core of public services and concepts of public intervention ... [they] attract social stability and order' (146). Ultimately, embracing complexity is about 'serving the community and the public interest' (149).

This reference to values is clear but its reasonableness risks clashing with the dominant administrative logics which, as shown by the exemplary case of the SUAP programme, usually manage to ride out the storms without feeling the need to update the credo of 'how' to do reform. In other words, the case evidences that none of the governmental systems made any attempt to learn, that their response was merely to adapt, and that the stacking up of laws, rules, and regulations only further complicated matters. Moreover, the public managers continue to be trained in mostly legal–formal aspects of the national administrative tradition. Paradoxically, in legalistic administrative contexts like Italy, the law takes precedence over the value generated by the effectiveness of local emergent solutions. The government's reforms are seen as rigid obligations, not as opportunities to drive major change, which is what set Italy's one-stop business shop reform on a turbulent journey that lasted almost 20 years.

Conclusions and further research directions

The paper goes against the grain of the metaphorical use of complexity principles in the mainstream literature to highlight the value of applying a complexity-based lens to the analysis of the implementation of a nationwide public reform. This initial scoping of the three concepts of emergence, co-evolution, and self-organization has flagged the potential threats to the operational success of such a programme unless it is recognized as a self-organizing system that breeds emergence and co-evolution.

The study's findings point to a more pragmatic and advantageous way to deal with the non-negotiable issue of the complex nature of multi-organizational environments, making a strong argument for the policymakers and the public managers to step off the merry-go-round of reducing complexity and to strategically engage with complexity.

This tentative bid to build a bridge between generalized complexity concepts and a specific case does not deliver absolute answers to the puzzling question of how to apply complexity theories to the public domain; it offers no direct guidance on how large-scale programmes can be implemented; nor does it provide evidence of the effectiveness of implementation (outcomes). Rather, the study sets the start line from which to develop complexity assessment systems capable of managing the instability of the external world effectively, and not to mirror (or co-align) it (à la Lawrence and Lorsh).

The overarching aim of the paper is to advance our current thinking by integrating different disciplinary perspectives that identify key interlinked factors worthy of further investigation. In particular, the authors acknowledge the paper's limitations, which translate into the need to develop the framework of the conceptual clarification (merely outlined here, also due to lack of space); test the list of Table 1 for both comprehensiveness and parsimony; make a more in-depth analysis of the connections between emergence, co-evolution, and self-organization to help improve the descriptive scope of the model in Figure 1; and use other case studies to test and validate the proposed heuristic approach. Future research projects also will enquire more deeply into how the strategy of engaging with complexity ties in with Haynes's (2015) proposal of 'managing for values.'

Ultimately, the fact that the 'generalizability of the information about complex systems is problematic' (Morçöl 2012, 247) means that empirical studies are needed to expand the knowledge gained from the single case and single-country research, and to enable the comparison of the approaches and results of different countries and different policy domains.

The research approach adopted here is a contribution to what is necessarily a collective endeavour to glean useful insights from the application of a complexity-based lens.

Disclosure statement

No potential conflict of interest was reported by the authors.

ORCID

Walter Castelnovo ⓘ http://orcid.org/0000-0002-5741-5106

References

Anderson, P. 1999. "Complexity Theory and Organization Science." *Organization Science* 10 (3): 216–232. doi:10.1287/orsc.10.3.216.

Burnes, B. 2005. "Complexity Theories and Organizational Change." *International Journal of Management Reviews* 7 (2): 73–90. doi:10.1111/ijmr.2005.7.issue-2.

Butler, M. J. R., and P. M. Allen. 2008. "Understanding Policy Implementation Processes as Self-Organizing Systems." *Public Management Review* 10 (3): 421–440. doi:10.1080/14719030802002923.

Byrne, D. 1998. *Complexity Theory and the Social Sciences.* London: Routledge.

Cairney, P. 2012. "Complexity Theory and Political Science." *Political Studies Review* 10 (3): 346–358. doi:10.1111/j.1478-9302.2012.00270.x.

Cairney, P., and R. Geyer. 2017. "A Critical Discussion of Complexity Theory: How Does 'Complexity Thinking' Improve Our Understanding of Politics and Policymaking?" *Complexity, Governance and Networks* 3 (2): 1–11. doi:10.20377/cgn-56

Cairney, P., and R. Geyer. 2015a. "Introduction: A New Direction in Policymaking Theory and Practice?" In *Handbook on Complexity and Public Policy*, edited by P. Cairney and R. Geyer, 1–15. Cheltenham, UK: Edward Elgar.

Cairney, P., and R. Geyer. 2015b. "Conclusion: Where Does Complexity and Policy Go from Here?" In *Handbook on Complexity and Public Policy*, edited by P. Cairney and R. Geyer, 457–465. Cheltenham: Edward Elgar.

Capano, G. 2003. "Administrative Traditions and Policy Change: When Policy Paradigms Matter. The Case of Italian Administrative Reform during the 1990s." *Public Administration* 81: 781–801. doi:10.1111/padm.2003.81.issue-4.

Castelnovo, W., M. Sorrentino, and M. De Marco. 2016. "Italy's One-Stop Shop: A Case of the Emperor's New Clothes? In *Organizational Innovation and Change*, LNSIO 13, edited by C. Rossignoli, M. Gatti, and R. Agrifoglio, 27–39. Berlin: Springer.

Cherry, N. 2014. "Organisational Paradoxes of Local E-Government." *Journal of Contemporary Issues in Business and Government* 20 (1): 41–57. doi:10.7790/cibg.v20i1.19.

Christensen, T., and P. Lægreid. 2012. "Competing Principles of Agency Organization – the Reorganization of a Reform." *International Review of Administrative Sciences* 78 (4): 579–596. doi:10.1177/0020852312455306.

Duit, A., and V. Galaz. 2008. "Governance and Complexity—Emerging Issues for Governance Theory." *Governance* 21 (3): 311–335. doi:10.1111/gove.2008.21.issue-3.

Eppel, E. 2012. "The Application of a Complexity Analytical Lens to Understanding and Explaining Public Policy Processes." In *COMPACT I: Public Administration in Complexity*, edited by L. Gerrits and P. Marks, 174–197. Litchfeld Park: Emergent Publications.

Eppel, E. 2016. "Complexity Thinking in Public Administration's Theories-In-Use." *Public Management Review* 19 (6): 845–861.

Eppel, E., A. Matheson, and M. Walton. 2011. "Applying Complexity Theory to New Zealand Public Policy - Principles for Practice." *Policy Quarterly* 7 (1): 48–55.

Eppel, E., D. Turner, and A. Wolf. 2011. "Experimentation and Learning in Policy Implementation: Implications for Public Management." Institute of Policy Studies Working Paper 11/04. Wellington, NZ: Victoria University of Wellington

Forti, A. 2000. "Reduction of Administrative Burden for Enterprises – the One Stop Shop Experience in Italy." European Commission Peer Review Programme. http://pdf.mutual-learning-employ ment.net/pdf/ind-exp-paper-it-nov00-p.pdf

Gerrits, L., and J. W. Meek. 2011. "Propositions for Complexity Science." In COMPACT I: Public Administration in Complexity, edited by L. Gerrits and P. Marks, 350–363. Litchfeld Park: Emergent Publications.

Haveri, A. 2006. "Complexity in Local Government Change." Public Management Review 8 (1): 31–46. doi:10.1080/14719030500518667.

Haynes, P. 2015. Managing Complexity in the Public Services. 2nd ed. Abingdon: Routledge.

Head, B. W., and J. Alford. 2015. "Wicked Problems: Implications for Public Policy and Management." Administration and Society 47 (6): 711–739. doi:10.1177/0095399713481601.

Houchin, K., and D. MacLean. 2005. "Complexity Theory and Strategic Change: An Empirically Informed Critique." British Journal of Management 16 (2): 149–166. doi:10.1111/bjom.2005.16. issue-2.

Jacobs, A. M., and R. K. Weaver. 2010. "Policy Feedback and Policy Change." Paper presented at the APSA 2010 Annual Meeting, Washington, DC, September 2–5.

Jacobs, A. M., and R. K. Weaver. 2015. "When Policies Undo Themselves: Self-Undermining Feedback as a Source of Policy Change." Governance 28 (4): 441–457. doi:10.1111/gove.2015.28. issue-4.

Jones, B. D., and F. R. Baumgartner. 2012. "From There to Here." Policy Studies Journal 40: 1–19.

Klijn, E. H. 2008. "Complexity Theory and Public Administration." What's New? Public Management Review 10 (3): 299–317. doi:10.1080/14719030802002675.

Krolczyk, A., C. Senf, and N. Cordes. 2010. "Construction of a Complex Adaptive Systems Pattern as an Epistemological Lens for E-Government Systems." In Proceedings of the 43rd Hawaii International Conference on System Sciences (HICSS-43), edited by Ralph H. Sprague, Jr., 1–10. Piscataway, NJ: IEEE.

Kuhlmann, S., and H. Wollmann. 2014. Introduction to Comparative Public Administration. Cheltenham: Edward Elgar.

Langley, A. 1999. "Strategies for Theorizing from Process Data." Academy of Management Review 24 (4): 691–710. doi:10.5465/amr.1999.2553248.

Levy, D. L. 2000. "Applications and Limitations of Complexity Theory in Organization Theory and Strategy." In Handbook of Strategic Management, 2nd ed., edited by J. Rabin, G. J. Miller, and W. B. Hildreth, 67–87. New York: Marcel Dekker.

Lichtenstein, B. 2011. "Complexity Science Contributions to the Field of Entrepreneurship." In The SAGE Handbook of Complexity and Management, edited by P. Allen, S. Maguire, and B. McKelvey, 471–493. London: Sage.

Lichtenstein, B. B., and B. McKelvey. 2011. "Four Types of Emergence: A Typology of Complexity and Its Implications for a Science of Management." International Journal of Complexity in Leadership and Management 1 (4): 339–378. doi:10.1504/IJCLM.2011.046439.

Lissack, M. R. 1997. "Mind Your Metaphors: Lessons from Complexity Science." Long Range Planning 30 (2): 294–298. doi:10.1016/S0024-6301(96)00120-3.

Maguire, S., P. Allen, and B. McKelvey. 2011. "Complexity and Management: Introducing the SAGE Handbook." In Complexity and Management, edited by S. Maguire, P. Allen, and B. McKelvey, 1–26. Los Angeles, CA: Sage.

Marks, P. K., and L. M. Gerrits. 2013. "Approaching Public Administration from a Complexity Perspective." Public Administration Review 73 (6): 898–903. doi:10.1111/puar.2013.73.issue-6.

Mathews, K. M., M. C. White, and R. G. Long. 1999. "Why Study the Complexity Sciences in the Social Sciences?" Human Relations 52 (4): 439–462. doi:10.1177/001872679905200402.

Morçöl, G. 2012. A Complexity Theory for Public Policy. New York: Routledge.

OECD. 2009. "Better Regulation to Strengthen Market Dynamics – Italy 2009." http://www.oecd-ilibrary.org/governance/oecd-reviews-of-regulatory-reform-italy-2009_9789264067264-en

Ongaro, E. 2004. "Process Management in the Public Sector: The Experience of One-Stop Shops in Italy." International Journal of Public Sector Management 17 (1): 81–107. doi:10.1108/09513550410515592.

Peters, B. G. 2008. "The Napoleonic Tradition." *International Journal of Public Sector Management* 21 (2): 118–132. doi:10.1108/09513550810855627.

Peters, B. G. 2015. *Advanced Introduction to Public Policy*. Cheltenham: Edward Elgar.

Plowman, D. A., L. T. Baker, T. E. Beck, M. Kulkarni, S. T. Solansky, and D. V. Travis. 2007. "Radical Change Accidentally: The Emergence and Amplification of Small Change." *Academy of Management Journal* 50 (3): 515–543. doi:10.5465/AMJ.2007.25525647.

Rhodes, M. L. 2008. "Complexity and Emergence in Public Management: The Case of Urban Regeneration in Ireland." *Public Management Review* 10 (3): 361–379. doi:10.1080/14719030802002717.

Rhodes, M. L., J. Murphy, J. Muir, and J. Murray. 2011. *Public Management and Complexity Theory: Richer Decision Making in Irish Public Services*. New York: Routledge.

Richardson, K. A. 2008. "Managing Complex Organizations: Complexity Thinking and the Science and Art of Management." *Emergence: Complexity and Organization* 10 (2): 13–26.

Stacey, R. D. 1995. "The Science of Complexity: An Alternative Perspective for Strategic Change Processes." *Strategic Management Journal* 16 (6): 477–495. doi:10.1002/(ISSN)1097-0266.

Teisman, R. G. 2008. "Complexity and Management of Improvement Programmes." *Public Management Review* 10 (3): 341–359. doi:10.1080/14719030802002584.

True, J.L., B. D. Jones, and F. R. Baumgartner. 2007. "Punctuated Equilibrium Theory." In *Theories of the Policy Process*, 2nd ed., edited by P. Sabatier, 155–189. Cambridge, MA: Westview Press.

von Ghyczy, T. 2003. "The Fruitful Flaws of Strategy Metaphors." *Harvard Business Review*, (Sep.): 86–94.

Bridging complexity theory and hierarchies, markets, networks, communities: a 'population genetics' framework for understanding institutional change from within

Tim Tenbensel

ABSTRACT

Complexity theory is highly compatible with institutionalist approaches to analysing governance. This article develops a 'population genetics' account of governance dynamics using complexity concepts. This framework joins 'hierarchy, markets, networks and communities' (HMNC) with concepts of endogenous change, genetic recombination, and fitness landscapes. Institutional environments comprise 'populations' that contain a range of genetic profiles. Change and stability are shaped by nesting and abrasion of alternative combinations within a governance field. This framework can help researchers understand how agents attempt to transform meso-level institutions from within, using the field of primary medical care governance in Auckland as an example.

Introduction

Institutions – the relatively hard-wired, formal and informal rules that govern public management practices – are (by definition) difficult things to change. When they do change, according to much public policy literature of the past 30 years, it is because of 'external perturbations' – policy equivalents of meteorites wiping out dinosaurs. This does not give much hope to policy actors operating within institutional environments that they may see as problematic and in need of change. Yet institutions do change from within, and many authors more recently have highlighted the role of endogenous processes in generating institutional change (Streeck and Thelen 2005; Mahoney and Thelen 2010). Nevertheless, there are challenges in understanding the ways in which 'intentional agents' attempt, instigate and/or enact institutional change. Part of the challenge here is that institutional change in public management is commonly conceptualized in terms of abstract ideal types such as hierarchies, markets, networks, and communities (HMNC). While these concepts have proven to be useful, if broad-brush, descriptive analytical categories, they have not proven particularly amenable to the development of theories of institutional change, or how actors attempt to generate change within their institutional settings.

By contrast, the emerging public management literature that draws on complexity theory purports to theorize dynamics of endogenous change, and the role of agents in these change processes (Bovaird 2008; Rhodes et al. 2011; Haynes 2015). A number of influential authors have expounded the argument that the most important contribution that can be made by complexity theory to public policy will be based on 'theoretical partnerships' with more established bodies of public policy and public management theory (Pollitt 2009; Room 2011; Cairney 2012). While I have argued elsewhere that the complexity-inspired approaches to public policy and governance could benefit from sustained engagement and cross-fertilization with HMNC concepts (Tenbensel 2015), there is also a great deal that complexity theory can offer in return.

The purpose of this article is to provide a new lease of life to the HMNC by infusing it with concepts drawn from complexity theory. More specifically, I develop a 'population genetics' framework for analysing institutional change in public management, and the role of agents in that change, from materials that have been provided by Colin Crouch in his discussion of the role of 'institutional entrepreneurs' in the process of 'recombinant governance' (Crouch 2005; Room 2011), and the concept of rugged institutional landscapes adapted by Graham Room (2011) from Stuart Kauffman (1995). By using these concepts drawn from complexity theory, it is possible to infuse some dynamism and a clear actor-centred focus into what has been a predominantly static and descriptive HMNC approach.

I start by outlining the key principles of the HMNC approach and the limitations that have emerged. The second section draws on the work of Crouch, Room and Kaufmann to address these limitations and put actors in the forefront of processes of institutional change, and a third section applies the resultant approach – what I refer to as a 'population genetics' approach – to a New Zealand health policy case study which tracks the attempts of policy actors to transform their institutional environment. In doing so, I aim to provide a framework which draws from complexity concepts which can be useful to actors engaging in institutional change.

Hierarchy, Market, Network, Community (HMNC)

HMNC literature has been applied extensively to public management cases in two ways. The first way is to make broad generalizations about the tide of history in public management turning from hierarchical to market governance, and subsequently (perhaps) to network governance. Such approaches are broad-brush and are problematic because they apply HMNC teleologically and/or normatively to argue that public management is progressing (or should progress) or is regressing from one ideal type to another (Osborne and Gaebler 1992; Goldsmith and Eggers 2004). This is characteristic of a great deal of New Public Management (NPM) literature, as well as much New Public Governance (NPG) literature. These approaches often neglect the significant degree of 'network-type' governance that did exist in the so-called hierarchial mid-twentieth century (cf. Le Grand 2007), as well as the persistence and reinventions of hierarchical tropes and techniques over recent decades (Lynn 2011).

Others (including this author) have adopted a more agnostic approach (Davies and Spicer 2015) to applying HMNC. Here, HMNC is primarily used as a language of classification. The basic principles of this more agnostic HMNC literature can be identified:

(1) Hierarchies, markets, networks, and communities are ideal types of social co-ordination generally. As such, they are also ideal types of institutional designs that can be harnessed by governmental and non-governmental actors to govern policy problems. As ideal types, they provide a way of mapping governance types analogous to the way that compass points of north, west, south and east provide a foundation for mapping geographical space.

(2) Most governance arrangements involve combinations of these ideal types. This idea first articulated in sociological literature by Bradach and Eccles (1989) quickly became widely accepted and adopted in public management literature since the late 1990s (Rhodes 1997; Exworthy, Powell, and Mohan 1999; Considine and Lewis 2003; Keast, Brown, and Mandell 2007; Lewis 2009). 'Hybridity' has become a common term for describing combined types of co-ordination and governance (Ranade and Hudson 2003; Lewis 2009; Byrkjeflot and Guldbrandsøy 2013)

(3) Those who use HMNC in this way are agnostic about whether specific modes are normatively preferable to others. A common argument is that all have specific congenital strengths and weaknesses, and that the appropriateness of the use of any mode is largely shaped by contextual factors (Rhodes 1997; Tenbensel 2005; Bouckaert, Peters, and Verhoest 2010).

(4) There is also widespread agreement that governance combinations are not static and change over time. Again, there are many empirical studies that interpret change in terms of the evolution of new governance mixes (Lowndes and Skelcher 1998; Lance, Georgiadou, and Bregt 2009).

For the most part, this use of HMNC in public management literature is predominantly pragmatic and primarily descriptive, and not particularly ambitious theoretically. Unless it is tied to a broader historical institutionalist framework (e.g. Tuohy 1999; Helderman 2007; Van De Bovenkamp et al. 2013), the HMNC categorization is rarely elaborated and used as a theoretical framework. While it offers some potential for understanding how agents might initiate, sustain, or even resist changes in governance, there are a number of conceptual issues that require clarification if HMNC is to be useful for understanding processes of institutional change, and for generating insights about how institutional change could be catalyzed by agents in the worlds of public policy and management.

Is there a fixed quantum of governance?

One assumption often built into analyses that use HMNC is that of a 'fixed quantum' of governance. This is the idea that if new modes of governance become important, they do so *at the expense of* another mode. As applied to the analysis of governance, this implicit assumption is that as one type increases in its scope, another (or others) must decrease (Byrkjeflot and Guldbrandsøy 2013). A move *towards* a new destination is always a move *away* from another. A variation of the 'fixed quantum' assumption, is that 'extra' governance entails redundancy that is inefficient. This argument is made by Entwistle et al. who posit that 'it must … be true, at least in purely theoretical terms, that the duplication or triplication of a single act of co-ordination is wasteful of resources' (Entwistle et al. 2007, 66).

However, this 'fixed quantum' view is challenged by a growing base of empirical work that highlights the presence of 'positive-sum' rather than 'zero-sum' relationships between governance modes. A study of frontline welfare staff across four nations found that Australian practices of welfare governance involved *higher levels* of hierarchy, *more* network and *more* market than practices in other countries (Considine and Lewis 2003). The use of control (hierarchy) and trust (network) can be seen as supplementing each other (the existence of one underpinning the existence of the other) creating a 'reinforcing cycle' (Edelenbos and Eshuis 2009; Six 2013). Similarly, it may also be possible that there may be 'not enough governance' in that co-ordination of any sort between actors is absent or minimal (Tenbensel, Mays, and Cumming 2011). This question is important because it has implications for agents intentionally seeking to change how things are governed – particularly whether or not existing institutional structures need to be intentionally dismantled.

Are all governance 'hybrids' the same?

Widespread use of the term 'hybrid' with regards to governance modes has the potential to obscure rather than enlighten. In public management literature, there have been countless studies of specific governance arrangement consists of a combination of hierarchy and network. However, to paraphrase Leo Tolstoy, each example of hybrid governance is hybrid in its own way. This issue is analogous to that raised by Skelcher and Rathgeb Smith (2015) regarding hybridity of organizational types.

In health sector examples from Israel and New Zealand (Sax 2014; Tenbensel, Mays, and Cumming 2011), the mixes are those in which the hierarchical control is over policy direction and network collaboration comes into play in implementation. By contrast, Moynihan (2008) provides an account of the USA's Incident Command System (ICS), in which there are networking relationships between a range of different government organizations in planning system responses, but a hierarchical chain of command in response to national emergencies and crises. Treating these examples as members of the same analytic category of hierarchy-network hybrids may not be that useful or meaningful. For agents seeking to change institutional rules and conditions, thinking in terms of hybrids is therefore problematic and vague.

Under what conditions are co-existing modes compatible or incompatible?

There are many examples in the literature in which writers attribute the coexistence of different modes to the fact that one or both is present in order to make up for the deficiencies (perceived and/or real) of the other(s). If we focus our attention on the co-existence of hierarchy and network, a number of studies reveal examples in which hierarchical and network co-ordination coexist in complementary ways. These examples traverse a wide range of contexts ranging from the management of geographic data (Lance, Georgiadou, and Bregt 2009), health service delivery (Currie, Grubnic, and Hodges 2011); pharmaceutical benefits systems (Sax 2014) and crisis response (Moynihan 2008). Many of these are examples of 'mandated networks' in which governments use authority (hierarchy) to stimulate the development of network co-ordination where it is regarded as necessary to achieve policy goals (Rodríguez et al. 2007; Elst and Rynck 2013).

There are also many examples in which the coexistence of different modes is regarded as a source of incoherence, tension, and conflict. Jonathan Davies (2005) emphasizes the inherent conflict in attempts to blend networks with hierarchy and/or markets, as do Entwistle et al. (2007). Conflicting modes is also a prominent theme in the work of Bode (Bode 2006; Bode and Firbank 2009). Many studies of mandated networks diagnose failure due to the inherent contradiction entailed in enforcing co-operation between organizations (Addicott et al. 2007). In addition, a number of studies readily identify both conflict and complementarity within the same case, or across multiple cases (Addicott 2008; Ferlie et al. 2011; Sax 2014). The theoretical challenge, therefore, is to develop a more general language that aims to understand/explain why (the same) combinations of governance types are conflictual in some contexts and complementary in others. The conflict/compatibility question is parti-cularly pertinent for agents attempting some form of institutional change, as it raises the question of whether attempted changes will be resisted or accommodated by other actors. Being able to distinguish between actions and interventions that set off vicious cycles of conflict between institutional principles from those that trigger virtuous cycles of improvements in governance could constitute a 'high-level' capa-city of public managers.

How can we understand the dynamics of change?

Combinations of governance modes do change over time, and can change regularly, and these changes are often driven endogenously. Thus, co-ordination and/or governance in a particular field can move from one admixture of hierarchy and network to another, different, mix of the two. Again, the metaphor of 'hybrid' governance is ill-suited for this purpose, as hybridity (for individual organisms) is static, rather than changeable.

Bringing together HMNC and complexity concepts – a 'population genetics' approach

Each of these weaknesses of the HMNC conceptual repertoire can be addressed by turning to complexity literature. Genetic metaphors and concepts have been touch-stones for a range of complexity theorists, and have also been fruitfully applied to institutional analyses. The key is to shift from thinking of institutional arrangements as 'individual units' that may exhibit 'purebred' or 'hybrid' characteristics to imagin-ing them as 'populations' of governance arrangements. The foundation of such a 'population genetics' approach to governance can be found in Colin Crouch's book, *Capitalist diversity and change: recombinant governance and institutional entrepre-neurs* (2005). Graham Room (2011) has argued strongly that Crouch's approach should be at the heart of any approach incorporating complexity and institutionalism.

Crouch and the genetics of institutional change

Crouch's framework emerged from a critique of the way ideal types were applied in the 'varieties of capitalism' (VOC) literature. Specifically, he took issue with the implicit (and sometimes explicit) argument that there were 'pure' types of capitalism that were coherent packages, and that examples that did not fit these pure types were problematic/unlikely to be viable. For Crouch, ideal types should be seen as reference points, but many permutations of governance (institutions) are actually possible in the past, present, and future. Some may be realized, others not. The primary task of analysis is to understand how and why particular empirical forms develop in particular circumstances, rather than assessing governance arrangements in terms of proximity to ideal types.

Crouch starts by introducing the concept of 'fields' of governance. Fields, according to Crouch can be 'anything from the production of innovative biopharmaceutical products to organizing a religion' (Crouch 2005, 101). He then proceeds to provide a way of mapping the particular governance arrangements that take place in particular fields. Governance for Crouch is social co-ordination generally, which includes, but is not limited to, governmental attempts to steer. Crouch specifies a list of nine governance (institutional) attributes (see Table 1) that may be relevant to any form of social co-ordination. Each attribute distinguishes between two contrasting capacities. We can think of these capacities as particular 'allele' expressions of specific genes. Crouch's nine attributes (genes) of governance are outlined in Table 1 below.

Any specific capacity (allele) may be more or less relevant in different fields. Just as webbed feet may be particularly useful in a swampy environment but not in a desert, dialogue as communication capacity may be useful in some contexts, while 'signalling' (non-dialogical communication) might be useful in another. Crouch then suggests which specific permutations characterize particular ideal types of governance, including state hierarchy, markets, networks, communities, guilds, and associations (Crouch 2005, 100–109).

Crouch regards his list of attributes as a starting point for discussion rather than the final word. For the purposes of applying the argument to policy implementation and public management in a parsimonious way, I suggest we start with six attributes of Crouch's framework. For present purposes, I restrict the list to those public management

Table 1. Crouch's attributes of governance.

1. *Exogeneity* versus *endogeneity*. A governance mechanism may be either external to the institution being governed or internal to it.
2. *Formality* versus *informality*. The character of the rules through which governance is expressed can be either formal (that is explicit, in principle clearly specifiable) or informal (implicit, subject to nuance and variable mutual understanding).
3. *Substance* versus *procedure*. In the former, there is direct intervention by agents responsible for governance to give incentives to behaviour by allocating resources. In the latter, a set of procedures affects the behaviour of ordinary actors within the institution.
4. *Signalling* versus *dialogue*. Signalling simply indicates what constitutes compliant behaviour (as in the pure market). Dialogue provides for complex exchanges of speech acts and negotiation of terms (as in most other governance forms, particularly at the local level).
5. *Verticality* versus *horizontality*. Communication also has a directional dimension. Vertical communication implies an authority centre (as in an association, or a corporate hierarchy). Horizontality presupposes a system of rules in place, enabling communication itself to be lateral and not itself embodying a command structure.
6. *Strong* versus *weak enforcement*. Fundamental to governance is enforcement capacity: How effective is the governance mechanism in ensuring compliance? We can initially model this capacity simply as being either strong or weak.
7. *Extensive* versus *limited reach*. There is a second aspect of enforcement: its reach. Do the enforcement mechanisms in question extend generally across the society or indeed the world, or are they limited to those directly connected to the institution?
8. *Difficult* versus *easy exit*. Related to the strength and reach of enforcement capacity is the possibility of exit from the institution. This can be difficult, leaving units and individuals trapped within the enforcement scope of the governance mechanism, or easy.
9. *Public* versus *private goods*. All governance provides goods for a collectivity of some kind, but the character of the collectivity so served can vary from a pure public one (in the economist's sense) to a private, defined group.

Source: (Crouch 2005, 109)

contexts in which governance is endogenous – defined within territorial boundaries of the state (cf. Crouch's first attribute), noting that exogenous constraints would need to be included where there is multilevel governance. Second, all public management, by definition, involves public goods (attribute 9) so all institutional forms will feature this capacity. Finally, I have omitted attribute 7 – reach of enforcement – from the discussion because in public management, strength (attribute 6) and reach of enforcement are largely synonymous. This leaves six attributes:

- (2) **Formal** versus informal governance rules
- (3) **Substance** versus procedure
- (4) **Signalling** communication v dialogue
- (5) **Vertical** vs. horizontal communication
- (6) **Strong** vs. weak enforcement of rules
- (8) **Difficult** vs. easy exit from relationships

Table 2 plots Crouch's genetic profiles of hierarchies, markets, networks and communities across these six attributes (2005, 110–11). The value '1' denotes the first pole of each attribute from Table 1, the value '0' represents the second term.

In Table 2, note that hierarchies and networks have opposing capacities for five of the six selected public management attributes in this attenuated version of Crouch's table

This offers a way of understanding the range of possible hybrids. Table 3 identifies two hybrids of hierarchy and network (HN Hybrids A & B). Leaving aside attribute 3 in which hierarchy and network have the same value, Hybrid A shares three capacities with 'pure' hierarchy (formal rules, vertical communication, strong enforcement) and two with 'pure' network (dialogical communication, easy exit). Hybrid B is the opposite of Hybrid A on these five attributes.

However, the usefulness of Crouch's framework goes well beyond this more fine-grained taxonomy of governance institutions. This genetic approach also enables a

Table 2. Genetic profiles of public management governance modes.

	2 Formal (1) vs. informal (0) governance	3 Substance (1) vs. procedure (0)	4 Signalling (1) vs. Dialogue (0)	5 Vertical (1) vs. horizontal (0) communication	6 Strong (1) vs. weak (0) enforcement	8 Difficulty (1) vs. ease (0) of exit
Hierarchy	1	1	1	1	1	1
Market	1	0	1	0	0	0
Network	0	1	0	0	0	0
Community	0	0	0	0	1	1

Table 3. Genetic profiles of hierarchy-network hybrids.

	2 Formal (1) vs. informal (0) governance	3 Substance (1) vs. procedure (0)	4 Signalling (1) vs. Dialogue (0)	5 Vertical (1) vs. horizontal (0) communication	6 Strong (1) vs. weak (0) enforcement	8 Difficulty (1) vs. ease (0) of exit
Hierarchy	1	1	1	1	1	1
Network	0	1	0	0	0	0
HN Hybrid A	1	1	0	1	1	0
HN Hybrid B	0	1	1	0	0	1

dynamic, evolutionary understanding of governance modes. To see how Crouch does this, we revisit the issue of conflict vs. compatibility. Crouch's critique of the VOC literature took issue with the assumption that ideal types of governance were necessarily more coherent than mixtures. He distinguished between logics of similarity and complementarity. The logic of complementarity entails a preference for 'mongrel' forms that 'appear more balanced', whereas the logic of similarity entails the superiority of 'purebred' ideal types that have 'exaggerated characteristics' that enable these institutions to 'do some things particularly well' (2005, 55).

Crouch is particularly interested in complementarity which can take a number of forms. A dominant institutional form may contain, nested within it, a complementary, 'recessive' institutional form. This recessive form may be present, protected, latent, and ready to emerge under different environmental conditions. The recessive, complementary form could also arise as a consequence of exogenous punctuations which suddenly render the dominant form less effective. This resonates with the concept of 'bifurcation' in the complexity literature in that movement away from one relatively stable state to another requires the availability of the alternative state (Rhodes et al. 2011). The presence of a ready-made alternative creates institutional arrangements that are more robust in the face of major external changes. But contrasting institutional forms can also result in abrasions (see also Room 2011) in which the differing institutional principles reflect competing logics of adaptation when there is no form that is clearly optimal.

While an individual of any species carries a finite amount of genetic material, the population of that species can express a narrow or a broad range of genetic diversity. In the same way, the amount of governance (and available institutional forms) can vary enormously from a limited genetic pool to a highly diversified species. Within this genetic diversity, particular expressions may be dominant in the population at a particular time, but the population may carry within it other patterns that may come to be dominant under quite different environmental conditions. Institutional change can involve changing just a single allele, while more far-reaching institutional change would involve the switching of multiple alleles (attributes).

The key point of Crouch's approach is that it brings agents back in to the picture of institutional change. In circumstances in which agents perceive problems and limitations in established institutional arrangements, agents can attempt to shape institutions by drawing from complementary institutional capacities which could be found 'within' the field, or could be borrowed, copied or adapted from 'adjacent' fields (see Crouch 2005, Chapters 6–7). Similarly, Room (2012) emphasizes the importance of 'artificial selection' (rather than Darwinian natural selection), in order to emphasize the role of human agents in deliberately attempting to craft institutional arrangements from available materials. For both Crouch and Room, 'recombination', both large scale and small scale, is the driving force of institutional change.

Fitness and fields/landscapes

Change and recombination are oriented to achieving better 'fitness' of the institutional arrangements in the particular field of governance. But what does fitness mean? To begin to answer this question, imagine a public management field in which a particular genetic combination of Crouch's institutional capacities is unambiguously superior to any other combination (see Kauffman 1995, 173–4). This would entail that there was one allele of each public management gene which was clearly superior to the other. Under these conditions, the optimal solution would be the combination of the six superior alleles. For example, in James Q Wilson's typology of organizational activities (Wilson 1989), 'production' activities such as the delivery of mail may be best co-ordinated under an ideal type hierarchical mode (formal rules, substantive governance, vertical relationships, signalling communication, strong enforcement, and difficulty of exit). If there was a particular example of mail delivery governance that included some '0' settings (i.e. network alleles), any move from '0' to '1' (the hierarchical alleles) would result in superior fitness.

However, there are no guarantees that innovations or mutations will actually achieve improved fitness. An important concept in complexity literature is that of 'fitness landscapes' which can vary from 'smooth' to 'rugged' (Kauffman 1995; McKelvey 1999; Room 2011). Here, the term landscape can be regarded as synonymous with Crouch's 'fields'. To illustrate this, first imagine a scenario in which the optimal institutional form is a specific combination of hierarchy and network alleles (0s and 1s), such that any move towards this combination would unambiguously result in better fitness. In this field/landscape there is no inter-dependency between the hierarchical (1s) and network (0s) components in the optimal institutional arrangement. They are entirely compatible. This describes a 'smooth' landscape.

In most public management contexts, however, there is much less clarity around optimal institutional arrangements, and no arrangement is likely to fit 'perfectly' in a given field/landscape. Where the fitness of one allele is dependent on the expression of other alleles, a mutation from one allele to its alternative will often result in reduced overall fitness. This is what Kauffman (1995) describes as a rugged land-scape. The higher the level of interdependency there is between alleles, the more rugged the landscape. This means that trade-offs are required because there are multiple and potentially conflicting possibilities of 'better' governance.

Under such conditions, agents seeking to change institutional arrangements (alleles) do so in an inherently risky environment. In some landscapes, there may be strong imperatives to change, particularly if actors experience and interpret existing institutional arrangements as sub-optimal. Yet, agents attempting institutional change do not know what the results of their innovations will be.

Summary of the population genetics approach

By drawing on the ideas of Crouch, combined with the idea of rugged and smooth landscapes, we have developed a 'population genetics' approach that deals with the limitations of HMNC literature outlined earlier. First, the framework provides a way of moving beyond a 'zero-sum' view of the quantum of governance. The population genetics framework conceptualizes 'more governance' in terms of greater diversity of institutional genetics within a particular field, even though this may generate conflict between institutional forms.

Second, through the identification of the specific institutional genes relevant to public management, it is possible to distinguish between different institutional combinations of the same set of governance ideal types. This can stimulate more sophisticated comparisons between governance arrangements. Hierarchies, markets, networks, and communities remain as useful concepts for understanding governance forms as 'aids to navigation' or reference points analogous to north, south, east, and west as points of the compass. Following Crouch, however, it is important not to treat hierarchy, market, network and community as 'pure-bred' ideal types that are inherently more coherent or better adapted than 'mongrels'.

Third, the population genetics framework allows for a sophisticated analysis of conflict and compatibility between governance modes. By adopting Crouch's concepts of complementarity, nesting and abrasion, and Kauffman's concept of rugged landscapes based on interdependency between genes, we have developed a conceptual language that explores the dynamics of conflict and compatibility in a given field. Conflict between institutional forms is a highly likely feature of rugged landscapes.

Finally, and most importantly, the framework develops a conceptual language for understanding the dynamics of governance through processes of natural and artificial selection. It is an approach that can be applied at micro, meso, and macro levels of analysis, and through the concept of nesting, allows for analytical movement between these levels.

Applying the population genetics approach: governing after-hours medical care in Auckland, New Zealand

To show the analytical possibilities of this population genetics approach, we apply these concepts to an example of institutional innovation in primary medical care in the city of Auckland, New Zealand. The specific dynamics involve attempts to change the inter-organizational arrangements (contracting, accountability, and collaboration) pertaining to the availability and affordability to patients of medical care on evenings and weekends that were developed by the Auckland After-Hours Network (ARAHN). The data for this case study analysis was drawn from two evaluations of these initiatives (Tenbensel et al. 2013; Tenbensel et al. 2014). The primary focus of the evaluations was the effectiveness of specific initiatives to improve patient access to after-hours care. However, over the two phases of evaluation, investigators conducted 28 interviews with key informants from the range of organizations involved, were non-participant observers at some network meetings, and conducted analysis of network, agendas, minutes and contracts. A substantial portion of these data sources contained information on the formation and maintenance of ARAHN, its governance and its processes of decision-making. This data provided rich information about existing institutional arrangements, and attempts to transform them by some agents at the centre of ARAHN. Fuller summaries and interpretations of this data can be found in the evaluation reports (Tenbensel et al. 2013, 10–18, 24–28, 62–63; Tenbensel et al. 2014, 38–41, 175–183).

In order to show how actors actively attempt to reshape their institutional environment, and the ways these attempts play out, the following account draws from the above exposition of Crouch's approach. We first identify the specific institutional field (landscape) of interest, then define the public management problem that agents seek to address. The third step is to pin down the institutional 'genetic profile' that characterizes this field, and the fourth is to show how particular agents attempted to alter this profile in their 'sub-field'. Finally, we trace the dynamics of nesting and abrasion between the pre-existing institutional form and the 'challenger'.

Step 1: identify the institutional field/landscape

The institutional field in this analysis is primary medical care in Auckland. As a consequence of health system restructuring in the early 2000s, two types of organization became the central actors in New Zealand's primary care system. District Health Boards (DHBs) are public sector organizations responsible for planning and funding health services in a geographical district, and they directly provide publicly funded hospital services, and a range of other health services. Primary Health Organizations (PHOs) are non-government organizations of primary care providers, publicly funded by capitated budgets per enrolled patient (Cumming and Mays 2008). PHOs enter into contractual service agreements with DHBs. In New Zealand, most patients also pay a co-payment when they visit a primary care practitioner. While New Zealand's health system is organized centrally, there are distinct differences in the configuration of organizations and services at the local level, which have been shaped by local, historical contingencies. An important development specific to Auckland was the proliferation of PHOs, and the fact that their boundaries were not contiguous with DHB geographic catchments (Tenbensel 2016). Even since a period of PHO consolidation in 2009–10, the Auckland region has been served by 3 DHBs and 6–7 PHOs. Another largely unique feature for Auckland is that since the 1980s, a different model of after-hours service provision, known as Accident & Medical (A&M) clinics, became established (Hider, Lay-Yee, and Davis 2007). Most of these after-hours providers are not part of PHOs, and therefore are not funded by government to provide medical services. Primary care providers (general practices) in Auckland have long regarded A&Ms as competitors.

Step 2: identify the problem that policy actors are attempting to address

The problem at the centre of this case study is access to medical care in evenings and weekends (after-hours) in the city of Auckland. In 2010, the cost for many patients visiting a doctor after-hours was around $90 NZD (far more than most 'within-hours' co-payments). For some policy actors, this highlighted a large problem of unmet need in primary care, particularly for patients such as young children whose conditions often manifest or worsen after-hours. For others, including the DHBs themselves, this situation contributed to a broader problem of increasing demand on hospital emergency departments for patients for whom non-hospital after-hours care was unaffordable (Tenbensel et al. 2013).

Step 3: specify the dominant genetic code of the field

Despite some examples of collaborative relationships across the health sector at the local level (Tenbensel, Mays, and Cumming 2011), Auckland's health sector in the 2000s quickly settled into a set of institutional arrangements in which contractual and principal-agent relationships came to be dominant. This institutional dynamic was underpinned by a legislative and regulatory framework that emphasized accountability for the use of government funds and responsiveness to government policy priorities (Hood 1991; Boston et al. 1996; Ashton and Tenbensel 2010).

In terms of Crouch's attributes (see Table 4), the relationship between DHBs and PHOs was characterized by **formality** rather than **informality**, primarily in the form

Table 4. Pre-existing governance of primary medical care in Auckland.

	2 Formal (1) vs. informal (0) governance	3 Substance (1) vs. procedure (0)	4 Signalling (1) vs. Dialogue (0)	5 Vertical (1) vs. horizontal (0) communication	6 Strong (1) vs. weak (0) enforcement	8 Difficulty (1) vs. ease (0) of exit
Pre 2010	1	1	1	1	0	1

of the PHO Service Agreement. Governance was **substantive** in that central government policy specified what should be done. Communication more commonly took the form of **signalling** rather than dialogue, because DHBs were legislatively bound to implement central government policy, such that PHOs came to be seen as agents of implementation. PHOs in Auckland saw each other as competitors for enrolled patients. Where there was additional funding available, such processes were contestable, invoking the signalling mechanisms of the market. DHB–PHO relationships under this contractual model were predominantly **vertical**. By-and-large, it was **difficult** for DHBs and PHOs to exit relationships with each other if they occupied the same or similar geographical territory. However, there was one key attribute according to which DHB-PHO arrangements did not fit the hierarchical ideal type. In some key areas of the PHO Service Agreement, the DHBs were often unable and/or unwilling to enforce the terms of the contract, a situation of **weak** enforcement.

This profile was particularly evident in the area of after-hours medical care. Under the PHO Service Agreement, PHOs are contracted by their local DHBs to provide 'access to first-level services 24 h a day, seven day a week basis for 52 weeks a year for all service users' (After Hours Primary Health Care Working Party 2005). However, from the establishment of PHOs there was considerable ambiguity in the interpretation of the clause from the PHO Service Agreement. A Ministry of Health report noted that GPs that were not contributing to after-hours care and did not experience any imposition of penalties. PHOs and GPs claimed that service agreements were not funded sufficiently to cover after-hours care (Verstappen 2011).

In Auckland, DHBs thought that they were paying for after-hours care through the PHO Service Agreement, but this was not enforced in any meaningful way. Subsequently, in 2009 the Ministry of Health provided extra funding for DHBs, requiring them to take on the specific responsibility of reducing barriers of access to after-hours medical care in their district.

Step 4: trace policy actors attempts to create a new institutional form

In 2010, the three DHBs in metropolitan Auckland agreed to take a regional approach to the issue. They circulated a request for proposals (RFP), and a consortium of some A&M clinics developed a proposal. However, some PHOs objected to this process and threatened to challenge it. Consequently, the original RFP process was abandoned and a 'working group' of health provider organizations (DHBs, PHOs, A&M clinics) was established and a new 'alliancing' contracting process was initiated. In June 2011, this working group became formally constituted as the Auckland Regional After-Hours Network (ARAHN) (Tenbensel et al. 2013).

After an intensive 3-month process in mid-2011, ARAHN members agreed on specific initiatives to be funded, and the mechanisms by which the initiatives would be funded. The most prominent initiative was the subsidization of A&M co-payments for young children, the elderly and other high-needs categories for after-hours medical services. This initiative was paid for jointly by DHBs and PHOs (Tenbensel et al. 2013). The development of ARAHN was one example of many attempts by government to stimulate more collaborative relationships between health sector players, and was arguably more successful in forging these relationships than other attempts in Auckland in the two years prior. ARAHN was chaired by a retired general practitioner who was also the chair of one of the smaller PHOs. An Auckland-based health sector consultancy organization was funded by the network to provide logistical support for the development of network activities.

The emergence of ARAHN provides a clear example of an attempt to alter the genetic profile of governance in the field of after-hours care. Crouch's institutional attributes help us to chart how policy actors – in this case, the ARAHN chair, the consultant agency employee and some key representatives of A&Ms, PHOs and DHBs engaged in 'artificial selection' regarding the governance arrangements. The new arrangements developed as part of ARAHN differed across three of the six attributes of governance used in this framework. Most clearly, there were shifts from signalling to **dialogue**, and from vertical to **horizontal** relationships. There was considerable investment of time and resources in *processes* (meetings, negotiations, face-to-face consultation), which required considerable energy, leadership and consistency of key personnel, to build and maintain. The chair of ARAHN estimated that 90 meetings took place over a three month period in mid-2011 (Tenbensel et al. 2013). DHB representatives attended as network members, rather than as principals of an agency relationship. The development of the ARAHN initiatives required significant compromises between participants which would not have been reached without a commitment to dialogue and horizontal communication (Tenbensel et al. 2013). The third shift (mutation) was from from weak to strong enforcement. Network members signed up to a set of obligations of which they were accountable to fellow members. A&Ms were required to reduce fees for targeted groups and keep specific opening hours. PHOs and DHBs were committed to contributing to the pool of funds. These contractual requirements were regularly reported on and reviewed at network meetings.

This also indicates that there was no change on the attribute of **formality**, a new agreement (the network contract) was highly formal, and the focus of sustained effort from ARAHN participants. There was also no change regarding **difficulty of exit**, and new actors (A&Ms) were drawn into the alliance contracting process.

The contrast between pre-ARAHN and ARAHN institutional arrangements is highlighted in Table 5. Here, we can see that the ARAHN arrangements were not 'pure' networks as defined by Crouch's attributes. Indeed, they comply with the network ideal type (i.e. values of 0, aside from dimension 3) in only two of the five

Table 5. Contrast between pre-ARAHN and ARAHN governance of after-hours medical care.

	2 Formal (1) vs. informal (0) governance	3 Substance (1) vs. procedure (0)	4 Signalling (1) vs. Dialogue (0)	5 Vertical(1) vs. horizontal (0) communication	6 Strong (1) vs. weak (0) enforcement	8 Difficulty (1) vs. ease (0) of exit
Pre ARAHN	1	1	1	1	0	1
ARAHN	1	1	0	0	1	1

attributes in which pure hierarchy and pure network types differ – namely the two attributes (dialogue and horizontal communication) that are most frequently emphasized in network literature.

In this example, it is also clear that key participants in ARAHN acted as institutional entrepreneurs by crafting these new arrangements. This institutional array can be seen as an attempt to mitigate the effects of the dominant institutional mode (111,101). PHOs in particular appreciated the move to more horizontal relationships based on dialogue and good-faith negotiation. This produced a number of negotiated solutions to various sticking points. For example, a system of variable co-payment levels for A&Ms participating in the initiative was devised in order to address concerns raised by some of the PHOs and their member practices that after-hours co-payments at A&Ms would be cheaper for patients than in-hours co-payments charged by GPs located nearby participating A&Ms. The eventual solution was to set co-payment levels for each eligibility category at the '80th percentile' of GP charges within a 5-km radius of the A&M. This meant that the agreed co-payment level for A&Ms were the same or more than the fees charged by 80per cent of GPs within that radius (Tenbensel et al. 2013).

DHB participants in the network were pleased to see the shift to an arrangement with more teeth (a sense that they might now actually get what they were paying for). For these participants, the move from weak to strong enforcement was the key motivation for supporting institutional innovation. Thus, the innovation involves a new combination of attributes drawn from both the network and hierarchical ideal types.

Step 5: analyse the dynamics of abrasion, nesting

This new institutional arrangement (110,011) was specific to after-hours medical care. The overall institutional environment of health services governance in Auckland, however, followed the overarching institutional form (111,101). Thus, the new after-hours institutional forms could be seen as 'nested' within the more encompassing regime of primary care governance. There are some important consequences of this nesting.

First, there is abrasion between the dominant and the nested institutional arrangements. ARAHN and its approach to governing after-hours care were not universally welcomed in the Auckland primary health sector. Some key actors within DHBs defended the integrity and appropriateness of the dominant mode, and argued that the new collaborative arrangements between providers violated the principles of efficiency, contestability, and value for money (Tenbensel et al. 2013). For these actors, a move from principal-agent **signalling** could stimulate 'provider-capture' and the formation of provider cartels.

In another example of abrasion, when ARAHN institutional entrepreneurs attempted to expand the scope of ARAHN from after-hours care to all 'urgent care', encompassing an even broader range of services and providers beyond primary care, there was significant pushback and resistance from more senior DHB management who were instrumental in reasserting the predominant institutional approach in response to ARAHN's attempted expansion (Tenbensel, Dwyer, and Lavoie 2014).

Third, ARAHN's continued existence was governed by the rules of the dominant institutions. As the network's activities are predominantly funded by DHBs, continued funding was subject to yearly renewal in which the ARAHN enters into a relationship defined in principal-agent contractual terms with the three DHBs (Tenbensel et al. 2014). DHB senior managers were able to act simultaneously within the pre-existing and new institutional forms. As a consequence of all these factors, the new institutional forms developed within ARAHN were fragile, and vulnerable to changes to local and national priorities.

Ultimately, the ARAHN initiative to subsidise after-hours services broke down in 2015. After all parties had agreed to a comprehensive agreement for funding after-hours services, DHB board members and senior management put the contract on ice in response to an internally (DHB) sought legal opinion that deemed the agreement to be in breach of New Zealand's Commerce Act (Taylor 2015). One example of a supposed breach was the '5km radius' agreement outlined above. At the time of writing, it appeared that the DHBs would unilaterally determine contracts for after-hours service, marking a return to the traditional 'principal-agent' institutional form (Taylor 2016). This amounts to a rejection of the **dialogue** element of ARAHN governance by the broader institutional parameters of public management in New Zealand.

Our example indicates that Auckland's health service governance is arguably a rugged institutional landscape, in which there appear to be strong interdependencies between 'genes'. Relationships between the actors in the after-hours space (DHBs, PHOs, A&M clinics) are contingent upon multiple institutional arrangements of neighbouring and overarching governance spaces. For example, the feasibility of horizontal communication was dependent on the setting of the 'signalling/dialogue' gene. If contracting for after-hours services must be commercially contestable, then horizontal communication between organizations becomes (or remains) problematic. In this environment, attempts to introduce innovations such as those developed by ARAHN trigger the cascade of consequences for primary care governance beyond the after-hours subfield, which then have the consequences for ARAHN that were outlined above.

The analysis of the Auckland primary care field provides the basis of a deeper understanding of how actors' attempts to create and strengthen alternative institutional forms fare in an institutionally dynamic setting. Actors clearly have some scope to develop alternative institutional forms, but ultimately the ruggedness of the landscape is largely beyond their control. Nevertheless, there may be scope for central government actors to 'tune' the parameters that give the landscape its shape (Room 2011). In this example, loosening or tightening the requirements around competitive contracting in the health sector are possible ways in which the parameters can be tuned. While this article has focused primarily on the meso-level of analysis, this 'macro' question of how to tune landscapes in order to reduce the complexity of interdependencies emerges as a central issue for both public management theorists and practitioners.

Conclusion

The population genetics framework based on the work Colin Crouch draws from complexity theory in order to provide a language for understanding the dynamics of institutional change. HMNC concepts, which are widespread in institutionalist literature, provide a viable starting point for this conceptual bridge between complexity theory and institutionalist analysis. This population genetics approach points to a type of advice in which practitioners have some concrete options for influencing institutional dynamics. The first possibility is to actively scan their governance field/landscape for alternative, recessive institutional forms and seek to widen their reach.

A second possibility is to 'pilot' new institutional forms within their field. These new forms need not be polar opposites of dominant forms. Instead, they may only involve switching two or three capacities (alleles) identified by Crouch. Such a targeted approach could well be useful in limiting the scope of resistance from dominant institutional forms. Ultimately, the success of local attempts to change institutions may be beyond the control of the practitioners that initiate them, as exemplified by the Auckland after-hours care case. However, it is possible that many other public management stories of successful institutional change at the local level can be easily interpreted in terms of the population genetics framework.

As a contribution to public management theory, this fusion of concepts addresses respective weaknesses in complexity theory and HMNC. On the one hand, it addresses the predominantly descriptive character and the lack of dynamism in HMNC. It does this by treating HMNC ideal types as a small subset of a much larger range of empirically possible governance forms defined in terms of dimensions of genetic variation. In doing so, we are able to avoid the conceptual dead-end of 'hybrid governance'. By seeing governance forms as genetic expressions which can be subject to mutation and selection, the range of possibilities for understanding governance evolution is significantly expanded beyond broad-brush narratives of change from hierarchy to market to network. Crouch's approach then allows us to understand the dynamics of change and attempted change in terms of competition and/or synergy between contrasting governance modes characterized by processes of nesting, abrasion and recombination.

The population genetics approach also enhances the application of complexity concepts to public management by utilizing more established policy and public management concepts, in this case, hierarchies, markets, networks and communities, to underpin complexity-inspired analyses. An important benefit of this move is that it counteracts the tendency in complexity literature to regard hierarchical governance as antithetical to complexity-informed 'good practice', a stance that is distinctly unhelpful in understanding public management and policy dynamics in parliamentary democracies (Tenbensel 2015). More broadly, it provides an example of a bridge between complexity theory and more established conceptual and theoretical repertoires. Following the recommendations of Room, Cairney, and Pollitt, this is the most promising way to develop the analytical and practical utility of complexity theory.

The Auckland primary care example sketches out the analytical possibilities of a population genetics approach, but also highlights areas for further empirical and conceptual development. First, a more sustained development of the approach would require a methodology for mapping the genetic profile of governance arrangements. There needs to be a reliable and plausible method for empirically distinguishing between capacities on each of Crouch's dimensions. This challenge could possibly be addressed through development of interview schedules, surveys or Delphi processes designed to unpack these dimensions. In doing so, it will be important to be cognisant of a key limitation of the metaphor in that gene alleles are 'digital' (either/or) states, whereas possible positions on Crouch's dimensions may be analogue (more of/less of). Indeed, in Crouch's application of his own framework, he allows for ambiguity and variation on specific genes within defined modes (Crouch 2005, Chapter 5). Another metaphorical limitation is that real genes often have more than two alleles, and therefore variation might not be one dimensional. However, moving beyond Crouch's unidimensional representation of capacities would add considerably to the complexity of the framework itself and could reduce its parsimony.

Second, if the concept of rugged landscapes is to be useful, there needs to be a way to map the interdependencies between genes. This is a considerably more difficult challenge, because in order to demonstrate interdependencies one would need to explore and map a range of governance possibilities in a single field/landscape. The best that might be possible is to develop 'thought experiments' and scenarios to draw out these (possibly hidden) interconnections and interdependencies from participants in governance arrangements.

Even if such challenges prove difficult to address methodologically, the conceptual language of population genetics can still provide useful metaphors that can be used to construct plausible accounts of governance dynamics. In this way, it already provides a novel and potentially powerful way to understand the role of agents in attempting institutional change from within.

Disclosure statement

In accordance with Taylor & Francis policy and the author's ethical obligation as a researcher, the author reports having received funding from Auckland Regional After-Hours Network through a research contract administered via one of its constituent organisations (the National Hauora Coalition). The author has disclosed those interests fully to Taylor & Francis, and has placed an approved plan for managing any potential conflicts arising from that involvement.

Funding

This work was supported by New Zealand Health Research Council [grant number 12-940].

References

Addicott, R. 2008. "Models of Governance and the Changing Role of the Board in the "Modernised" UK Health Sector." *Journal of Health, Organisation and Management* 22 (2): 147–163. doi:10.1108/14777260810876312.

Addicott, R., G. McGivern, and E. Ferlie. 2007. "The Distortion of a Managerial Technique? The Case of Clinical Networks in UK Health Care." *British Journal of Management* 18 (1): 93–105. doi:10.1111/bjom.2007.18.issue-1.

After Hours Primary Health Care Working Party. 2005. *Towards Accessible, Effective and Resilient after Hours Primary Health Care Services: Report of the after Hours Primary Health Care Working Party*. Wellington: Ministry of Health.

Ashton, T., and T. Tenbensel. 2010. "Reform and Re-reform of the New Zealand System." In *Six Countries, Six Reform Models: The Healthcare Reform Experiences of Israel, The Netherlands, New Zealand, Singapore, Switzerland and Taiwan*, edited by K. G. H. Okma and L. Crivelli, 83–110. Singapore: World Scientific Publishing.

Bode, I. 2006. "Co-Governance within Networks and the Non-Profit-For-Profit Divide. A Cross-Cultural Perspective on the Evolution of Domiciliary Elderly Care." *Public Management Review* 8 (4): 551–566. doi:10.1080/14719030601022932.

Bode, I., and O. Firbank. 2009. "Barriers to Co-Governance: Examining the "Chemistry" of Home-Care Networks in Germany, England, and Quebec." *Policy Studies Journal* 37 (2): 325–351. doi:10.1111/psj.2009.37.issue-2.

Boston, J., J. Martin, J. Pallot, and P. Walsh. 1996. *Public Management, the New Zealand Model.* Auckland: Oxford University Press.

Bouckaert, G., B. G. Peters, and K. Verhoest. 2010. *The Coordination of Public Sector Organizations: Shifting Patterns of Public Management.* Basingstoke: Palgrave.

Bovaird, T. 2008. "Emergent Strategic Management and Planning Mechanisms in Complex Adaptive System." *Public Management Review* 10 (3): 319–340. doi:10.1080/14719030802002741.

Bradach, J. L., and R. G. Eccles. 1989. "Price, Authority, and Trust: From Ideal Types to Plural Forms." *Annual Review of Sociology* 15 (1): 97–118. doi:10.1146/annurev.so.15.080189.000525.

Byrkjeflot, H., and K. Guldbrandsøy. 2013. "Hierarchical Steering and Networks. A Study of How the Steering of the Norwegian Hospitals Has Developed." *Tidsskrift for Samfunnsforskning* 54 (4): 463–491.

Cairney, P. 2012. "Complexity Theory in Political Science and Public Policy." *Political Studies Review* 10 (3): 346–358. doi:10.1111/j.1478-9302.2012.00270.x.

Considine, M., and J. M. Lewis. 2003. "Bureaucracy, Network, or Enterprise? Comparing Models of Governance in Australia, Britain, the Netherlands, and New Zealand." *Public Administration Review* 63 (2): 131–140. doi:10.1111/puar.2003.63.issue-2.

Crouch, C. 2005. *Capitalist Diversity and Change: Recombinant Governance and Institutional Entrepreneurs.* Oxford: Oxford University Press.

Cumming, J. M., and N. Mays. 2008. "Reforming Primary Health Care: Is New Zealand's Primary Health Care Strategy Achieving Its Early Goals?" *Australia-New Zealand Health Policy* 5: 24. doi:10.1186/1743-8462-5-24.

Currie, G., S. Grubnic, and R. Hodges. 2011. "Leadership in Public Services Networks: Antecedents, Process and Outcome." *Public Administration* 89 (2): 242–264. doi:10.1111/padm.2011.89.issue-2.

Davies, J. S. 2005. "Local Governance and the Dialectics of Hierarchy, Market and Network." *Policy Studies* 26 (3–4): 311–335. doi:10.1080/01442870500198379.

Davies, J. S., and A. Spicer. 2015. "Interrogating Networks: Towards an Agnostic Perspective on Governance Research." *Environment and Planning C: Government and Policy* 33 (2): 223–238. doi:10.1068/c11292.

Edelenbos, J., and J. Eshuis. 2009. "Dealing with Complexity through Trust and Control." In *Managing Complex Governance Systems: Dynamics, Self-organization and Coevolution in Public Investments*, edited by G. Teisman, A. van Buuren and L. Gerrits, 193–212. New York: Routledge.

Elst, S. V., and F. D. Rynck. 2013. "Will Mandated Network Steering Do the Trick? A Balanced Assessment of the Belgian Network "Crossroads Bank for Enterprises"." *International Review of Public Administration* 18 (2): 47–63. doi:10.1080/12294659.2013.10805252.

Entwistle, T., G. Bristow, F. Hines, S. Donaldson, and S. Martin. 2007. "The Dysfunctions of Markets, Hierarchies and Networks in the Meta-Governance of Partnership." *Urban Studies* 44 (1): 63–79. doi:10.1080/00420980601023836.

Exworthy, M., M. Powell, and J. Mohan. 1999. "The NHS: Quasi-Market, Quasi-Hierarchy and Quasi-Network?" *Public Money and Management* 19 (4): 15–22. doi:10.1111/pmam.1999.19.issue-4.

Ferlie, E., L. Fitzgerald, G. McGivern, S. Dopson, and C. Bennett. 2011. "Public Policy Networks and 'Wicked Problems': A Nascent Solution?" *Public Administration* 89 (2): 307–324. doi:10.1111/padm.2011.89.issue-2.

Goldsmith, S., and W. Eggers. 2004. *Governing by Network: The New Shape of the Public Sector.* Washington, DC: Brookings Institute.

Haynes, P. 2015. *Managing Complexity in the Public Services.* Abingdon: Routledge.

Helderman, J.-K. 2007. "Bringing the Market Back In? Institutional Complementarity and Hierarchy in Dutch Housing and Health Care." PhD diss., Erasmus University Rotterdam.

Hider, P., R. Lay-Yee, and P. Davis. 2007. "Practitioners, Patients, and Their Visits: A Description of Accident and Medical (A & M) Clinics in New Zealand, 2001/2." *New Zealand Medical Journal* 120 (1254). http://journal.nzma.org.nz/journal/120-1254/2538/

Hood, C. 1991. "A Public Management for All Seasons?" *Public Administration* 69: 3–20. doi:10.1111/j.1467-9299.1991.tb00779.x.

Kauffman, S. 1995. *At Home in the Universe: The Search for Laws of Self-Organization and Complexity*. New York: Oxford University Press.

Keast, R., K. Brown, and M. Mandell. 2007. "Getting the Right Mix: Unpacking Integration Meanings and Strategies." *International Public Management Journal* 10 (1): 9–33. doi:10.1080/10967490601185716.

Lance, K. T., Y. Georgiadou, and A. K. Bregt. 2009. "Cross-Agency Coordination in the Shadow of Hierarchy: 'Joining Up' Government Geospatial Information Systems." *International Journal of Geographical Information Science* 23 (2): 249–269. doi:10.1080/13658810801909615.

Le Grand, J. 2007. *The Other Invisible Hand*. Princeton, NJ: Princeton University Press.

Lewis, J. M. 2009. "The Why and How of Partnerships: Policy and Governance Foundations." *Australian Journal of Primary Health* 15 (3): 225–231. doi:10.1071/PY09001.

Lowndes, V., and C. Skelcher. 1998. "The Dynamics of Multi-Organizational Partnerships: An Analysis of Changing Modes of Governance." *Public Administration* 76 (2): 313–333. doi:10.1111/padm.1998.76.issue-2.

Lynn L. E. 2011. "The Persistence of Hierarchy." In *The SAGE Handbook of Governance*, edited by M. Bevir, 218–236. London: SAGE Publications.

Mahoney, J., and K. A. Thelen. 2010. *Explaining Institutional Change: Ambiguity, Agency, and Power*. Cambridge: Cambridge University Press.

McKelvey, B. 1999. "Avoiding Complexity Catastrophe in Coevolutionary Pockets: Strategies for Rugged Landscapes." *Organization Science* 10 (3): 294–321. doi:10.1287/orsc.10.3.294.

Moynihan, D. P. 2008. "Combining Structural Forms in the Search for Policy Tools: Incident Command Systems in U.S. Crisis Management." *Governance* 21 (2): 205–229. doi:10.1111/j.1468-0491.2008.00395.x.

Osborne, D., and T. Gaebler. 1992. *Reinventing Government: How the Entrepreneurial Spirit Is Transforming the Public Sector*. New York: Plume.

Pollitt, C. 2009. "Complexity Theory and Evolutionary Public Adminsitration: A Sceptical Afterword." In *Managing Complex Governance Systems: Dynamics, Self-Organization and Coevolution in Public Investments*, edited by G. Teisman, A. Van Buuren, and L. Gerrits, 213–230. New York: Routledge.

Ranade, W., and B. Hudson. 2003. "Conceptual Issues in Inter-Agency Collaboration." *Local Government Studies* 29 (3): 32–50. doi:10.1080/03003930308559378.

Rhodes, M. L., J. Murphy, J. Muir, and J. A. Murray. 2011. *Public Management and Complexity Theory: Richer Decision-Making in Public Services*. New York: Routledge.

Rhodes, R. A. W. 1997. "From Marketisation to Diplomacy: It's the Mix that Matters." *Australian Journal of Public Administration* 56 (2): 40–53. doi:10.1111/j.1467-8500.1997.tb01545.x.

Rodríguez, C., A. Langley, F. Béland, and J.-L. Denis. 2007. "Governance, Power, and Mandated Collaboration in an Interorganizational Network." *Administration and Society* 39 (2): 150–193. doi:10.1177/0095399706297212.

Room, G. 2011. *Complexity, Institutions and Public Policy: Agile Decision-Making in a Turbulent World*. Cheltenham: Edward Elgar.

Room, G. 2012. "Evolution and the Arts of Civilisation." *Policy and Politics* 40 (4): 453–471. doi:10.1332/030557312X13323392627832.

Sax, P. 2014. "The Shaping of Pharmaceutical Governance: The Israeli Case." *Israel Journal of Health Policy Research* 3 (1): 16. doi:10.1186/2045-4015-3-16.

Six, F. 2013. "Trust in Regulatory Relations: How New Insights from Trust Research Improve Regulation Theory." *Public Management Review* 15 (2): 163–185. doi:10.1080/14719037.2012.727461.

Skelcher, C., and S. Rathgeb Smith. 2015. "Theorizing Hybridity: Institutional Logics, Complex Organizations, and Actor Identities: The Case of Nonprofits." *Public Administration* 93 (2): 433–448. doi:10.1111/padm.12105.

Streeck, W., and K. Thelen. 2005. "Introduction: Institutional Change in Advanced Political Economies." In *Beyond Continuity*, edited by W. Streeck and K. Thelen, 1–39. Oxford: Oxford University Press.

Taylor, C. 2015. "Back to Drawing Board for Auckland After-Hours Plan: Open RFP to Come." *New Zealand Doctor*, October 14. https://www.nzdoctor.co.nz/in-print/2015/october-2015/14-october/back-to-drawing-board-for-auckland-after-hours-plan-open-rfp-to-come.aspx

Taylor, C. 2016. "Auckland DHBs Circle the Wagons on After-Hours Plan, GPs Left in the Dark." *New Zealand Doctor*, November 23. http://www.nzdoctor.co.nz/news/2016/november-2016/23/auckland-dhbs-circle-the-wagons-on-after-hours-plan,-gps-left-in-the-dark.aspx

Tenbensel, T. 2005. "Multiple Modes of Governance." *Public Management Review* 7 (2): 267–288. doi:10.1080/14719030500091566.

Tenbensel, T. 2016. "Health System Regionalization - The New Zealand Experience." *Healthcare Papers* 16 (1): 27–33. doi:10.12927/hcpap.

Tenbensel, T., J. Dwyer, and J. Lavoie. 2014. "How Not to Kill the Golden Goose: Reconceptualizing Accountability Environments of Third-Sector Organizations." *Public Management Review* 16 (7): 925–944. doi:10.1080/14719037.2013.770054.

Tenbensel, T., N. Mays, and J. Cumming. 2011. "A Successful Mix of Hierarchy and Collaboration? Interpreting the 2001 Reform of the Governance of the New Zealand Public Health System." *Policy and Politics* 39 (2): 239–255. doi:10.1332/030557310X519678.

Tenbensel, T., R. Edlin, A. Field, L. Walton, P. Neuwelt, R. McNeill, and D. Rees. 2013. *Evaluation of Auckland Regional After-Hours Network and the After-Hours Initiative.* Auckland: Uniservices, University of Auckland. https://researchspace.auckland.ac.nz/handle/2292/20823

Tenbensel, T., R. Edlin, L. Wilkinson-Meyers, A. Field, L. Walton, S. Appleton, K. Dowson, R. Lee, J. Snapp, and A. Old. 2014. *Evaluation of A&M, HML Telephone Triage, and St John Transport Initiatives.* Auckland: Uniservices, University of Auckland. https://researchspace.auckland.ac.nz/handle/2292/22918

Tenbensel, T. 2015. "Complexity and Health Policy." In *Handbook on Complexity and Public Policy,* edited by R. Geyer and P. Cairney. Cheltenham: Edward Elgar.

Tuohy, C. H. 1999. *Accidental Logics: The Dynamics of Change in the Health Care Arena in the United States, Britain and Canada.* New York: Oxford University Press.

Van De Bovenkamp, H. M., M. De Mul, J. G. U. Quartz, A. M. J.W.M. Weggelaar-Jansen, and R. Bal. 2013. "Institutional Layering in Governing Healthcare Quality." *Public Administration* 92 (1): 208–223. doi:10.1111/padm.2014.92.issue-1.

Verstappen, A. 2011. "Falling between the Cracks: Access to After-Hours Primary Health Care in New Zealand, Auckland." Honours diss., University of Auckland.

Wilson, J. Q. 1989. *Bureaucracy: What Government Agencies Do and Why They Do It.* New York: Basic Books.

Utilizing complexity theory to explore sustainable responses to intimate partner violence in health care

Claire Gear, Elizabeth Eppel and Jane Koziol-Mclain

ABSTRACT

Implementing effective and sustainable health care responses to intimate partner violence (IPV) is a complex public health problem internationally. Increasingly scholars are recognizing that research methods which explore health-system responses to IPV obscure the complexity of the problem. This paper discusses the use of complexity theory for researching sustainable responses to IPV within New Zealand primary health care. We reconceptualize IPV responses as complex adaptive systems and propose a complexity-friendly methodology to explore interactions within and between the problem (IPV), intervention (IPV response), and the setting (health care).

Introduction

Current approaches to public health policy are being challenged to address the increasing complexity of health care service delivery (Ellis 2013; Martin and Felix-Bortolotti 2010). Despite debates on how to apply it, the use of complexity theory for exploring and describing health care organization and behaviour is increasing (McDaniel, Driebe, and Lanham 2013; Thompson et al. 2016). Complexity theory reconceptualizes health care systems as dynamic and non-linear, highlighting characteristics disregarded by other perspectives and providing rich and nuanced accounts of health service delivery and policy (Tenbensel 2013; Thompson et al. 2016).

Intimate partner violence (IPV) is often referred to as a complex problem, alluding to the entanglement of personal, socio-economic, and cultural factors which contribute to and sustain violence in people's lives (Family Violence Death Review Committee 2014; Gulliver and Fanslow 2016; O'Campo et al. 2011; Taft et al. 2009; Spangaro, Zwi, and Poulos 2009). The effects of IPV result in adverse health outcomes, leading women who experience IPV to utilize health care services more often than women who have not been exposed to IPV (Garcia-Moreno et al. 2015; Bonomi et al. 2009). As one in three women worldwide experience violence by an intimate partner, IPV is a global public health problem of epidemic proportions (World Health Organisation 2013).

Internationally, implementing effective sustainable responses to IPV within health care systems and settings has proven challenging and the best evidenced-based model is still unknown (Garcia-Moreno et al. 2015; O'Campo et al. 2011; Hegarty et al. 2012). Until recently, research exploring responses to IPV have tended to apply theoretical perspectives and methodologies which obscure the complexities arising from interactions within and between the problem and the response settings (Garcia-Moreno et al. 2015; Kevin, Rhodes, and Brown 2015; O'Campo et al. 2011). In recognition, research designs are seeking to capture and value different types of knowledge, a wider range of meaningful outcomes for women, and different process information (Decker et al. 2012; Spangaro, Koziol-McLain et al. 2016; Spangaro, Zwi, and Poulos 2011; Goicolea et al. 2015a). Conceptualizations of sustainability in health care are also trending towards an ecological or complex-systems approach, emphasizing how different influences interact with complex interventions over time (Fleiszer et al. 2015; Mohrman, Shani, and McCracken 2012; Wiltsey Stirman et al. 2012). The blending of these emerging bodies of knowledge opens new opportunities for improving our understanding of what impacts sustainable responses to IPV in health care, utilizing research approaches designed to work with such complexity.

This paper presents complexity theory as a methodology for researching the complex problem of responding sustainably to IPV. We begin by providing an overview of complexity theory use in health care and its implications for how we conceptualize sustainability for complex systems. We then describe the New Zealand health care response to IPV as an example of a complex adaptive system (CAS) in action, before proposing a complexity-friendly methodology for research into exploring sustainable responses to IPV. In the conclusion, we consider how this approach may be applicable for other complex social systems.

Complexity theory application in health care

Theory-informed approaches to health care are increasingly demanded to make explicit the assumptions underpinning health-system investments (Martin and Felix-Bortolotti 2010; Thompson et al. 2016). Complexity theory calls attention to how different theoretical perspectives and assumptions underpin how we understand and interpret the behaviour of health care organizations and their interaction with complex interventions (Felix-Bortolotti 2011; Jordon et al. 2010; Kernick 2006). How IPV responsiveness in health care is conceptualized plays a big role in how we attempt to address the problem and our choices of intervention (Thurston and Eisener 2006). Studies testing different models of health-system approaches to IPV have traditionally used reductionist research methods, such as randomized controlled trials (RCTs). While these reductionist approaches have offered an understanding of the system components needed to support an effective health care response (O'Campo et al. 2011), there is increasing recognition these methods obscure the complexity of the problem (Ghandour, Campbell, and Lloyd 2015).

A recent scoping review of complexity theory use in health services research found the theory is especially appropriate in allowing researchers to conceptualize a system as dynamical and non-linear, rather than reducible and predictable (Thompson et al. 2016). The review found complexity theory is primarily used as an explanatory tool to describe or explore system interactions and relationships and how they may contribute to system change (Thompson et al. 2016). Rather than presenting a prescribed methodology, complexity theory provides a set of concepts which enable a different way of viewing phenomena. The scoping review identified 18 complexity concepts in use; the most common being relationships, self-organization, and diversity, though there is wide variation in conceptual definition (Thompson et al. 2016; Tenbensel 2015). A strength of complexity theory lies in its ability to bring together different combinations of concepts to provide an analytical framework. Moreover, this framework can be applied in combination with other theoretical frameworks (Tenbensel 2015). Complexity theory can provide new insight into the complexity of a problem through understanding the patterns of interactions taking place between system elements at different levels and times (McDaniel, Driebe, and Lanham 2013). Such complexity is often obscured by reductionist methods, which tends to analyse individual system elements, overlooking the reflexive, non-linear relationship between them, thereby concealing the whole (Thompson et al. 2016).

Health care, CASs and sustainability

Complexity theory is often used to reconceptualize health care systems as CASs (Ellis 2013; McDaniel and Driebe 2001; McDaniel, Driebe, and Lanham 2013; Mohrman and Kanter 2012). A CAS perspective focuses attention on the interactions between agents within a system (Ellis 2013). In primary health care, an agent may be an individual such as a general practitioner or a patient, a collective such as a group of nurses or general practice, or an entire primary health care organization. Each of these agents hold information about the part of the system they exist within, but do not hold knowledge of the entire system. As agents interact with one another they generate knowledge which they learn from and respond to, acting and reacting to other agent actions. This process facilitates agent mutual adaptation and co-evolution as agent actions alter the landscape they operate within, as well as their relationships with other agents. The repeated patterns of interaction between agents as they co-evolve generate self-organization – new forms or behaviours which spontaneously emerge within the system. Over time, repeated self-organization results in the emergence of new system properties, such as responsiveness to IPV, or intervention sustainability (Jordon et al. 2010; McDaniel, Driebe, and Lanham 2013). Likewise, agent interactions may result in unintended consequences leading to the emergence of system properties which challenge effective and sustainable practices.

Complexity arises from simple causes (interactions between agents) which generate complex effects (health care organization structure) (Phelan 2001). The structure of a CAS cannot be understood through an understanding of individual agent actions in isolation, but as emerging from the continuous non-linear interaction between agents (McDaniel, Driebe, and Lanham 2013). Ellis (2013) shows how this perspective provides insight into the 'subjective and socially constructed nature of primary care' resulting from the patient community's interaction with the wider environment (489). Patients present to general practices with issues which are important to them, stemming from unique sociocultural, economic, and political conditions of their community (Ellis 2013). Similarly, complexity theory can provide us with insight into what agent interactions influence IPV responsiveness.

The way sustainability is conceptualized has implications for how we design and conduct research, and the possible conclusions which can be made (Wiltsey Stirman et al. 2012; Gruen et al. 2008). Current approaches to IPV responsiveness often conceptualize sustainability as a focal point of interest (e.g. was the original intervention sustained 2-years post implementation and initial funding?) (Blasinsky, Goldman, and Unützer 2006; Bond et al. 2014; Swain et al. 2010). However, as we become more aware of the different influences which interact with complex interventions and affect sustainability, ecological and complex-systems models of sustainability are becoming more useful (Fleiszer et al. 2015; Mohrman, Shani, and McCracken 2012; Wiltsey Stirman et al. 2012). From a complexity perspective, applying standardized responses or interventions restricts long-term sustainability due to the continuous non-linear interactions between diverse agents (Booth, Zwar, and Harris 2013; Felix-Bortolotti 2009). This unpredictability means sustainability is not an outcome which can be achieved in perpetuity, but a continuous evolving process dependent on the interactions between multiple factors at different levels of analysis, points in time, and settings (Fleiszer et al. 2015; Gruen et al. 2008; Martin et al. 2011; Morden et al. 2015; Wiltsey Stirman et al. 2012; Scheirer 2005). For example, the implementation and sustainability of a complex intervention is understood as an adaptive process (Wiltsey Stirman et al. 2012). As an intervention adapts to its local setting, it may take different forms (Shani and Mohrman 2012; Willis, Small, and Brown 2012). This reflects a period of mutual adaptation between implementation and sustainability, where individual agents in the CAS find accommodations between maintaining intervention fidelity and promoting sustainability, mediated by stakeholder expectations (Wiltsey Stirman et al. 2012; Gruen et al. 2008; Hawe 2015; Hawe, Shiell, and Riley 2009; Shiell, Hawe, and Gold 2008; Young-Wolff, Kotz, and McCaw 2016). This theoretical position leads to the conclusion that intervention sustainability is an emergent phenomenon which arises from these interactions between the agents (Bender and Judith 2015; Mohrman, Shani, and McCracken 2012). Complexity theory then becomes fundamentally useful in studying the complex and dynamic nature of sustainability. This approach allows strategic intervention in future interactions to accelerate self-organization and the emergence of system structures which support effective sustainable responses to IPV (Thompson et al. 2016; Ellis 2013; Mohrman, Shani, and McCracken 2012).

The New Zealand health care response to IPV

New Zealand's Violence Intervention Programme (VIP) was established by the Ministry of Health (MOH) in 2007 to 'reduce and prevent the health impacts of violence and abuse through early identification, assessment and referral of victims presenting to designated District Health Board (DHB) services' (Koziol-McLain and McLean 2015, 1). The comprehensive, health-system approach to family violence (including IPV and child abuse and neglect) is supported by guidelines, funding, standardized training, material and technical resources, and ongoing monitoring and evaluation (Fanslow 2002; Fanslow and Kelly 2016; Koziol-McLain and McLean 2015).

In the New Zealand health system, DHBs are responsible for planning, funding, and providing health services under the stewardship of the MOH. DHBs provide public funding for the delivery of primary health care services through service agreements with regional Primary Health Organizations (PHOs). These agreements require PHOs to deliver essential primary health care services to their enrolled patient population, largely through private general practices (Ministry of Health Primary Care Team 2015; Ministry of Health 2001, 2016). World Health

Organization (2013) guidelines strongly recommend health professionals offer first-line support to victims of IPV including facilitating disclosure, offering support, and referral, providing medical treatment and follow-up care, and documenting evidence. It is also strongly recommended primary health care is prioritized for training and service delivery. However in New Zealand, implementation of VIP has largely occurred within hospital-based services. While efforts are increasing to engage primary health care providers (Fanslow and Kelly 2016), New Zealand currently does not formally provide adequate policy, funding or resources for a health-system response to family violence within primary health care, leaving room for extreme variation, and potentially harmful, responses to victims. (Gear et al. 2016).

Nevertheless, a small network of volunteer primary health care professionals are developing local responses to family violence, supported by limited resources (Gear et al. 2012, 2016; Ministry of Health 2000, 2003). Tenbensel (2016) observes three structural tensions of the health care system which may increase the complexity of responding sustainably to IPV within primary health care settings. First, PHOs are focused on improving the health of a population, while general practitioners focus on the health of individuals; second, state-funded DHB-contracted outputs are difficult to enforce within primary health care private business models; and third, system hierarchy is undermined by the tacit power of health professionals to adapt health policy through implementation. Gear et al. (2016) reported the experience of a small group of New Zealand primary health care settings that embarked on developing responses to family violence. The study identified system elements which supported or challenged response development, but found further work was needed to understand how complex health care system relationships could be utilized to effect sustainable responses to IPV in primary health care. The New Zealand health care response to IPV exemplifies a CAS in action. The interactions between system agents (such as the World Health Organization, MOH, DHB, PHO, general practice, VIP, primary health care volunteer network and resources) are continuously enabling or constraining the potential actions of other agents in the system. These interactions are generating the structure within which the agents operate – the health care system.

Reconceptualizing primary health care IPV responsiveness as a CAS

Complexity theory enables a reconceptualization of IPV responsiveness as a CAS, in which interactions within and between the problem (IPV), intervention (IPV response), and the setting (health care) become a primary focus. In this section, we develop a complexity-friendly methodology for research into sustainable IPV responses in primary health care settings based on a literature review. The discussion contrasts the features and issues of the current approach to IPV responsiveness with a complexity theory approach with respect to (a) the problem frame, (b) the setting, (c) research approaches, (d) outcome measures, and (e) sustainability. A summary of the discussion is provided within Table 1. In the conclusion, we discuss how, as an example of particularly complex intervention design and implementation, this conceptualization may provide transferable knowledge to other complex interventions and policy domains.

Table 1. Reconceptualising primary health care IPV responsiveness as a complex adaptive system.

Feature	Current approach	Issue	Complexity approach
The problem frame	Health care professionals are well placed to respond to the global public health problem of IPV.	Responses to IPV are often not recognized or implemented. Implementing and sustaining current health-system approaches has proven challenging.	Health care responsiveness to IPV represents a complex problem, requiring a complex intervention, in a complex setting.
The health care setting	Health care organizations are mechanistic and Newtonian in their approach and delivery of care.	Understandings of health care organizations are inconsistent with the complexity of health care. A shift in the models used to frame our thinking is needed.	Health care organizations are complex adaptive systems involving many diverse agents which interact recursively and non-linearly.
Research approaches to problem	Post-positivist, reductionist methods such as RCTs which assume a direct relationship between cause and effect.	The complexity of responding to IPV has been obscured by use of reductionist methods typical of traditional research.	Applies complexity concepts to explore or describe patterns of agent interaction which lead to self-organization and emergence of new system properties.
Outcome measures	Applies a range of outcomes to reflect IPV intervention effects. No consensus on what measures should be used.	Often conceptualized as an end point of linear cause and effect measured at a fixed point in time, which obscures the myriad of factors between the intervention and a reduction in violence.	Complex intervention rationale or ontology shapes its methods, components, and outcomes, affecting the scope and level of knowledge that can be understood and described.
Sustainability	Standardized health-system approach supports effective response but presents challenges for sustainability. Conceptualized as a focal point of interest or state of being.	Current research methods provide little implementation, contextual and process information to support sustainable integration. Increasing awareness of different influences which interact with complex interventions and affect sustainability.	Sustainability is a continuous evolving and adaptive process based on the interactions between multiple diverse agents, at different levels of analysis, points in time, and settings.

The problem frame

Despite wide recognition that health care professionals are well placed to respond to those experiencing IPV, the need for a response is often not recognized or implemented (Garcia-Moreno et al. 2015). A comprehensive health-system approach, as part of a multi-sectorial response, is advocated to support effective and sustainable health care responses (O'Campo et al. 2011). However, implementing and sustaining these models has proven challenging, resulting in poor integration and wide variation across health systems and settings (Garcia-Moreno et al. 2015; Hegarty et al. 2012; O'Campo et al. 2011; Colombini, Mayhew, and Watts 2008). Increasingly, scholars are beginning to identify the complexities which arise from the interaction of many different agents involved in responding to IPV in primary health care (Ghandour, Campbell, and Lloyd 2015; Goicolea et al. 2015b), but we have yet to understand how these complexities interact with, and influence, the sustainability of a health-system response to IPV (Willis, Small, and Brown 2012; Goicolea et al. 2015a; O'Doherty et al. 2015). A complexity theory approach emphasizes health care responsiveness to IPV as representing a complex problem, requiring a complex intervention, in a complex setting (Family Violence Death Review Committee 2014; O'Campo et al. 2011; Spangaro, Zwi, and Poulos 2009). Reframing IPV responsiveness as a CAS allows us to explore the complexities which arise from the interaction between system elements which challenge the implementation and sustainability of an effective response to IPV.

Health care settings

Health care system designers, policymakers, and guideline authors often conceptualize health care organizations as Newtonian and mechanistic, inconsistent with direct observations and experiences (McDaniel, Driebe, and Lanham 2013). There is a growing recognition we need a shift in the models used to frame our thinking to understand the complexity of responding to IPV (Family Violence Death Review Committee 2014; McDaniel, Driebe, and Lanham 2013; Young-Wolff, Kotz, and McCaw 2016). Complexity theory allows conceptualization of health care systems as complex and adaptive involving a large number of elements which interact dynamically and non-linearly (McDaniel, Driebe, and Lanham 2013).

Research approaches to the problem

Cognizant of the biomedical model of health and traditional scientific research approaches, RCTs are consistently recommended to test the effectiveness of IPV interventions, assuming a direct relationship between cause and effect (Ramsay, Rivas, and Feder 2005; Bonds et al. 2006; Hegarty et al. 2013; McFarlane et al. 2006; Taft et al. 2011; Ambuel et al. 2013; MacMillan et al. 2009). Often, women are 'screened' (asked direct questions about different types of violence) to facilitate disclosure of IPV, yet RCTs and other quantitative studies have encountered difficulties in producing positive and consistent findings on the effectiveness of interventions like screening (Kevin, Rhodes, and Brown 2015; MacMillan et al. 2009; Wathen and MacMillan 2003). A lack of context appreciation in these studies is cited as a reason why little impact is found, highlighting a need for qualitative methods to inform and complement quantitative study findings and offer a wider perspective of whether screening is effective (Kevin, Rhodes, and Brown 2015; Garcia-Moreno et al. 2015; O'Campo et al. 2011; Decker et al. 2012). Qualitative studies emphasize influences on IPV responses such as the individual motivation and ideology of the health professional (Goicolea et al. 2013, 2015b; O'Campo et al. 2011; Tower 2007), or response champion (Goicolea et al. 2015a, 2016), how women themselves respond to violence (Ghandour, Campbell, and Lloyd 2015; Kelly 2011; Narula, Agarwal, and McCarthy 2012; Nicolaidis and Touhouliotis 2006; Spangaro, Herring, et al. 2016; Spangaro, Koziol-McLain, et al. 2016) and wider systemic and societal influences (Garcia-Moreno et al. 2015; Goicolea et al. 2013; Kelly 2011; Thurston and Eisener 2006; Tower 2007). This suggests the need for a more complex research design to capture the complexity of intervening in IPV in health care settings (Goicolea et al. 2015a).

Complexity theory theorizes that in order to understand the complexity of a problem, we need to understand the patterns of interactions which are taking place between agents of the system at different levels and times (McDaniel, Driebe, and Lanham 2013). Moreover, we must consider the heterogeneity of agents and their influence on those interactions. Agents are not all the same, they hold both different micro-diversities (e.g. the mix of health professionals which constitute a general practice) and macro-diversities (e.g. different specialities of general practices) which influence their ability to respond to change in their environment (Boulton, Allen, and Bowman 2015). Viewing health care as a CAS shows how both agent heterogeneity and their patterns of interaction lead to self-organization and the emergence of new system properties. The non-linearity of interactions between diverse agents means there is irreducible uncertainty about how things will unfold. Small changes may lead to big effects and vice versa (McDaniel, Driebe, and Lanham 2013; Ellis 2013). The implications of this unpredictability are illustrated in the next section which considers complex interventions.

Complex interventions

A complexity-informed view of a primary health care response to IPV understands intervention outcomes as 'co-created' by the different agents in the system (Thompson and Clark 2012). No two interventions can be the same, even if strictly controlled, due to the unique interaction between parts at different levels which contribute to the intervention (McDaniel, Driebe, and Lanham 2013). Each part of the intervention is underpinned by tacit ontological assumptions, which influences its interaction with other parts (Clark 2013). The degree of complexity generated by interactions between parts at the time of the intervention influences intervention outcomes, and further, how we interpret and value those outcomes (Thompson and Clark 2012, 278; Clark 2013). This unpredictability raises significant problems for integrating a standardized intervention, as cause and effect will always be uncertain (Ellis and Herbert 2011; McDaniel, Driebe, and Lanham 2013). As Goicolea et al. (2015b) found, 'adequate detection of women suffering from IPV is a complex process that requires more than asking questions and following the steps of a protocol' (9). Complexity theory allows us to explore or describe this behaviour by applying selected complexity concepts (Tenbensel 2015; Thompson et al. 2016). These concepts can be applied alongside other theoretical frameworks such as critical realism (Clark 2013), realist evaluation, action research, or systems dynamic mapping (Best et al. 2016) creating potential to engage in cross-discipline research, overcome knowledge dichotomies, and foster interdisciplinary collaboration (Martin and Felix-Bortolotti 2014).

Outcome measures

A range of outcome measures are used to reflect the impact of IPV interventions. Outcome measures are widely debated in the literature with no consensus on what is most appropriate (Wathen and MacMillan 2003; Goicolea et al. 2015a; Bair-Merritt et al. 2014; Nicolaidis and Touhouliotis 2006; Spangaro, Zwi, and Poulos 2011).

Quantitative studies tend to use outcomes as the end point of a linear cause and effect intervention measured at a fixed point in time (such as 're-abuse' or 'violent events'), obscuring the myriad of factors between screening and a reduction in violence (O'Campo et al. 2011; Thurston and Eisener 2006). In contrast, qualitative studies tend to acknowledge the problematic nature of outcome measures in accounting for the complexities of responding to IPV and work towards identifying and measuring other valuable outcomes such as reduced isolation, naming abuse (Spangaro, Zwi, and Poulos 2011), or disclosure and safety planning (Taft et al. 2015).

Current methods testing complex interventions, such as RCTs, do not account for the complexity of diverse concepts and multiple outcomes (Martin and Felix-Bortolotti 2014). Further, the complexity of the interactions between agents contributing to a complex intervention causes uncertainty for predicting outcomes (Paterson et al. 2009). Complexity theory emphasizes how the rationale or ontology of a complex intervention shapes the methods, components, and outcomes, affecting the scope and level of knowledge that can be understood and described (Paterson et al. 2009; Clark et al. 2012). Recognising this complexity can facilitate a different interpretation of outcomes for complex interventions which address aspects of process (such as new meaning and understanding) and longer term changes in health and well-being (Paterson et al. 2009).

Sustainability

As argued earlier, complexity theory conceptualizes sustainability not as an outcome state, but as an ongoing dynamic process which arises from the interactions between multiple agents within a system. Research designs often provide limited information on how a comprehensive health-system response can be integrated into practice sustainably (Decker et al. 2012; Hooker et al. 2015; O'Doherty et al. 2016). RCTs provide little implementation information as it occurs (O'Doherty et al. 2016) and research methodologies which account for the impact of contextual factors and sustainability are scarce (Goicolea et al. 2015a). Often, the distinction between implementation and sustainability is blurry (Willis, Small, and Brown 2012; Fleiszer et al. 2015). Using complexity theory, these processes may be better understood as agents which interact with one another in a complex system (e.g. implementation affects sustainability and if the intervention is not sustained, implementation fails) though this interaction needs further research (Willis, Small, and Brown 2012; Martin et al. 2012).

Increasingly, attention is being paid to process information. This includes the multistep process of the comprehensive health-system response to IPV (O'Campo et al. 2011), the process of disclosing IPV (Goicolea et al. 2015b; Kelly 2011; McFarlane et al. 2006; Spangaro, Herring, et al. 2016; Spangaro, Koziol-McLain, et al. 2016), clinical system processes such as scheduling of appointments or care continuity (Narula, Agarwal, and McCarthy 2012), implementation processes such as provider screening or comfort, or the identification pathway (Decker et al. 2012), research process effects such as unintentional intervention (Hamberger et al. 2014; O'Doherty et al. 2016), and women's progress following IPV screening (Decker et al. 2012; Koziol-McLain et al. 2008; Spangaro, Zwi, and Poulos 2011). This process information reflects what is emerging from the interactions between different agents. Traditional conceptualizations of sustainability often obscure this dynamic and emergent nature of knowledge.

Complexity theory is fundamental in understanding sustainability as an evolving and adaptive process generated by the interaction between agents (Bender and Judith 2015; Mohrman, Shani, and McCracken 2012). A sustainable health care response to IPV relies on the interaction between the complex world in which the women lives and the complex health care system. For example, a woman entrapped by IPV seeks health care for the effects of the violence, where she interacts with the complex health-system response to IPV. An effective and sustainable health care response to IPV emerges when the interaction between the two complex systems (the women and the health care setting) causes each to mutually adapt in ways which generate positive outcomes for both the woman (e.g. reduced violence) and the health professional (e.g. increased confidence and capability in responding). Utilizing complexity theory enables us to conceptualize sustainability as an emergent phenomenon which occurs when a sufficient level of interactive engagement between the complex worlds generates mutual understanding, adaptation, and solutions, increasing the likelihood of positive outcomes.

Conclusions

Use of complexity theory is increasing in health care research, calling our attention to new ways of thinking about complex problems. Responding sustainably to IPV in health care is a persistent problem of particular complexity for public health policy internationally. We know what is needed for an effective health care response to IPV, yet the complexity of the problem continues to challenge sustainable integration in health care systems. There is increasing recognition the research methods which test health-system responses are obscuring the complexity of the problem. Scholars are beginning to pay more attention to what contextual factors influence IPV responses and how they work in tandem with health-system components.

The utilization of complexity theory for researching this complex problem contrasts with the current approach by creating greater fidelity between the nature of the system under investigation and the research methodology. As we begin to acknowledge the complexity of health and social systems, complexity theory facilitates a blending of multiple actor's knowledge enabling new insights into complex emergent phenomena like sustainability. In addition, the focus on emerging outcomes over time that are systemic and evolving provides a more holistic and sustainable basis for assessing interventions. Understanding that there cannot be a single definitive 'solution' to the complex problem naturally arises from this perspective. Instead the system must be continuously directed towards the desired state, through strategic intervention in agent interactions. This requires a significant shift in how we engage with systems that exhibit the features of CAS.

The next steps are to apply this theoretical framework to diverse New Zealand primary health care settings to explore agent interactions which promote or challenge sustainable responses to IPV in primary health care. This innovative use of complexity theory as a research methodology necessitates careful, clear, and deliberate selection of research methods to both identify and explore relevant agent interactions as well as understand the scope of knowledge which can be understood and described. It also requires an adaptive study design which allows responsiveness to findings as they emerge. In particular, the conceptualization of complex system's sustainability as an emergent phenomenon will be explored. Finally, the proposed framework lends itself to adaptation for researching other complex social interventions exhibiting multiple interacting elements generating complex problems.

Acknowledgement

The first author is thankful for the support of an Auckland University of Technology Vice-Chancellor Doctoral Scholarship (no grant number).

Disclosure statement

No potential conflict of interest was reported by the authors.

References

Ambuel, B., L. Hamberger, C. Guse, M. Melzer-Lange, M. B. Phelan, and A. Kistner. 2013. "Healthcare Can Change from Within: Sustained Improvement in the Healthcare Response to Intimate Partner Violence." *Journal of Family Violence* 28 (8): 833–847. doi:10.1007/s10896-013-9550-9.

Bair-Merritt, M. H., A. Lewis-O'Connor, S. Goel, P. Amato, T. Ismailji, M. Jelley, P. Lenahan, and P. Cronholm. 2014. "Primary Care-Based Interventions for Intimate Partner Violence: A Systematic Review." *American Journal of Preventive Medicine* 46 (2): 188–194. doi:10.1016/j.amepre.2013.10.001.

Bender, H., and K. Judith. 2015. "Does Sustainability Emerge from between the Scales?" *Emergence: Complexity and Organization* 17 (1): 10.

Best, A., A. Berland, C. Herbert, J. Bitz, M. W. van Dijk, C. Krause, D. Cochrane, et al. 2016. "Using Systems Thinking to Support Clinical System Transformation." *Journal of Health Organization and Management* 30 (3): 302–323. doi:doi:10.1108/JHOM-12-2014-0206.

Blasinsky, M., H. H. Goldman, and J. Unützer. 2006. "Project IMPACT: A Report on Barriers and Facilitators to Sustainability." *Administration and Policy in Mental Health and Mental Health Services Research* 33 (6): 718–729. doi:10.1007/s10488-006-0086-7.

Bond, G. R., R. E. Drake, G. J. McHugo, A. E. Peterson, A. M. Jones, and J. Williams. 2014. "Long-Term Sustainability of Evidence-Based Practices in Community Mental Health Agencies." *Administration and Policy in Mental Health Services Research* 41 (2): 228–236. doi:10.1007/s10488-012-0461-5.

Bonds, D. E., S. D. Ellis, E. Weeks, S. L. Palla, and P. Lichstein. 2006. "A Practice-Centered Intervention to Increase Screening for Domestic Violence in Primary Care Practices." *BMC Family Practice* 7: 63. doi:10.1186/1471-2296-7-63.

Bonomi, A. E., M. L. Anderson, F. P. Rivara, and R. S. Thompson. 2009. "Health Care Utilization and Costs Associated with Physical and Nonphysical-Only Intimate Partner Violence." *Health Services Research* 44 (3): 1052–1067. doi:10.1111/j.1475-6773.2009.00955.x.

Booth, B. J., N. Zwar, and M. F. Harris. 2013. "Healthcare Improvement as Planned System Change or Complex Responsive Processes? A Longitudinal Case Study in General Practice." *BMC Family Practice* 14: 51. doi:10.1186/1471-2296-14-51.

Boulton, J. G., P. M. Allen, and C. Bowman. 2015. *Embracing Complexity: Strategic Perspectives for an Age of Turbulence*. Oxford: University Press.

Clark, A. M. 2013. "What are the Components of Complex Interventions in Healthcare? Theorizing Approaches to Parts, Powers and the Whole Intervention." *Social Science Medicine* 93: 185–193. doi:10.1016/j.socscimed.2012.03.035.

Clark, A. M., T. G. Briffa, L. Thirsk, L. Neubeck, and J. Redfern. 2012. "What Football Teaches Us about Researching Complex Health Interventions." *British Medical Journal* 345: e8316. doi:10.1136/bmj.e8316.

Colombini, M., S. Mayhew, and C. Watts. 2008. "Health-Sector Responses to Intimate Partner Violence in Low- and Middle-Income Settings: A Review of Current Models, Challenges and Opportunities." *Bulletin of the World Health Organization* 86 (8): 635–642. doi:10.2471/BLT.07.045906.

Decker, M. R., S. Frattaroli, B. McCaw, A. L. Coker, E. Miller, P. Sharps, W. G. Lane, et al. 2012. "Transforming the Healthcare Response to Intimate Partner Violence and Taking Best Practices to Scale." *Journal of Women's Health* 21 (12): 1222–1229. doi:10.1089/jwh.2012.4058.

Ellis, B. 2013. "An Overview of Complexity Theory: Understanding Primary Care as a Complex Adaptive System." In *Handbook of Systems and Complexity in Health*, edited by J. P. Sturmberg and M. M. Martin, 485–494. New York: Springer.

Ellis, B., and S. I. Herbert. 2011. "Complex Adaptive Systems (CAS): An Overview of Key Elements, Characteristics and Application to Management Theory." *Informatics in Primary Care* 19 (1): 33–37.

Family Violence Death Review Committee. 2014. *Fifth Report: January 2014 to December 2015*. Wellington: Health Quality & Safety Commission.

Fanslow, J. 2002. *Family Violence Intervention Guidelines: Child and Partner Abuse*. Wellington: Ministry of Health.

Fanslow, J., and P. Kelly. Ministry of Health. 2016. *Family Violence Assessment and Intervention Guideline: Child Abuse and Intimate Partner Violence*. Wellington: Ministry of Health.

Felix-Bortolotti, M. 2009. "Part 1 - Unravelling Primary Health Care Conceptual Predicaments through the Lenses of Complexity and Political Economy: A Position Paper for Progressive Transformation." *Journal of Evaluation in Clinical Practice* 15 (5): 861–867. doi:10.1111/j.1365-2753.2009.01274.x.

Felix-Bortolotti, M. 2011. "Part 2 - Primary Health Care Workforce Policy Intricacies: Multidisciplinary Team Case Analysis." *Journal of Evaluation in Clinical Practice* 17 (2): 400–404. doi:10.1111/j.1365-2753.2011.01647.x.

Fleiszer, A. R., S. E. Semenic, J. A. Ritchie, M.-C. Richer, and J.-L. Denis. 2015. "The Sustainability of Healthcare Innovations: A Concept Analysis." *Journal of Advanced Nursing* 71 (7): 1484–1498. doi:10.1111/jan.12633.

Garcia-Moreno, C., K. Hegarty, A. F. d'Oliveira, J. Koziol-McLain, M. Colombini, and G. Feder. 2015. "The Health-Systems Response to Violence against Women." *The Lancet* 385 (9977): 1567–1579. doi:10.1016/s0140-6736(14)61837-7.

Gear, C., J. Koziol-McLain, D. Wilson, and F. Clark. 2016. "Developing a Response to Family Violence in Primary Health Care: The New Zealand Experience." *BMC Family Practice* 17: 115. doi:10.1186/s12875-016-0508-x.

Gear, C., J. Koziol-McLain, D. Wilson, N. Rae, H. Samuel, F. Clark, and E. McNeill. 2012. "Primary Healthcare Response to Family Violence: A Delphi Evaluation Tool." *Quality in Primary Care* 20 (1): 15–30.

Ghandour, R. M., J. C. Campbell, and J. Lloyd. 2015. "Screening and Counseling for Intimate Partner Violence: A Vision for the Future." *Journal of Women's Health* 24 (1): 57–61. doi:10.1089/jwh.2014.4885.

Goicolea, I., E. Briones-Vozmediano, A. Ohman, K. Edin, F. Minvielle, and C. Vives-Cases. 2013. "Mapping and Exploring Health Systems' Response to Intimate Partner Violence in Spain." *BMC Public Health* 13: 1162. doi:10.1186/1471-2458-13-1162.

Goicolea, I., A. K. Hurtig, M. San Sebastian, B. Marchal, and C. Vives-Cases. 2015a. "Using Realist Evaluation to Assess Primary Healthcare Teams' Responses to Intimate Partner Violence in Spain." *Gaceta Sanitaria* 29 (6): 431–436. doi:10.1016/j.gaceta.2015.08.005.

Goicolea, I., A. K. Hurtig, M. San Sebastian, C. Vives-Cases, and B. Marchal. 2015b. "Developing A Programme Theory to Explain How Primary Health Care Teams Learn to Respond to Intimate

Partner Violence: A Realist Case-Study." *BMC Health Services Research* 15: 228. doi:10.1186/s12913-015-0899-8.

Gruen, R. L., J. H. Elliott, M. L. Nolan, P. D. Lawton, A. Parkhill, C. J. McLaren, and J. N. Lavis. 2008. "Sustainability Science: An Integrated Approach for Health-Programme Planning." *The Lancet* 372 (9649): 1579–1589. doi:10.1016/s0140-6736(08)61659-1.

Gulliver, P., and J. Fanslow. 2016. *Understanding Research on Risk and Protective Factors for Intimate Partner Violence*. Auckland: New Zealand Family Violence Clearinghouse, University of Auckland.

Hamberger, L. K., B. Ambuel, C. Guse, M. B. Phelan, M. Melzer-Lange, and A. Kistner. 2014. "Effects of a Systems Change Model to Respond to Patients Experiencing Partner Violence in Primary Care Medical Settings." *Journal of Family Violence* 29 (6): 581–94 14. doi:10.1007/s10896-014-9616-3.

Hawe, P. 2015. "Lessons from Complex Interventions to Improve Health." In *Annual Review of Public Health*, edited by J. E. Fielding, 307–323. Doi:10.1146/annurev-publhealth-031912-114421

Hawe, P., A. Shiell, and T. Riley. 2009. "Theorising Interventions as Events in Systems." *American Journal of Community Psychology* 43 (3/4): 267–276. doi:10.1007/s10464-009-9229-9.

Hegarty, K., L. O'Doherty, A. Taft, P. Chondros, S. Brown, J. Valpied, J. Astbury et al. 2013. "Screening and Counselling in the Primary Care Setting for Women Who Have Experienced Intimate Partner Violence (WEAVE): A Cluster Randomised Controlled Trial." *The Lancet* 382 (9888): 249–258. DOI:10.1016/S0140-6736(13)60052-5.

Hegarty, K., L. O. O'Doherty, J. Astbury, and J. Gunn. 2012. "Identifying Intimate Partner Violence When Screening for Health and Lifestyle Issues among Women Attending General Practice." *Australian Journal of Primary Health* 18 (4): 327–331. doi:10.1071/py11101.

Hooker, L., R. Small, C. Humphreys, K. Hegarty, and A. Taft. 2015. "Applying Normalization Process Theory to Understand Implementation of a Family Violence Screening and Care Model in Maternal and Child Health Nursing Practice: A Mixed Method Process Evaluation of a Randomised Controlled Trial." *Implementation Science* 10 (1): 39. doi:10.1186/s13012-015-0230-4.

Jordon, M., H. J. Lanham, R. A. Anderson, and R. R. McDaniel Jr. 2010. "Implications of Complex Adaptive Systems Theory for Interpreting Research about Health Care Organizations." *Journal of Evaluation in Clinical Practice* 16 (1): 228–231. doi:10.1111/j.1365-2753.2009.01359.x.

Kelly, U. A. 2011. "Theories of Intimate Partner Violence: From Blaming the Victim to Acting against Injustice Intersectionality as an Analytic Framework." *Advances in Nursing Science* 34 (3): E29–E51. doi:10.1097/ANS.0b013e3182272388.

Kernick, D. 2006. "Wanted - New Methodologies for Health Service Research. Is Complexity Theory the Answer?" *Family Practice* 23 (3): 385–390. doi:10.1093/fampra/cml011.

Kevin, H. L., K. Rhodes, and J. Brown. 2015. "Screening and Intervention for Intimate Partner Violence in Healthcare Settings: Creating Sustainable System-Level Programs." *Journal of Women's Health (15409996)* 24 (1): 86–91 6. doi:10.1089/jwh.2014.4861.

Koziol-McLain, J., L. Giddings, M. Rameka, and E. Fyfe. 2008. "Intimate Partner Violence Screening and Brief Intervention: Experiences of Women in Two New Zealand Health Care Settings." *Journal of Midwifery Women's Health* 53 (6): 504–510. doi:10.1016/j.jmwh.2008.06.002.

Koziol-McLain, J., and C. McLean. 2015. *Hospital Responsiveness to Family Violence: 120 Month Follow-Up Evaluation*. Auckland: Interdisciplinary Trauma Research Centre, Auckland University of Technology.

MacMillan, H. L., C. N. Wathen, E. Jamieson, M. H. Boyle, H. S. Shannon, M. Ford-Gilboe, A. Worster, et al. 2009. "Screening for Intimate Partner Violence in Health Care Settings: A Randomized Trial." *Jama* 302 (5): 493–501. doi:10.1001/jama.2009.1089.

Martin, C. M., and M. Felix-Bortolotti. 2010. "W(H)ither Complexity? the Emperor's New Toolkit? or Elucidating the Evolution of Health Systems Knowledge?" *Journal of Evaluation in Clinical Practice* 16 (3): 415–420. doi:10.1111/j.1365-2753.2010.01461.x.

Martin, C. M., and M. Felix-Bortolotti. 2014. "Person-Centred Health Care: A Critical Assessment of Current and Emerging Research Approaches." *Journal of Evaluation in Clinical Practice* 20 (6): 1056–1064. doi:10.1111/jep.12283.

Martin, G. P., G. Currie, R. Finn, and R. McDonald. 2011. "The Medium-Term Sustainability of Organisational Innovations in the National Health Service." *Implementation Science* 6 (1): 1–7. doi:10.1186/1748-5908-6-19.

Martin, G. P., S. Weaver, G. Currie, R. Finn, and R. McDonald. 2012. "Innovation Sustainability in Challenging Health-Care Contexts: Embedding Clinically Led Change in Routine Practice." *Health Services Management Research* 25 (4): 190–199. doi:10.1177/0951484812474246.

McDaniel Jr., R. R., and D. J. Driebe. 2001. "Complexity Science and Health Care Management." In *Advances in Health Care Management*, edited by L. H. Friedman, J. Goes and G. T. Savage, 11–36. Bingley: Emerald Group Publishing Limited.

McDaniel Jr., R. R., D. J. Driebe, and H. J. Lanham. 2013. "Health Care Organizations as Complex Systems: New Perspectives on Design and Management." *Advances in Health Care Management* 15: 3–26.

McFarlane, J. M., J. Y. Groff, J. A. O'Brien, and K. Watson. 2006. "Secondary Prevention of Intimate Partner Violence: A Randomized Controlled Trial." *Nursing Research* 55 (1): 52–61. doi:10.1097/00006199-200601000-00007.

Ministry of Health. 2016. *New Zealand Health Strategy: Future Direction*. Wellington: Ministry of Health.

Ministry of Health. 2000. *Recommended Referral Process for General Practitioners: Suspected Child Abuse and Neglect*. Wellington: Ministry of Health.

Ministry of Health. 2001. *The Primary Health Care Strategy*. Wellington: Ministry of Health.

Ministry of Health. 2003. *Recognising and Responding to Partner Abuse: A Resource for General Practice*. Wellington: Ministry of Health.

Ministry of Health Primary Care Team. 2015. *Primary Health Care Services Funding and Contracting*. Accessed May 2016. http://www.health.govt.nz/system/files/documents/pages/primary-care-funding-flows-3sept2015v2.pdf.

Mohrman, S. A., and M. H. Kanter. 2012. "Designing for Health: Learning from Kaiser Permanente." In *Organizing for Sustainable Health Care*, edited by S. A. Mohrman and A. B. Shani, 77–111. Bingley: Emerald Group Publishing House.

Mohrman, S. A., A. B. Shani, and A. McCracken. 2012. "Organizing for Sustainable Health Care: The Emerging Global Challenge." In *Organizing for Sustainable Health Care*, edited by S. A. Mohrman and A. B. Shani, 1–39. Bingley: Emerald Group Publishing Limited.

Morden, A., L. Brooks, C. Jinks, M. Porcheret, B. N. Ong, and K. Dziedzic. 2015. "Research "Push", Long Term-Change, and General Practice." *Journal of Health Organization and Management* 29 (7): 798–821. doi:10.1108/jhom-07-2014-0119.

Narula, A., G. Agarwal, and L. McCarthy. 2012. "Intimate Partner Violence: Patients' Experiences and Perceptions in Family Practice." *Family Practice* 29 (5): 593–600. doi:10.1093/fampra/cms008.

Nicolaidis, C., and V. Touhouliotis. 2006. "Addressing Intimate Partner Violence in Primary Care: Lessons from Chronic Illness Management." *Violence Victims* 21 (1): 101–115. doi:10.1891/vivi.21.1.101.

O'Campo, P., M. Kirst, C. Tsamis, C. Chambers, and F. Ahmad. 2011. "Implementing Successful Intimate Partner Violence Screening Programs in Health Care Settings: Evidence Generated from a Realist-Informed Systematic Review." *Social Science Medicine* 72 (6): 855–866. doi:10.1016/j.socscimed.2010.12.019.

O'Doherty, L., K. Hegarty, J. Ramsay, L. L. Davidson, G. Feder, and A. Taft. 2015. "Screening Women for Intimate Partner Violence in Healthcare Settings." *Cochrane Database of Systematic Reviews* 7: CD007007. doi:10.1002/14651858.CD007007.pub3.

O'Doherty, L., A. Taket, J. Valpied, and K. Hegarty. 2016. "Receiving Care for Intimate Partner Violence in Primary Care: Barriers and Enablers for Women Participating in the Weave Randomised Controlled Trial." *Social Science Medicine* 160: 35–42. doi:10.1016/j.socscimed.2016.05.017.

Paterson, C., C. Baarts, L. Launsø, and M. J. Verhoef. 2009. "Evaluating Complex Health Interventions: A Critical Analysis of the 'Outcomes' Concept." *BMC Complementary and Alternative Medicine* 9: 18. doi:10.1186/1472-6882-9-18.

Phelan, S. E. 2001. "What Is Complexity Science, Really?" *Emergence* 3 (1): 120–136. doi:10.1207/S15327000EM0301_08.

Ramsay, J., C. Rivas, and G. Feder. 2005. *Interventions to Reduce Violence and Promote the Physical and Psychosocial Well-Being of Women Who Experience Partner Violence: A Systematic Review of Controlled Evaluations*. London: Barts and The London Queen Mary's School of Medicine and Dentistry.

Scheirer, M. A. 2005. "Is Sustainability Possible? A Review and Commentary on Empirical Studies of Program Sustainability." *American Journal of Evaluation* 26 (3): 320–347. doi:10.1177/1098214005278752.

Shani, A. B., and S. A. Mohrman. 2012. "Learning to Organize for Sustainable Health Care: Rigor, Reflection and Relevance." In *Organizing for Sustainable Health Care*, edited by S. A. Mohrman and A. B. Shani, 227–249. Bingley: Emerald Group Publishing Limited.

Shiell, A., P. Hawe, and L. Gold. 2008. "Complex Interventions or Complex Systems? Implications for Health Economic Evaluation." *BMJ* 336 (7656): 1281–1283. doi:10.1136/bmj.39569.510521.AD.

Spangaro, J., S. Herring, J. Koziol-Mclain, A. Rutherford, M. Frail, and A. B. Zwi. 2016. "'They Aren't Really Black Fellas but They are Easy to Talk to': Factors Which Influence Australian Aboriginal Women's Decision to Disclose Intimate Partner Violence during Pregnancy." *Midwifery* 41: 79–88. //dx.doi.org/10.1016/j.midw.2016.08.004.

Spangaro, J., J. Koziol-McLain, A. Zwi, A. Rutherford, M. Frail, and J. Ruane. 2016. "Deciding to Tell: Qualitative Configurational Analysis of Decisions to Disclose Experience of Intimate Partner Violence in Antenatal Care." *Social Science and Medicine* 154: 45–53. doi:10.1016/j.socscimed.2016.02.032.

Spangaro, J., A. B. Zwi, and R. Poulos. 2009. "The Elusive Search for Definitive Evidence on Routine Screening for Intimate Partner Violence." *Trauma Violence Abuse* 10 (1): 55–68. doi:10.1177/1524838008327261.

Spangaro, J. M., A. B. Zwi, and R. G. Poulos. 2011. "'Persist. Persist.': A Qualitative Study of Women's Decisions to Disclose and Their Perceptions of the Impact of Routine Screening for Intimate Partner Violence." *Psychology of Violence* 1 (2): 150–162. doi:10.1037/a0023136.

Swain, K., R. Whitley, G. J. McHugo, and R. E. Drake. 2010. "The Sustainability of Evidence-Based Practices in Routine Mental Health Agencies." *Community Mental Health Journal* 46 (2): 119–129. doi:10.1007/s10597-009-9202-y.

Taft, A. J., L. Hooker, C. Humphreys, K. Hegarty, R. Walter, C. Adams, P. Agius, and R. Small. 2015. "Maternal and Child Health Nurse Screening and Care for Mothers Experiencing Domestic Violence (MOVE): A Cluster Randomised Trial." *BMC Medicine* 13 (1): 150. doi:10.1186/s12916-015-0375-7.

Taft, A. J., R. Small, K. L. Hegarty, J. Lumley, L. F. Watson, and L. Gold. 2009. "MOSAIC (Mothers' Advocates in the Community): Protocol and Sample Description of a Cluster Randomised Trial of Mentor Mother Support to Reduce Intimate Partner Violence among Pregnant or Recent Mothers." *BMC Public Health* 9: 159. doi:10.1186/1471-2458-9-159.

Taft, A. J., R. Small, K. L. Hegarty, L. F. Watson, L. Gold, and J. A. Lumley. 2011. "Mothers' AdvocateS in the Community (Mosaic)–Non-Professional Mentor Support to Reduce Intimate Partner Violence and Depression in Mothers: A Cluster Randomised Trial in Primary Care." *BMC Public Health* 11: 178. doi:10.1186/1471-2458-11-178.

Tenbensel, T. 2013. "Complexity in Health and Health Care Systems." *Social Science and Medicine* 93: 181–184. doi:10.1016/j.socscimed.2013.06.017.

Tenbensel, T. 2015. "Complexity and Health Policy." In *Handbook on Complexity and Public Policy*, edited by R. Geyer and P. Cairney. Cheltenham: Edward Elgar Publishing.

Tenbensel, T. 2016. "Health System Regionalization – the New Zealand Experience." *HealthcarePapers* 16 (1): 27–33. doi:10.12927/hcpap.

Thompson, D. R., and A. M. Clark. 2012. "The Complexity Conundrum: Nursing Interventions for Complex Health Problems." *Contemporary Nurse* 40 (2): 277–280. doi:10.1080/10376178.2012.11002593.

Thompson, D. S., X. Fazio, E. Kustra, L. Patrick, and D. Stanley. 2016. "Scoping Review of Complexity Theory in Health Services Research." *BMC Health Services Research* 16. doi:10.1186/s12913-016-1343-4.

Thurston, W. E., and A. C. Eisener. 2006. "Successful Integration and Maintenance of Screening for Domestic Violence in the Health Sector: Moving beyond Individual Responsibility." *Trauma, Violence, & Abuse* 7 (2): 83–92. doi:10.1177/1524838005285915.

Tower, M. 2007. "Intimate Partner Violence and the Health Care Response: A Postmodern Critique." *Health Care for Women International* 28 (5): 438–452. doi:10.1080/07399330701226404.

Wathen, C. N., and H. L. MacMillan. 2003. "Interventions for Violence against Women: Scientific Review." *JAMA* 289 (5): 589–600. doi:10.1001/jama.289.5.589.

Willis, K., R. Small, and S. Brown. 2012. "Using Documents to Investigate Links between Implementation and Sustainability in a Complex Community Intervention: The PRISM Study." *Social Science and Medicine* 75 (7): 1222–1229. doi:10.1016/j.socscimed.2012.05.025.

Wiltsey Stirman, S., J. Kimberly, N. Cook, A. Calloway, F. Castro, and M. Charns. 2012. "The Sustainability of New Programs and Innovations: A Review of the Empirical Literature and Recommendations for Future Research." *Implementation Science* 7: 17. doi:10.1186/1748-5908-7-17.

World Health Organisation. 2013. *Global and Regional Estimates of Violence against Women: Prevalence and Health Effects of Intimate Partner Violence and Non-Partner Sexual Violence.* Geneva: World Health Organization.

World Health Organization. 2013. *Responding to Intimate Partner Violence and Sexual Violence against Women: WHO Clinical and Policy Guidelines.* Geneva: World Health Organization.

Young-Wolff, K. C., K. Kotz, and B. McCaw. 2016. "Transforming the Health Care Response to Intimate Partner Violence: Addressing "Wicked Problems"." *JAMA* 315 (23): 2517–2518. doi:10.1001/jama.2016.4837.

Sustainability of collaborative networks in higher education research projects: why complexity? Why now?

Amanda Scott, Geoff Woolcott, Robyn Keast and Daniel Chamberlain

ABSTRACT
This article outlines the potential of complexity theory as a framework for understanding collaborative project networks and their sustainability within cross-institutional funded projects, responding to funders' interest in projects that deliver public value. Preliminary analysis from an educational project suggests that complexity thinking may be useful also in examining attributes of sustainable networks. The article argues for new measures that shed light on how and why (or why not) collaborative project networks achieve sustainability, removing the current reliance on conventional, linear management and evaluation approaches.

Introduction

For some time now there has been increased attention and public funding directed towards cross-disciplinary projects designed to address contemporary societal challenges (Provan, Fish, and Sydow 2007). Such projects are widely understood to rely heavily on a collaborative approach for their realization (Gajda and Koliba 2007; Huxham 1996) in order to create the 'new whole' or system change (Innes and Booher 2010), often allied to intractable or persistent societal problems. Project collaboration is a sought-after objective, and when done well can bring about significant change. The complex, uncertain or turbulent conditions around which a collaboration often forms and operates (Head 2008), however, means that the structural and/or functional collaborative networks required for project success are difficult to achieve and challenging to sustain (Huxham 2003; Keast 2011; Le Pennec and Raufflet 2016).

A collaborative project network (CPN) is characterized by the bringing together of diverse groups of people and resources to form closer, more interdependent relationships and interactions, and through these, shaping new thinking and behaviours (Keast 2011; Keast et al. 2004). CPNs are different from many other ways of working together, for example, cooperative or coordinative networks, partnerships or alliances, in that such networks are a high-risk, high return working environment where participants are required to change how they think, behave and work (Gray 1985; Huxham 1996; Keast, Brown, and Mandell 2007; Alford and O'Flynn 2009). Furthermore, collaboration via CPNs is not cost free. It takes a significant investment of time and effort to build capacity. Many resources, both physical and material, are required for its composition and operation as well as to sustain their effects beyond the initial funding or support contributions (Willard and Creech 2006).

A substantial allocation of public funds is often coupled with a growing demand to demonstrate 'good investment' to deliver public value in collaborative projects (Scheirer 2005). Given that there is also an understanding that solving intractable or persistent problems is generally a long-term commitment, there appears a recent and growing interest in the concept of project sustainability. While productive and sustained collaboration is increasingly sought after by funding bodies, it is difficult to locate practical and relevant resources to inform practices supporting sustainability within collaborative projects, or their underlying CPNs. There is also limited theoretical knowledge about how the sustainability of such CPNs is defined, what it looks like, how it can be achieved, and what useful measures might be.

This gap in knowledge and the lack of practical tools supporting sustainability of CPNs is not necessarily due to the societal problems being addressed by collaborative projects, but arises also from the limitations of conventional research as applied to collective entities. Conventional methodologies are grounded in linear, rational and predictable models of operation and understanding (Rogers 2008; Sarriot et al. 2014) but these are not conducive to capturing the complexity arising from the dynamic, unpredictable and emergent properties of many CPNs (Patton 2011).

Furthermore, while collaborative projects may seek system change and therefore may give rise to emergent and unpredictable outcomes, conventional research methodologies are more directed towards the execution of predetermined activities, leading to the delivery of planned outcomes. There is, in addition, an expectation that in achieving these outcomes, the relationships established, and associated joint programmes of work, will continue after funding ceases (Frey et al. 2006). Conventional approaches may also demand and impose simple solution frameworks onto complex problems (Kania, Kramer, and Russell 2014) which, in their application, commonly only address the concept of sustainability towards the end of a project's life. These solution frameworks rarely consider a collaborative project as an evolving and changing dynamic environment, where the history of the CPN influences the future state of the collaboration, and thus the capacity for project sustainability. Such conventional methodologies do not fully acknowledge, or account for the resources and supporting infrastructure required over the life of a project, and that is required to build capacity to a level that facilitates sustainability.

If collaborative projects can be considered as complex systems, then the assumptions we have held around conventional management of such projects for their sustainability are open to reconsideration; sustainability is a long-term, ongoing and complex change process (Hall and Hord 2006) that should be considered from project outset, and without pre-established expectations. Complexity thinking (Innes and Booher 2010), therefore, may be useful in offering a way of understanding CPNs and by extension, a better understanding of CPN and project sustainability.

Studies of various collaborative forms, where people work together towards a common goal, have delivered important insights into the unique characteristics of collaborative projects as complex systems, including the dynamic inter-relational processes and interactions associated with such systems, and the different processes and management required for their optimal functioning (Eppel 2012; Keast 2016; Provan and Lemaire 2012; Provan and Milward 1995; Mitleton-Kelly 2003). There is limited theoretical research, however, that considers the CPNs themselves in this complex system context. Furthermore, there are few ways of capturing and measuring complex information to use in order to set up sustainable processes from project inception and the establishment of a CPN.

This article contributes to the growing interest in the concept of sustainability of CPNs as a critical component of the public value of collaborative projects. In doing so, it highlights the current gap in knowledge at both the theoretical level and as applied knowledge. The article contends that a complexity lens can help to better understand the design and operation of CPNs, including the delivery of insights into collaborative project sustainability. The article begins with a definition of sustainability of CPNs, followed by an outline of complexity thinking and complex systems. The article then describes the characteristics of CPNs using a complexity lens, and considers the challenges related to examination of CPN sustainability. Next the research approach is articulated, the findings are presented and discussed, and finally, some conclusions and implications are drawn.

CPN sustainability defined

A CPN is considered sustainable if collaborative effects are continued beyond the resource (funding) allocation and timeframe; and, both the CPN and/or its related effects are deemed to have value by relevant stakeholders. This means that a collaborative network supporting/facilitating the project 'continues to function until it achieves its goals, or until its members are no longer willing or able to continue, or until it becomes irrelevant' (Wind 2004, 12), or, it has the capacity to can be called upon and leveraged on future occasions as needed (Jacobus, Baskett, and Bechstein 2011).

Complexity as a bridge

Complexity theory is multidisciplinary in origin, but has evolved over time to be considered a conceptual lens that provides a perspective through which to see both the world and its interactions (Mitleton-Kelly 2003). Seen through a complexity lens, the world consists of multiple systems, which are complex in their interaction and which are constantly learning from and adapting to their environment.

Although there is no single unified complexity perspective, there is general agreement on the core characteristics being explored through complexity (Teisman and Klijn 2008). This article builds on such core characteristics as applied in collaborative project contexts, such as those outlined and Teisman and Klijn (2008), as well as Laszlo and Krippner (1998), Mitleton-Kelly (2003), Eppel (2009, 2012) and Akkerman and Bakker (2011). The study also draws on the Innes and Booher (2010) study on the alignment of collaborative governance and complex adaptive systems within collaborative projects (Table 1). These core characteristics form the analytical framework used in this study to support a case for CPN in a higher education research project to be considered as a complex system.

Table 1. Characteristics of a complex system, drawn from Laszlo and Krippner (1998), Mitleton-Kelly (2003), Teisman and Klijn (2008), Innes and Booher (2010), Akkerman and Bakker (2011) and Eppel (2009), 2012).

Characteristics of a complex system	Explanation of characteristics
1. Consists of a large numbers of elements	Large number of actors connecting and intersecting within larger system, actors bound by socially constructed boundaries and the open system is shaped by interaction and exchange (relationships)
2. Elements interact dynamically	Interaction is constant and iterative and influences subsequent behaviours
3. Interactions are non-linear	Actors in the system are not aware of the behaviour of the system as a whole, and respond only to what is available or known locally in a non-linear pattern
4. Feedback loops are operating	Multiple interacting (nested) systems create feedback mechanisms with and between actors and systems, with direct and indirect feedback loops
5. Functions under conditions far from equilibrium	If actors are working together in situations operating outside of established norms, a system can be said to be functioning far from equilibrium. These systems, although often appearing stable, can undergo radical unpredicted changes, disproportionate to small stimulus, when tensions or paradoxes occur
6. Actors and the system have history	The history of the actors and the system influences the system's starting point for change, shaping present and future behaviour
7. The system is a whole	The combined effect on the system of the interactions between actors (relationships) is greater than the sum of their actions. Exploration of coherent and novel emergent patterns informs system understanding
8. Self-organization and co-evolution	Without hierarchy of command, a system continuously self-organizes to best respond to, and change with environment. The system can learn from adaptation to evolve more effectively over time (co-evolution)
9. Emergence	Emergence is a process by which new order is generated through self-organization and co-evolution, arising from the actor interaction, but affecting the system as a whole

Collaborative projects, and by extension CPNs, are known to share similarities with complex systems: they comprise multiple actors working together in a dynamic way, they are constantly evolving and/or co-evolving, and they demonstrate self-organization and emergence (Innes and Booher 2010; Keast et al. 2004; Koppenjan and Koliba 2013; Rhodes 2008). Importantly, strong resonance exists between complexity theory and sustainability, since sustainability concepts may be grounded in notions of interconnectedness, dynamic interaction, constant change, adaption and co-evolution (Peter and Swilling 2014).

Given these similarities, it is proposed that the application of a complexity theoretic approach may contribute new insight into the conceptualization and measurement of CPN sustainability, bridging the gap from conventional methodologies. A complexity lens may also provide an opportunity for development of a more comprehensive and nuanced understanding of how and why (or why not) CPNs become sustainable.

A complexity framework for understanding sustainability

Two attributes of complex systems, flexibility and adaptability, are inherent to sustainability of a collaborative project, and by implication of CPNs. Flexibility represents the property of a system that can be changed easily, with low effort and without undesired effects, through intrinsic modification (for example through actor interactions). Adaptability characterizes a system's ability to maintain its goals while adapting itself towards changing environments, through extrinsic modifications (Kissel, Schrieverho, and Lindemann 2012; Schulz, Fricke, and Igenbergs 2000). This is sometimes seen collectively as the flexibility to adapt (Uhl-Bien, Marion, and McKelvey 2007).

Resonating with concepts underpinning complexity theory and complex systems (Newman and Dale 2005), adaptability and flexibility of a CPN stem from the capacity to sense and learn from the project environment and, as a result, either act or react appropriately, in a timely manner, displaying resilience (Eppel 2012; Magis 2010) or opportunism (Newman and Dale 2005). A system, which can flex and adapt as needed, continually exploring the space of possibilities and responding to shock or opportunity by being resilient or opportunistic, will co-evolve within and across systems, and emerge along new trajectories. This means that the system continuously creates new structures and ways of working in order to continue to function, that is, to be sustainable. Thus, sustainability could be considered an emergent property in and of itself.

Resilience

The concept of resilience appears to be linked (explicitly or inferred) to sustainable collaborative projects, and CPNs, throughout the collaboration literature, regardless of context or goal (Bakker, Raab, and Milward 2012; Jacobus, Baskett, and Bechstein 2011; Magis 2010; Milward and Provan 2006). Resilience relates to a system's ability to adjust activity and retain functionality during change (Axelrod and Cohen 2000). Within this notion of resilience, two conditions are present: exposure to some kind of stress or shock; and, the ability to survive and recover despite the event (Vogus and Sutcliffe 2003).

The ability of a CPN to absorb shock and continue to function, its robustness (Walker et al. 2004), is essentially resumption of function, structure and identity exhibited prior to the event. Rebounding is the capacity of a CPN to transform itself (structures or processes) in order to promote competence, restore efficiency and/or encourage growth (Vogus and Sutcliffe 2003) and enables the CPN to retain and continue its function and productivity under varying operating conditions (Schulz Fricke, and Igenbergs 2000). CPNs can be seen as resilient, therefore, in responding through robustness, by rebounding, or by doing both. In this way, exposure to perturbation can have a positive function for sustainability.

Opportunism

The responses to system change discussed above can be considered reactive. It is argued here, however, that sustainable CPNs must also have proactive traits (Newman and Dale 2005). These would include the ability to pre-empt potential shock, and to act in advance to either reduce the impact the shock will have on the network, or take opportunist action (opportunism) in order to maximize the positive influence of the potential shock.

Stability versus change

While a CPN, to be sustainable, must be able to adapt, evolve and change by responding in real time in an ever-changing environment, not all elements of a collaborative network must be changing, and such change does not need to be constant. Some level of stability within a collaborative network is essential to foster the development of relationships based on trust, mutuality and reciprocity required for authentic collaborative interaction, and to also maintain processes that are working well (Burt 2005).

Research approach

Using examples from a case study of a collaborative network research project in Higher Education: *It's part of my life: Engaging university and community to enhance science and mathematics education* (IPOML), this article presents a first-cut analysis argument for consideration of this exemplar project as a complex system. It also establishes a relationship between characteristics of a CPN as a complex system and CPN sustainability through the identification of the sustainability attributes of resilience and opportunism in the case study project. This relationship highlights the potential suitability of a complexity approach in shedding new light on sustainability of CPNs and collaborative projects.

Methodology

An in-depth single case study of the IPOML project was used as the research methodology to capture CPN and project evolution (Yin 2013), examining the dynamic and emergent nature of the CPN, including changes to trajectory, as the project unfolded (time dimension, see e.g. Marshall and Rossman 1989). A purposeful case selection (Patton 2011) was applied focusing on a government-funded collaborative project, and its CPN, in a higher education setting with sustainability as an outcome, and with a conventional evaluation framework initiated by the funding body.

Both primary and secondary qualitative data sources informed the construction of the case study. Secondary data included information collected as part of the everyday management and evaluation practices within the project, and included quarterly reports from partners and project reports sent to the funding body, daily internal correspondence, project evaluation feedback surveys from partners, and minutes from monthly meetings with project partners. Primary data was collected in the form of an introductory network member survey, which included questions around if and how network members knew each other prior to their involvement in the project. A research journal was also a source of primary data. The journal was a weekly written reflection on the project, kept by the project manager, which documented project progress, opportunities and challenges. Together this mix of data sources provided for a range of perspectives.

All data collected or generated was subjected to manual thematic analysis and assessed against the (a) the complex systems characteristics framework outlined in Table 1 and (b) sustainability attributes related to complexity. Social network analysis was selectively applied to confirm presence of interaction and communication connections and flows (Scott et al. 2016). The study followed conventional ethical protocol, including the de-identification of respondents.

Findings

The following section reports the data related to the CPN against each of the nine characteristics in the analytical framework (Table 1).

Characteristic 1: consists of large numbers of elements

The CPN at project completion connected over 400 people across a broad diversity of environments, with connections recognized also to institutions. Interactions within and between multiple nested networks or hubs were designed to create a system whole that engendered university curriculum improvement in science and mathematics education for pre-service teachers.

The core hub comprised seven key actors, one team leader at each of the five university partner institutions, and the project leader and project manager at the lead institution. Each of these seven core members made connections to university and community mathematics, science and education experts, as well as school students, teachers and pre-service teachers. This created six nested hubs at each institutional location along the Australian eastern seaboard (Victoria, New South Wales and Queensland). Additional, largely peripheral hubs of the CPN included a network of representatives of the government funding body, an external evaluation team, and members of the project reference group. The IPOML CPN was also connected to a broader network that included members of four other related projects.

The CPN, therefore, operated through as a sizeable interconnected and dispersed network consisting of a large number of elements, with multiple degrees of connectivity. It had socially constructed boundaries determined by partner relationships and interactions but was, according to Eppel (2009), fundamentally an open system, with interaction and exchange between the actors within the system and the outside environment.

Characteristic 2: the elements interact dynamically

Several documentary sources, including the project manager journal and minutes from the regular partner meetings and Forums, highlighted the volume and dynamic nature of the interactions between IPOML members (as CPN elements). For example, journal entries show that, on an average day, the project manager received thirty emails and four phone calls from project partners, as well as additional enquiries from members of peripheral hubs such as the funding body, the external evaluation team or other mathematics and science education groups connected within the CPN. The dynamic interactivity characteristic is evident in return emails and telephone calls that included other CPN members, resulting in increased frequency and reach of discussion topics, and bringing more members into the decision-making and action process occurring between scheduled team meetings.

Further, the case data revealed that additional collaboration opportunities were facilitated annually through face-to-face and online forums or meetings in which partners came together and were encouraged to debate points of difference in order to develop alternative solutions in real time. As one institutional team leader commented after the November 2014 bi-annual Partner Forum:

> The capacity for the folks from the lead University to sit and allow others to express their, sometimes critical, views of the processes involved in the project has been excellent. This has been a highlight of the project in my view.

These data suggest that these Forums, and other regular meetings, gave project partners the opportunity to interact openly in a neutral space where opinions were valued and everyone had equal stake, thus building trust and mutuality between members as well as building commitment and engagement in a dynamic way (Provan and Lemaire 2012).

The data additionally showed that 'boundary crossing' (Akkerman and Bakker 2011) between project hubs was prompted by and further facilitated dynamic interaction. For example, the project leadership hub (the project leader, project manager and institutional team leaders) identified a need to moderate their role by ensuring that the project leader or project manager was more 'hands on' and onsite at partner universities. This led to the project manager interacting dynamically with institutional teams, modelling project processes and assisting in project implementation.

The results indicate that, in IPOML, the elements of the CPN interact dynamically as a system, with constant exchanges of information as well as continuous decision-making and action resulting in boosting combined effort across the network.

Characteristic 3: interactions are non-linear

Even though IPOML had a predetermined plan with defined activities and outcomes, unexpected challenges emerged, along with unpredictable outcomes and member interaction that was non-linear, aligning the CPN with complex system conditions as 'iterative, recursive and self-referential' (Innes and Booher 2010, 32).

As discussed in the previous section, CPN interactions were dynamic, and in the IPOML project context they were also non-linear. The interview data, for example, highlight a decision, promoted enthusiastically and spontaneously by an institutional team member, to introduce individual sub-project data collection instruments to boost confidence in the reliability and validity of data. This began as a linear connection by way of promotion of the instruments to a second team member, and other project partners were not aware of the behaviour until well after the event.

This response, recorded in the project Forum feedback survey May 2015 from a member of one of the other partner teams, highlights the dilemma and the value of non-linear dialogue:

> Discussion about team members regarding recruitment and data collection was helpful. Talking on numerous occasions with one team member about him feeling like the process wasn't working for him because he didn't believe the instruments we were using were reliable, so he has come up with his own process/instruments. He was torn between the importance of using what he thought were valid and reliable measures, and doing what everyone else was doing in the project. But now he sees how important it is to discuss these things with the group first.

All partner actions were in response only to what knowledge was available to them locally at the time, and they could not see the effects on the system as a whole. In the IPOML case, this action significantly and unpredictably impacted the project on several levels: affecting the comparability of trial data across the projects; causing other team members to question the lead institution's capabilities in developing valid and reliable instruments; and, impacting on the level of trust between group members.

Characteristic 4: feedback loops are operating

In the IPOML project, feedback loops were present and active within and across CPN hubs during opportunities to interact – ideas were tested and shared understandings found, and new ways to move forward identified, as is typical of complex systems (Eppel 2012).

The operational feedback loops were significant in the realization of positive outcomes despite differences of opinion was achieved through the introduction of such feedback opportunities as extra partner site visits, additional two-day face-to-face workshops, promoting activity and productivity as a natural outcome of the collaborative process, as evidenced by partner responses in the November 2014 bi-annual Partner Forum evaluation survey. This value-added outcome was demonstrated by, for example, the development of a model for cross-contextual embedding of project processes (in university curriculum) approved by team members within a week of the May 2015 Forum. For months prior to this Forum the models had been deemed 'too difficult' to develop and partners could not agree on the best approach.

Characteristic 5: functions under conditions far from equilibrium

As revealed from data in IPOML, one project partner's decision to deviate from the designed process, with minimal feedback across any of the hubs, led to a positive feedback loop that triggered generation of invalid data. This effect was amplified when another member, also without consultation across the CPN, adopted a similar process. The net result across the project was a disruption in the system, causing actors to question the suitability of the original process. When collaborative behaviour was re-established across the CPN, largely through a deliberate initiative of the project leader and manager team to instigate extra team meetings, common ground was found allowing new ideas to be tested and a suitable resolution to be developed as a recommendation from the October 2016 Annual Project Report indicates 'Development of clear trial protocol documents that allowed for flexibility for partners to meet the particular needs of their institution'.

Both positive and negative feedback loops played a role resolving such issues. The positive feedback loops that caused undesirable change were countered by other positive loops creating new process and structures, leading to negative feedback loops being established and maintained as stabilized patterns within the system. As the example illustrates, the project, and the CPN, demonstrated the characteristic of a system functioning under conditions far from equilibrium because, as Eppel (2012) suggests, complex systems that operate under these conditions are more easily exposed to perturbation creating feedback loops triggering transformation. In IPOML, this perturbation, which significantly disrupted the system, resulted in creation of something new (innovation).

Characteristic 6: actors and the system have history

Several data sources confirmed that several of the actors in the CPN had a prior working history, either directly or through associated networks, as determined by a survey administered early on in the project which sought information on the existence of professional and social relationships prior to the project within the network at the lead institution. The result of the survey, analysed using social network analysis (Scott et al. 2016), indicated that four out of fifteen members of the institutional lead team in the CPN knew at least one other person in the network socially prior to collaboration in this project. All fifteen members were connected with at least one other network member professionally prior to collaboration in this project.

Even though the IPOML model was developed specifically for science and mathematics pre-service teacher education, university CPN members with existing work history with others in different curriculum areas were able to leverage these relationships. In so doing, these CPN members were able to use the system model developed in the project to open up new opportunities for the project. This led to the establishment of emergent trajectories that would potentially support future sustainability of the CPN through expanded curriculum opportunities. This was most evident in curriculum innovation at one of the partner institutions, where the existing history of the actors within the CPN and across the entire system enabled them to build on existing networks, and expand the IPOML scope to include other subject domains, such as English and history.

Characteristic 7: the system is a whole

The IPOML data shows that the effects that arise from these interactions can be greater than the sum of the system's parts. Thus the system is a whole and its behaviour cannot be understood by looking at components individually (Eppel 2009; Kauffman 1993; Lewin and Bak 1993; Nicolis and Prigogine 1989).

There were initial issues with IPOML of protocols for trialling of developed processes. They were considered too rigid for successful implementation across varied partner contexts. The CPN members at partner institutions were encouraged to self-organize, trying out new ideas in local contexts and experiment with different trial processes or variations of existing processes. The intention was to develop trial protocols that supported better outcomes within their institution as well as for the project overall.

As evidenced by the following quotes from intuitional team leaders one and two respectively after the November 2014 bi-annual Partner Forum, these changes are encouraged and openly discussed with other CPN members, which in turn stimulated trialling of new ideas by some of those other members:

> Meeting everyone involved and having the time to think deeply and discuss issues together. Working together to plan the way forward was great. The different speakers talking about their local situation was great.

> Overview of strategies for implementation. Variety of excellent reports from different partner universities. Time to exchange ideas and review key instruments and plans.

This reciprocal influence facilitated a co-evolutionary process, leading to the development of new trial protocol not predicted at the start of the project.

Characteristic 8: self-organization and co-evolution

Self-organization and co-evolution was seen in CPN in response to opportunities identified through feedback mechanisms. As the IPOML case data showed, the two modules developed for science and mathematics education pre-service teachers were redeveloped into professional development modules for practising teachers. This occurred through CPN members discussing project development with actors outside their immediate CPN hub or cluster and, as a result, identifying an opportunity based on educational need in that outside group and leveraging from this in order to expand the scope and scale of the project modules. Although this extension of the project was not within the initial project plan, the unexpected output had positive consequences, delivering additional value through the potential project traction in new or different marketplaces.

Characteristic 9: emergence

The data reveals that over the course of the project there were changes in the CPN membership (although core membership did not change substantially), and multiple new and unexpected processes and products have emerged from collective interactions of CPN members. The benefit of this emergence is made apparent in the comments taken from the project manager's journal entry of 3 June 2015:

> The way the University has implemented their trials has interestingly led to the roles between educator and mathematician switching – crossing boundaries and breaking down silos. This is a really fascinating outcome and we can see its potential in the future of changing the culture in the mathematics and science faculties when it comes to education students. Other partners haven't had the same success as yet with this 'culture shift'.

As the above and other examples indicate, the IPOML project pathway was progressively adapted and redefined through the relationships and interactions between actors in the CPN, rather than through formalized or organizational hierarchal roles, processes or a predetermined trajectory. Thus individual and collective self-organization created a new order with knock-on effects on the system as a whole (Mitleton-Kelly 2003). Although the projected IPOML outcomes remained the same as originally drafted, evidence of emergence was viewed as an opportunity to rethink how a project CPN could modify its current processes in order to improve or add to those project outcomes.

Sustainability of the CPN in IPOML

Since the CPN could be considered in terms of complex systems, network interactions within the IPOML case study project were further examined to articulate the links between the CPN and sustainability viewed through a complexity lens. Table 2 summarizes findings related to links between the CPN system and the behavioural characteristics of sustainability, resilience and opportunism.

The findings in Table 2 suggest that when a collaborative network project is examined through a complexity theoretic lens, more nuanced insights, not afforded by a conventional lens, are illuminated. This is particularly true for flexibility and adaptability attributes, which are considered crucial for CPN sustainability. This conceptualization is developed further in the discussion section.

Discussion

A collaborative network considered as a complex system

Drawing from the case findings and analysis, Table 3 provides a summary of the ways in which the CPN in the IPOML case study demonstrated characteristics of a complex system.

Table 2. Sustainability attributes of the CPN in the IPOML project.

Behavioural characteristic demonstrated	Description of characteristic	Resulting action	System outcome
Resilience through rebounding	Realization that trials could not be successfully implemented as originally planned, as variation in context did not allow for implementation	Development of new a model for embedding and development of project resources, agreeable to all partners, but with sufficient emergent variability to accommodate differences	Emergence
Resilience through rebounding	Recognized that unhealthy system changes occurred due to system reinforcement caused by the practices of a few partners	New processes and structures supported by all project partners implemented to counteract undesirable behaviours	Emergence
Opportunism	Identified opportunity to implement new processes to boost combined benefit across project sites	Boundary crossing between the network hubs, as project partners swapped roles and/or joined peripheral hubs	Co-evolution
Opportunism	Identified that communication and productivity increased as a result of post partner forums because they facilitated opportunities for true collaboration	Initiation and implementation of additional opportunities for project partners to meet face-to-face	Emergence
Opportunism	Identified opportunity to extend the application of modules developed through the leveraging of one project partner's extended network	Extended project trials to include curriculum areas outside of project scope (English and history), establishing emergent system trajectories	Emergence
Opportunism	Identified opportunity to redevelop project modules for practising teacher professional development. Identified through a project partner's extended network – their becoming aware of soon-to-be-available funding for professional development	Modules developed for pre-service teachers redeveloped into professional development modules for practising teachers	Co-evolution

Table 3. Characteristics of a CPN as a complex system illustrated from the IPOML case study.

Characteristics of a complex system	Characteristics in practice – examples from CPNs in the IPOML case study
1. Consists of a large numbers of elements	• Educators and researchers from different institutions, fields of expertise, and different hierarchal positions formed a sizeable interconnected and dispersed set of nested CPNs within a larger IPOML system CPN • There were multiple degrees of connectivity within the CPN – it was well connected with both weak and strong ties within and across relevant hubs and clusters, for example across university hubs and school clusters
2. The elements interact dynamically	• Regular two-way and multi-directional emails and phone calls connecting the CPN members resulted in actors, such as the project manager and institutional team leaders, disseminating information dynamically and enacting decisions outside of formal project meetings • Face-to-face and online meetings and Forums of CPN members, for example those between project team leaders, or those between pre-service teachers and educators, in which partners came together, and were encouraged in order to discuss points of difference and develop resolutions in real time • Boundary crossing between the hubs occurred as the project manager swapped roles and/or joined other hubs, interacting dynamically with institutional teams, modelling project processes and assisting in project implementation
3. Interactions are non-linear	• Unpredictable actions of two CPN members adopting their own trial processes significantly impacted the project at the network level in a multitude of ways
4. Feedback loops operational	• Activity and productivity of the project team increasing as a result of feedback from partner meetings and Forums. The trust and motivation developed and supported through these events provide both stability and increased productivity of the CPN through stabilized feedback loops
5. Functions under conditions far from equilibrium	• CPN members working together in non-traditional ways, across organization/school boundaries and without hierarchal authority, for example, collaboration between scientists and educators in developing authentic science lessons for schools • System easily affected by perturbation. One CPN member deviating from the project plan caused a net disruption of the system, as other members questioned the suitability of the original process in their context
6. Actors and the system have history	• Existing relationship history within the core network and across peripheral networks combined with project history and developments, enabled the project to expand its scope to include other non-project subject domains, establishing emergent trajectories • Based on the leanings from issues with original processes and resources being implemented, new process and resources were developed during the project
7. The system is a whole	• Unpredictable actions of CPN members, for example in developing variations of IPOML protocols for their own local contexts, led to the development of systems level changes in processes and outputs not predictable at the start of the project, and not predictable by considering the individual actions of each individual partner

(Continued)

Table 3. (Continued).

Characteristics of a complex system	Characteristics in practice – examples from CPNs in the IPOML case study
8. Self-organization and co-evolution	• Application of project curriculum resources trialled in curriculum areas originally outside of the project scope, for example, in teacher professional development • Co-evolutionary process evidence by boundary crossing in IPOML between the network hubs, as project partners swapped roles and/or joined peripheral hubs, improving practice within hubs and across the system
9. Emergence	• Due to a realization that from that process variation is emergent, and that it can be considered as it occurs, CPN members acted on an opportunity to rethink how modifying current processes could improve project outcomes

As is evident from Table 3, the CPN of the IPOML project demonstrates the characteristics of a complex system and can, therefore, be considered as such a system. The large numbers of CPN actors connecting and interacting within and across nested hubs as part of a larger system corresponds well to the characteristics as described by Innes and Booher (2010). The CPN was also interacting within an open system where there is interaction and exchange between the actors within the system and the outside environment (Eppel 2009). The large number of actors in the CPN interacted constantly, with actors exchanging information and reacting to what other actors were doing, which in turn influenced behaviour and the network as a whole (Mitleton-Kelly 2003).

The non-linear interactions of the CPN, typical of complex systems (Innes and Booher 2010), mean small changes had large and unpredictable system effects. Actors in the system were not aware of the behaviour of the system as a whole and responded only to what was available or known locally in a non-linear pattern, with direct and indirect feedback loops. Any actor in the system was affected by, and affected several others, as well as the overall system, through direct or indirect influence (Eppel 2009). Documentation of the CPN interactions demonstrated that multifaceted and non-linear combinations of related and non-related mechanisms emerged over time as challenges were raised and addressed and tested in real time and the system operation adjusted accordingly. This way of working means that a system is more sensitive to perturbation, which can lead to either degradation of that system, or creation of something new this is underpinned by positive or reinforcing feedback loops, processes evident in the CPN.

The path to project outcomes as examined through CPN interactions remained emergent and unpredictable with complex interplay between actors, as well as self-organization and co-evolution of their relationships and interactions within the system. CPN actors were ignorant of the behaviour of the system, with little control or understanding of the system. Instead, self-organization of the CPN influenced the project environment through meditated changes in behaviour, while continuing to respond and change within the system. The effects that arise from actor interactions were greater than the sum of the system's parts, and thus the CPN can be considered as a system whole – its behaviour could not be understood by looking at components individually. Instead, coherent and novel patters that emerge needed to be explored in order to inform and understand project progress.

The CPN examined here, with its existing actor relationship history typical of complex systems (Eppel 2009; Mitleton-Kelly 2003), may be more likely to achieve system sustainability (Jacobus, Baskett, and Bechstein 2011). This is important for CPN sustainability because social connections can form some of the strongest relational bonds within a network (Borgatti et al. 2009). Since it is known that relationships take time and effort to develop and build capacity necessary for sustainability (Huxham 1996; Keast 2011; Keast et al. 2004), and CPN members in IPOML have significant relationship networks already established, there is a potentially provable link to the increased likelihood of achieving CPN sustainability.

Sustainability in a CPN

The argument presented here was developed on the basis of the close conceptual alignment between complexity theory and sustainability concepts (Peter and Swilling 2014). The complexity lens offers more nuanced insights into the connection of CPNs and sustainability and helps to illuminate the concepts of flexibility and adaptability. These two concepts are seen as critical for examining sustainability of a complex system, but the concepts are hard to account for using a more conventional lens.

Using the findings related to system attributes of sustainability (Table 2), the concepts of flexibility and adaptability were explored within the case study IPOML in relation to behavioural characteristics of resilience and opportunism, emphasizing also the significance of emergence and co-evolution. Within such a context, change needs to be seen in terms of co-evolution with all other related systems, rather than as adaptation to a separate and distinct environment (Chan 2001) – this is one way the system can affect flexibility.

In the CPN, flexibility and adaptability occurred most frequently when the IPOML project was in a position to redirect from predetermined activities and pathways (at a tipping point) due to perturbation or forthcoming opportunity. In IPOML, flexibility and adaptability was shown as opportunistic behaviour when the CPN members identified a chance to implement new processes, or redevelop modules, resulting in boundary crossing between the network hubs and peripherals, or modules redeveloped for a newly identified audience. On other occasions, flexibility and adaptability were shown as resilience when, for example, the network recognized unhealthy system changes occurring because of system reinforcement caused by the practices of a few partners, and in response, implemented new processes and structures to counteract undesirable system change.

The examples in Table 2 demonstrate flexible and adaptable behaviours that were underpinned in each instance by the CNP's capacity to share information, as knowledge and skills, for individual and collective learning. Throughout the project implementation, whenever an issue or opportunity arose, CPN members came together to share information, enabling real-time sense-making, and collective decision-making for action. This information sharing aligns with that described in Harris (2000), Mitleton-Kelly (2003) and Keast (2016), who all affirm that information sharing is fundamental for CPN sustainability. These scholars also emphasize the influence of the associated conditions, network structure, process mechanisms, and social (organizational) infrastructure that encourages and supports the complex and dynamic relationships, and interactions between network actors deemed necessary for information sharing.

The sustainability attributes of flexibility and adaptability appear to be evident from project beginnings, but most frequently occur when there is an opportunity or need to take an emergent trajectory. The ability of a complexity lens to facilitate and capture the dual nature of these central sustainability attributes in the CPN, and their link to both behaviours and complex characteristics, is an important finding.

If this is the case, then conventional methodological approaches, which commonly hold underlying assumptions around sustainability as an end-of-project consideration, and as part of a sequence of planned activities, may not capture critical sustainability attributes. Such approaches, therefore, may not provide an opportunity to better understand why and how some collaborative projects become sustainable, where others fail to last beyond their formal life. Examining CPN sustainability through a complexity theoretic lens may therefore set a new direction for the future study of sustainability, one that considers sustainability itself as an emergent property.

Conclusion and implications

This article aimed to contribute to the analytical and interpretative understanding of CPN sustainability, and the value of a complexity theoretic in offering new insights not provided by conventional approaches. From a preliminary analysis, the findings support the view for a CPN to be considered or equated with a complex system. The article also indicates that attributes of CPN sustainability, flexibility and adaptability, characterized by opportunistic and resilient behaviours, are more likely to be identified when a complexity theoretic lens is applied. This is an important contribution because it supports the need for new ways of capturing and measuring CPN sustainability.

A view of CPN sustainably as underpinned by a complexity theoretical position also legitimizes the need to address sustainability as an ongoing process, initiated from project outset, and one that is allowed to emerge, affording the time necessary to build this capacity.

These initial findings have implications for future research on collaborative projects and the CPNs that are integral to them. These findings suggest that project sustainability must be measured from project outset, through the establishment and use of a new set of variables and indicators for behavioural attributes of CPN sustainability. Through this new understanding there is potential to explore the conditions, network structure, contributing mechanisms, processes and infrastructure supporting sustainability, through longitudinal research.

In moving forward, the greatest challenge is in the development and application of management and evaluative tools that draw on a complexity approach for project sustainability. A contemporary framework for supporting sustainability would act as a dynamic sense-making tool, such as that described by Weick, Sutcliffe, and Obstfeld (2005), facilitating navigation through an ever-changing landscape of multiple perspectives, diverse stakeholders and accountabilities (Phelps and Graham 2012).

Similar to the work of Sarriot et al. (2009), we acknowledge the need for new approaches that will not be entirely controllable, and that will entail some sense of uncertainty. Although this may be an uncomfortable mind-set for some project stakeholders, if not considered there is a risk of continually creating solutions that are not contextually adaptive or flexible over time and space, meaning that projects will not achieve sustainability, and run the risk of not achieving their desired value through the interactions of their CPN.

Disclosure statement

No potential conflict of interest was reported by the authors.

References

Akkerman, S. F., and A. Bakker. 2011. "Boundary Crossing and Boundary Objects." *Review of Educational Research* 81 (2): 132–169. doi:10.3102/0034654311404435.

Alford, J., and J. O'Flynn. 2009. "Making Sense of Public Value: Concepts, Critiques and Emergent Meanings." *International Journal of Public Administration* 32 (3–4): 171–191. doi:10.1080/01900690902732731.

Axelrod, R., and M. D. Cohen. 2000. *Harnessing Complexity: Organizational Implications of a Scientific Frontier.* New York: Basic Books.

Bakker, R. M., J. Raab, and B. Milward. 2012. "A Preliminary Theory of Dark Network Resilience." *Journal of Policy Analysis and Management* 31 (1): 33–62. doi:10.1002/pam.20619.

Borgatti, S. P., A. Mehra, D. J. Brass, and G. Labianca. 2009. "Network Analysis in the Social Sciences." *Science* 323 (5916): 892–895. doi:10.1126/science.1165821.

Brinton, M. H., and K. G. Provan. 2006. *A Manager's Guide to Choosing and Using Collaborative Networks.* Vol. 8. Washington, DC: IBM Center for the Business of Government.

Burt, R. S. 2005. *Brokerage and Closure: An Introduction to Social Capital.* Oxford: Oxford University Press.

Chan, S. 2001. "Complex Adaptive Systems." Research Seminar in Engineering Systems. Accessed February 2, 2016. http://web.mit.edu/esd.83/www/notebook/Complex%20Adaptive%20Systems.pdf

Eppel, E. 2009. "The Contribution of Complexity Theory to Understanding and Explaining Policy Processes: A Study of Tertiary Education Policy Processes in New Zealand." PhD diss., University of Wellington.

Eppel, E. 2012. "What Does It Take to Make Surprises Less Surprising? The Contribution of Complexity Theory to Anticipation in Public Management." *Public Management Review* 14 (1): 881–902. doi:10.1080/14719037.2011.650055.

Frey, B. B., J. H. Lohmeier, S. W. Lee, and N. Tollefson. 2006. "Measuring Collaboration among Grant Partners." *American Journal of Evaluation* 27 (3): 383–392. doi:10.1177/1098214006290356.

Gajda, R., and C. Koliba. 2007. "Evaluating the Imperative of Intraorganizational Collaboration: A School Improvement Perspective." *American Journal of Evaluation* 28 (1): 26–44. doi:10.1177/1098214006296198.

Gray, B. 1985. "Conditions Facilitating Interorganizational Collaboration." *Human Relations* 38 (10): 911–936. doi:10.1177/001872678503801001.

Hall, G. E., and S. M. Hord. 2006. *Implementing Change: Patterns, Principles, and Potholes.* Boston: Pearson/Allyn & Bacon.

Harris, J. 2000. "Basic Principles of Sustainable Development." Working Paper. Medford: Tufts University.

Head, B. W. 2008. "Wicked Problems in Public Policy." *Public Policy* 3 (2): 101–118.

Huxham, C., ed. 1996. *Creating Collaborative Advantage.* California: Sage.

Huxham, C. 2003. "Theorizing Collaboration Practice." *Public Management Review* 5 (3): 401–423. doi:10.1080/1471903032000146964.

Innes, J. E., and D. E. Booher. 2010. *Planning with Complexity: An Introduction to Collaborative Rationality for Public Policy*. New York: Routledge.

Jacobus, M. V., R. Baskett, and C. Bechstein. 2011. "Building Castles Together: A Sustainable Collaboration as A Perpetual Work in Progress." *Gateways International Journal of Community Research and Engagement* 4: 65–82. doi:10.5130/ijcre.v4i0.1800.

Kania, J., M. Kramer, and P. Russell. 2014. "Strategic Philanthropy for a Complex World." *Stanford Social Innovation Review* Summer: 26–33. Accessed September 1 2015. http://www.ohio.edu/PEOPLE/paxton/WebPage/altruism/altruism/Strategic_Philanthropy.pdf.

Kauffman, S. A. 1993. *The Origins of Order: Self Organization and Selection in Evolution*. New York: Oxford University Press.

Keast, R. 2011. "Joined-Up Governance in Australia: How the Past Can Inform the Future." *International Journal of Public Administration* 34 (4): 221–231. doi:10.1080/01900692.2010.549799.

Keast, R. 2016. "Collaborative Research Networks Programme: Policy and Planning for Regional Sustainability, Southern Cross University." Final Report. Canberra: Australian Government.

Keast, R., K. Brown, and M. Mandell. 2007. "Getting the Right Mix: Unpacking Integration Meanings and Strategies." *International Public Management Journal* 10 (1): 9–33. doi:10.1080/10967490601185716.

Keast, R., M. P. Mandell, K. Brown, and G. Woolcock. 2004. "Network Structures: Working Differently and Changing Expectations." *Public Administration Review* 64 (3): 363–371. doi:10.1111/j.1540-6210.2004.00380.x.

Kissel, M., P. Schrieverho, and U. Lindemann. 2012. "Design for Adaptability Identifying Potential for Improvement on an Architecture Basis." In *DS 71: Proceedings of the 9th NordDesign Conference*, edited by P. A. Hansen, J. Ramussen, K. A. Jørgensen, and C. Tollestrup, 38. Aarlborg/Glasgow: Aarlborg University/University of Strathclyde.

Koppenjan, J., and C. Koliba. 2013. "Transformations Towards New Public Governance: Can the New Paradigm Handle Complexity?" *International Review of Public Administration* 18 (2): 1–8. doi:10.1080/12294659.2013.10805249.

Laszlo, A., and S. Krippner. 1998. "Systems Theories: Their Origins, Foundations, and Development." In *System Theories and a Priori Aspects of Perception*, edited by J. S. Jordan, 47–76. Amsterdam: Elsevier.

Le Pennec, M., and E. Raufflet. 2016. "Value Creation in Inter-Organizational Collaboration: An Empirical Study." *Journal of Business Ethics* 1–18. doi:10.1007/s10551-015-3012-7.

Lewin, R., and P. Bak. 1993. "Complexity: Life at the Edge of Chaos." *American Journal of Physics* 61 (8): 764–765. doi:10.1119/1.17163.

Magis, K. 2010. "Community Resilience: An Attribute of Social Sustainability." *Society & Natural Resources: An International Journal* 23 (5): 401–416. doi:10.1080/08941920903305674.

Marshall, C., and G. Rossman. 1989. *Designing Qualitative Research*. Thousand Oaks: Sage.

Mitleton-Kelly, E. 2003. "Ten Principles of Complexity and Enabling Infrastructures." In *Complex Systems and Evolutionary Perspectives on Organisations: The Application of Complexity Theory to Organisations*, edited by E. Mitleton-Kelly, 23–50. Oxford: Elsevier Science.

Newman, L., and A. Dale. 2005. "Network Structure, Diversity, and Proactive Resilience Building: A Response to Tompkins and Adger." *Ecology and Society* 10 (1): r2. doi:10.5751/ES-01396-1001r02.

Nicolis, G., and I. Prigogine. 1989. *Exploring Complexity: An Introduction*. New York: W.H. Freeman.

Patton, M. Q. 2011. *Developmental Evaluation: Applying Complexity Concepts to Enhance Innovation and Use*. New York: Guilford Press.

Peter, C., and M. Swilling. 2014. "Linking Complexity and Sustainability Theories: Implications for Modeling Sustainability Transitions." *Sustainability* 6 (3): 1594–1622. doi:10.3390/su6031594.

Phelps, R., and A. Graham. 2012. "Exploring Teacher Professional Development through the Lens of Complexity Theory: The Technology Together Story." In *The International Handbook of Cultures of Teacher Education: Comparative International Issues in Curriculum and Pedagogy*, edited by B. Boufoy-Bastick, 367–392. Strasbourg: Analytics.

Provan, K. G., A. Fish, and J. Sydow. 2007. "Interorganizational Networks at the Network Level: A Review of the Empirical Literature on Whole Networks." *Journal of Management* 33 (3): 479–516. doi:10.1177/0149206307302554.

Provan, K. G., and R. H. Lemaire. 2012. "Core Concepts and Key Ideas for Understanding Public Sector Organizational Networks: Using Research to Inform Scholarship and Practice." *Public Administration Review* 72 (5): 638–648. doi:10.1111/j.1540-6210.2012.02595.x.

Provan, K. G., and B. Milward. 1995. "A Preliminary Theory of Interorganizational Network Effectiveness: A Comparative Study of Four Community Mental Health Systems." *Administrative Science Quarterly* 40 (1): 1–33. doi:10.2307/2393698.

Rhodes, M. L. 2008. "Complexity and Emergence in Public Management: The Case of Urban Regeneration in Ireland." *Public Management Review* 10 (3): 361–379. doi:10.1080/14719030802002717.

Rogers, P. J. 2008. "Using Programme Theory to Evaluate Complicated and Complex Aspects of Interventions." *Evaluation* 14 (1): 29–48. doi:10.1177/1356389007084674.

Sarriot, E., M. Kouletio, S. Jahan, I. Rasul, and A. K. M. Musha. 2014. "Advancing the Application of Systems Thinking in Health: Sustainability Evaluation as Learning and Sense-Making in a Complex Urban Health System in Northern Bangladesh." *Health Research Policy and Systems* 12 (1): 12–45. doi:10.1186/1478-4505-12-45.

Sarriot, E., J. Ricca, L. Ryan, J. Basnet, and S. Arscott-Mills. 2009. "Measuring Sustainability as a Programming Tool for Health Sector Investments: Report from a Pilot Sustainability Assessment in Five Nepalese Health Districts." *The International Journal of Health Planning and Management* 24 (4): 326–350. doi:10.1002/hpm.v24:4.

Scheirer, M. A. 2005. "Is Sustainability Possible? A Review and Commentary on Empirical Studies of Program Sustainability." *American Journal of Evaluation* 26 (3): 320–347. doi:10.1177/1098214005278752.

Schulz, A. P., E. Fricke, and E. Igenbergs. 2000. "Enabling Changes in Systems Throughout the Entire Life-Cycle—Key to Success?" *INCOSE International Symposium* 10 (1): 565–573. doi:10.1002/j.2334-5837.2000.tb00426.x

Scott, A., R. Keast, G. Woolcott, and D. Chamberlain. 2016. "Sustainable Collaboration." Poster presented at the Australian Social Network Analysis Conference, Melbourne, November 16-17.

Teisman, G. R., and E.-H. Klijn. 2008. "Complexity Theory and Public Management: An Introduction." *Public Management Review* 10 (3): 287–297. doi:10.1080/14719030802002451.

Uhl-Bien, M., R. Marion, and M. Bill. 2007. "Complexity Leadership Theory: Shifting Leadership from the Industrial Age to the Knowledge Era." *The Leadership Quarterly* 18 (4): 298–318. doi:10.1016/j.leaqua.2007.04.002.

Vogus, T. J., and K. M. Sutcliffe. 2003. "Organizing for Resilience." In *Positive Organizational Scholarship: Foundations of a New Discipline*, edited by K. S. Cameron, J. E. Dutton, and R. E. Quinn, 94–110. San Francisco: Berrett-Koehler Publishers.

Walker, B., C. S. Holling, S. R. Carpenter, and A. Kinzig. 2004. "Resilience, Adaptability and Transformability in Social-Ecological Systems." *Ecology and Society* 9 (2): 5. doi:10.5751/ES-00650-090205.

Weick, K. E., K. M. Sutcliffe, and D. Obstfeld. 2005. "Organizing and the Process of Sensemaking." *Organization Science* 16 (4): 409–421. doi:10.1287/orsc.1050.0133.

Willard, T., and H. Creech. 2006. *Sustainability of International Development Networks: Review of IDRC Experience (1995–2005)*. Winnipeg: International Institute for Sustainable Development.

Wind, T. 2004. *Network Sustainability: Document Review for IDRC's Evaluation Unit and the Network*. Winnipeg: International Institute for Sustainable Development.

Yin, R. K. 2013. *Case Study Research: Design and Methods*. Thousand Oaks: Sage.

Cultivating resiliency through system shock: the Southern California metropolitan water management system as a complex adaptive system

Jack W. Meek ⓘ and Kevin S. Marshall

ABSTRACT

This study analyses the water management system in Southern California through the lens of complexity theory as it responds to system stressors and shock caused by severe and sustained draught. The study is grounded on the thesis that self-organization in the complex space of the water governance system creates the capacity to absorb spatial shock, and through this absorption process the space experiences resiliency. This paper identifies the attributes of spatial complexity of the Southern California metropolitan water management system, and analyses a spatial shock case that ignited stakeholder action that nurtured, promoted and furthered resiliency within the system.

1. Introduction – complexity theory as a referent frame for analysing Southern California metropolitan water governance

This study analyses – through the lens of complexity theory – the space where water management in Southern California manifests. The spatial complexity of the water management governance in Southern California – both in geo-governance expanse and stakeholder diversity – constitutes a unit of analysis that informs patterns of interaction among stakeholders. By spatial complexity we refer to the domain of interacting agents, networks, and systems influencing outcomes water management governance (Marshall 2014). The study further demonstrates that the space is resilient. Moreover, this study demonstrates that it is the spaces' complexity and the cultivation of that complexity that enhances its capacity to address and respond to the spatial-shock in a manner that ultimately advances both spatial-learning and comprehension.

We start by identifying the attributes of the system, its actors, and its stakeholders that render this system-space complex. We then re-direct the focus of the analysis on the case-specific actions of the City of Claremont (California) as it responds to both local and regional spatial-stressors and -shocks driven by severe water shortages and sustained drought conditions. The Claremont case illustrates that stakeholder action challenging the status quo is congruent with the maintenance of spatial-complexity, and that such spatial complexity fosters advancement, and ultimately resiliency. The Claremont case offers an illustration that complexity-informed and – friendly governance practices are to be embraced as a means for nurturing, promoting and maintaining spatial-complexity (and thereby nurturing, promoting and maintaining spatial-resiliency).

This study adopts the following methodological approach. First, we review and operationally define the constructs of 'complex-adaptive systems' and 'resiliency' and explore their reciprocating relevancy to one another (Section 2). It is against this backdrop that the analysis then focuses on understanding the water governance system in Southern California as a complex-adaptive system-seeking resiliency (Section 3). The analysis then proceeds by exploring a case study – the Claremont case – that illustrates the value of complexity-informed and – friendly governance practices and actions, as well as demonstrating that such practices and actions are congruent with theoretical expectations (Section 4). In our analysis of the Claremont case we retrieved and reviewed relevant court records, Claremont city records, policy statements, civic correspondences, as well as interviewed city officials, public administrators and managers within the Southern California water governance space. This study supports the thesis that the cultivation and maintenance of spatial-complexity influences spatial learning and comprehension both of which lead to spatial resiliency (Section 5). It is through spatial learning that the space achieves the capacity to progressively adapt and experience resiliency. As a space absorbs stressors and shocks, it is in a process of learning. And the absorption/learning process nurtures greater capacity for the space and its spatial actors to comprehend spatial strengths and weakness within the context of the spatial stressors or shock.

2. Complex space – identifying and assessing resilient space

Throughout the following discussion we use the term space to refer to the unit of analysis under examination. The use of the term is a way of conceptualizing a geopolitical space (with or without open boundaries) populated by stakeholders linked to a common interest or by a common issue. Such space may include individuals, organizations, and systems, all of whom have a stake in the how the space is formulated, manifested and administered. Fundamentally, the underlying thesis of this study is that if the space under examination is complex and adaptive, it is cultivating resiliency. Accordingly, it is important to understand resiliency as it is used in this paper.

As Boin, Comfort and Demchak observed: '[r]esilience has become a fashionable buzzword' (Boin, Comfort, and Demchack 2010, 19). Its usage generally refers to the 'capacity of a material person, or biotope survive sudden shocks.' (Boin, Comfort, and Demchack 2010, 36). In recent years, there has been an increased focus on what has been called 'societal resilience,' i.e. the ability for 'organizations, cities, and societies [to] bounce back in the face of a disturbance' (Boin, Comfort, and Demchack 2010, 37).

With respect to complex-adaptive spatial environments, resiliency means more than just being able to bounce back. Resilience refers to the space's ability to absorb and adapt to shock. (Dahlberg 2015, 544). The act of 'absorbing shock' suggests that the space is processing all the information that is being channelled through the shock. And the act of adapting to shock – through stakeholder actions – suggests that the space itself is evolving, progressing and advancing. As McMillan observes, 'a [complex] adaptive system is able to take advantage and learn from what the world around it is able to tell it.' (McMillan 2004, 32).

This ability to 'absorb and adapt' is the essence of resiliency in a complex spatial environment. The ability of a complex-space to adapt to (and not merely resist) spatial-stressors and -shocks drives the space's 'learning and transformational capabilities' (Dahlberg 2015, 545]. Thus, resilience, as it relates to complex spatial environments, 'is an emerging property [of complex space].' (Dahlberg 2015, 547). While resiliency cannot be designed, 'it can [nonetheless] be exercised and cultivated.' (Dahlberg 2015, 547). And it can be cultivated by complexity-informed and – friendly governance practices. Complexity-informed and – friendly governance practices acknowledge the self-organizing nature of the system's agents. Such practices are grounded on the assumption that 'the adaptive system has some ability to self-monitor its adaptive capacity ... and anticipate and learn so that it can modulate its adaptive capacity to handle future situations, events, opportunities, and disruptions' (Hollnagel et al. 2011, 128; Dahlberg 2015, 547). Complex spatial environments typically involve a pool of actors who are highly differentiated in tastes, preference, wants, needs, knowledge, background and experience, and who have the opportunity (and even motive) to engage in highly integrated and associative behaviour. Through the integration and (dis) integration of these differentiated actors, feedback loops emerge, ultimately leading to evolutionary and transformational progress and advancement.

In her work on complexity, organizations and change, Elizabeth McMillan observed:

> The concept of emergence is a main theme that flows through studies of complexity. It is a phenomenon of the process of evolving, of adapting and transforming spontaneously and intuitively to changing circumstances and finding new ways of being. And in doing this, something else, something complex, unexpected and enriching takes shape. Emergence is seen in the properties of ecosystems, food chains, embryo development, human societies, insect swarms, and especially in complex adaptive systems. (McMillan, 32)

It is in this context that complex space cultivates resilient space. Complex space often manifests 'a spontaneous, self-organizing dynamic' that 'stimulate[s] and energize[s]... change.' (McMillan, 11). It is the manifestation of this spontaneous, self-organizing dynamic that facilitates 'opportunities for learning both theoretical and experiential.' (McMillian, 11).

In contrast, simple space is not very differentiated nor is there much opportunity for integrative behaviour, and thus little opportunity for the manifestation of feed-back loops through which learning and comprehension is achieved. It is important to note that complex space experiences momentary states of equilibrium. While in simple space, states of equilibrium are sustainable for longer periods. Complex-space is in a persistent state of dynamic disequilibrium, but it is through this disequilibrium that the space maximizes its capacity to adapt. The research of Boin and Lodge (2016) illustrate how public administrative governance can respond to systems characterized by constant crisis conditions.

2.1. Cultivating complex space through complexity- informed/friendly governance practices

Complexity-informed and -friendly governance practices are practices that nurture, promote, embrace or enhance complexity within the relevant space under analysis. They are those practices that cultivate complexity with the intention that such complexity will create spaces that will self-organize in ways that will reveal the strengths and weakness of the space. And through such revelations, the space creates and invites opportunities for the spatial actors to address those revealed strengths and weaknesses.

Complexity-informed and – friendly governance practices acknowledge the self-organizing nature of system agents and assume that 'the adaptive system has some ability to self-monitor its adaptive capacity (reflective adaptation) and anticipate and learn so that it can modulate its adaptive capacity to handle future situations, events, opportunities and disruptions.' (Hollnagel et al. 2011, 128; Dahlberg 2015, 546). Such practices nurture complex, adaptive spatial environments. And according to the underlying thesis upon which complexity theory is framed, complex, adaptive spatial environments are resilient; that is, they have the capacity to absorb and adapt to system shock and stress (Dahlberg 2015: 545). The ability to absorb and adapt to shock and stress is essential for any space to persist and sustain itself. This is significantly relevant in the context of 'intergovernmental crisis management' (Comfort et al. 2010, 107).

Through complexity-informed or – friendly governance practices, we cultivate resiliency. Complexity-informed or -friendly governance practices are generally grounded on perspectives, policies and approaches that: (1) avoid simple reductionist approaches; (2) accommodate or facilitate the emergence of new structures and functions; (3) accommodate or facilitate differentiation, integration and feed-back loops; (4) accommodate or facilitate self-organization as a spatial driver, and (5) accommodate time and path dependencies. (Koliba, et. al. 2016)

At the macro-level, complex-space might appear to be in a state of equilibrium giving the appearance of stability. However, at the micro-level such space is in a constant state of disequilibria. Complex-space is constantly adjusting and responding to its evolving and shifting landscape fuelled by agent action. And while there is often temptation to 'resist' spatial-shock in furtherance of spatial-stability, this study demonstrates that a complexity-informed or – friendly practice is a practice that 'embraces' and 'absorbs' spatial-shock. It is the absorption of shock that ultimately furthers spatial-resiliency. A complexity-informed or friendly governance practice minimizes abstraction or simplification. Simplification stifles complexity and can render the space stagnate and jeopardize adaptation.

3. The spatial complexity of water governance

In assessing the governance of water management, this paper identifies the water management stakeholders and system characteristics as a complex adaptive system (CAS) seeking solutions to on-going, and now, dramatic challenges. An underlying message of the paper is that when we view water governance as a complex adaptive system, we move our analytic and administrative lens to a broader level of analysis. As noted by Bar Yam (2004), 'developing the ability to use a complex systems perspective requires new patterns of thinking' (2004, 19). This level of analysis – the systems level – offers a way to interpret the evolutionary nature of the system as a whole and how each stakeholder – from the individual water consumer to the federally funded infrastructure – contributes to the behaviour of the system. Each stakeholder plays a significant role in establishing the coherence of the system. Continuous change and emergence that evolve from stakeholder interaction from a large number of diverse stakeholders are important features of the adaptive nature of the complex system.

The spatial level of analysis also allows for a nuanced view of policy and administrative roles in water governance. Because there are multiple kinds of actors in the space – individual and household consumers, farmers, industries, housing units, regional water agencies – influencing behaviour and outcomes within the system, the governance of such a system is necessarily challenging because of the interconnected and conjoined participants. Water resource development, use, treatment and management are intertwined. From this perspective – the spatial perspective – research has observed from a systems theory perspective notable administrative behaviour that calls upon the need for enhanced trust among administrative units with the system and the necessity of 'system 'boundary spanners' or leaders (Edelenbos, Van Meerkerk, and Van Leeuwen forthcoming) that link administrative jurisdictions in water governance.

Stakeholders in this governance system include citizens, competing urban and rural water interests, as well as local, regional, state and federal water agencies and authorities. Combined, these stakeholders comprise of large number of diverse actors, interacting through multiple channels and responding with different forms of adaptations that characterize system learning. However, current system characteristics of Southern California, USA – increasing demand for water alongside extreme drought – has placed great stress on the governance system that call upon new forms of proposed or emergent and adaptive solutions designed for creating future resilient solutions for the future.

Previous research in regard to complex adaptive systems and complexity theory has been instructive in a number of governance concerns in particular in regard to metropolitan systems (Buijs et al. 2009; Innes and Booher 1999b) environmental protection (Hoffman et al. 2002), collaborative planning of water resources (Innes and Booher 1999a) and developing governance networks (Koliba, Meek and Zia 2011). Complexity theory has been usefully applied in examining governance systems (Teisman and Klijn 2008; Teisman, van Buuren and Gerritis 2009). Research on leadership theory in complex systems has been examined in collaborative networks (Keast and Mandell 2013) and in complex public sectors (Murphy et al. 2016).

Specific work on interpreting water governance as a complex adaptive system has been undertaken by Bohensky and Lynam (2005). This research found that in a water governance system with the possibility of many kinds of human interventions, stakeholder strategies that conceived of the whole system (scope of impact, awareness of impact and power distribution) allowed sufficient flexibility in responses in adapting to ever-evolving contexts. The work of Jiao and Boons (2017) similarly found policy fitness or durable governmental facilitation is established through an on-going translation process among diverse actors in differentiated contexts. The work of Dent (2012) argues that because water resource management necessarily involves multi-sector, multi-level stakeholders to collectively and wisely manage water resources, leadership development must match these demands. The work of van Buuren and Edelenbos (2006) found that the disciplinary variations of stakeholders call upon a new kind of communities of practice (COP) that recognize both internal and external realities and establish a more co-evolutionary character.

3.1. *Spatial stressors, shocks, and challenges*

Vital to both life and growth, control over water resources has become an issue that has affected many cities in the United States, dramatically so within the State of California. Within the world of water resource management, there is a very real struggle that is taking place in the management of water. In Southern California (United States), the management of water is exacerbated under the condition of scarcity and the recently released United States Drought Monitor – prepared by the National Drought Mitigation Center in conjunction with the Department of Agriculture and the National Oceanic and Atmospheric Administration – has shown increasingly dry conditions across the United States, and the state of California is currently classified as being in a severe or extreme drought. In combination with these dangerous conditions comes a continuous struggle to preserve water resources and water rights, while at the same time forming active and healthy relationships among a wide range of competing stakeholders – both urban and rural – entangled in the struggle.

For Southern California, similar to other areas in the world, the shock of sustained drought has heightened our understanding of our significant dependence on safe and secure water supplies and the web of agency connections that facilitate this security. For example, recognizing the need to deepen the capacity of supply water, California citizens passed the passage of Proposition 1 in 2014. The proposition identifies and funds a number of initiatives addressing drought, such as state water supply infrastructure projects, including public water system improvements, surface and groundwater storage, drinking water protection, water recycling and advanced water treatment technology, water supply management and conveyance, wastewater treatment, drought relief, emergency water supplies, and ecosystem and watershed protection and restoration. The proposition is a recognition of the large geospatial nature of the water supply system and its web of differentiated elements by addressing ten areas of water governance. This evolving stakeholder action is part of the absorption process that cultivates residency.

3.2. *Characteristics of complex adaptive systems – theory*

Drawing upon previous research on complex adaptive systems (Holland 1995; McMillan 2004), five characteristics of a complex adaptive system (CAS) are instructive in the application of constantly evolving governance systems. These characteristics are:

(1) *Network of many differentiated agents* – complex adaptive systems include a large number of differentiated agents (stakeholders or actors) that have the ability to influence the system;

(2) *Emergent quality* – agents (stakeholders or actors within the system) interact in a way to address collective concerns, agents have capacity to self-organize and have adaptive and emerging qualities;

(3) *No central control* – behaviour in the system is not a result of a central controlling agent that determines patterns of interaction. As a consequence, one feature of a complex adaptive systems is that behaviour in the system is not uniform (or linear) and can have significant impact on the system;

(4) *Multiplicity of interconnections/integrations/associative behaviours* – Another feature of a complex adaptive system is agents can interact in a number of ways and in a number of combinations. For example, in the water governance system, local water agencies can change patterns of control or alliance. These kinds of options – forming partnerships and alliances – can lead to new kinds of behaviour that influence the system.

(5) *Evidence of system learning* – Complex adaptive systems reveal an understanding of the system through interaction and demonstrate learning from the interaction. 'Learning may be simple or first level, such as the acquisition of new skills, or it may be complex or adaptive learning, such that mindsets are moved and people see the world afresh. These changes within an individual contribute significantly to the flow of change within an organization [or space] although they may be only observable over time. If sufficient learning takes place within a self-organizing system [or space] then it becomes a complex adaptive system [or space].' McMillian, 11.

In the following section, we analyse the Southern California Water Governance Space from a spatial-complexity perspective, ultimately concluding that it has all the attributes of a complex space, as well as demonstrating that as a complex space it exhibits spontaneous, self-organizing resiliency

3.3. Theory application – evidence of complexity within the southern California water governance space

3.3.1. Evidence of many differentiated agents

To frame the interconnected nature of water governance in California and the network of water agencies that influence the water governance system, it is useful to understand the diversity of challenges that confront the system and each region of the system. For example, statewide, 20% of the state's water supply goes to urban areas with 80% going to extremely productive agriculture areas – the most productive agriculture state in the union. Because of water interdependence, when the state is under extreme conditions – such as in this decade (2010s), farmers are asked to abandon cropland (400,000 acres in 2014, 1,000,000 in 2015). Water dependence by region varies according to groundwater basins in each region.

There are a number of water agencies that manage water in the Southern California region. Importantly, the water governance system attends to its dependence on water supplies from well outside of the metropolitan area. For example, Orange County in southern California imports 50% of its water and south Orange County is 100% dependent on water importation. Other regions of southern California have differentiated dependencies based upon naturally endowed groundwater capacities.

The role of managing geographically extended water demands has been played, in part, by a regional supplier of water – the Metropolitan Water District of Southern California (MWD) – an association of twenty-six member cities and water agencies serving nineteen million people in six counties. MWD has been granted rights (contracts) to water from the Colorado River as well as from the state water project in the Sierra-Nevada mountain ranges. An additional project that extends the region's reach for water is the Los Angeles Aqueduct, built in 1913 by the City of Los Angeles.

This project delivers water from the Owens's River and Mono Lake Basin reservoirs to the City. The mix of city, region, local dependence of water ranges significantly. The region as whole, however, depends on water imported from the mountains, Owen's Valley region and reservoirs and the Colorado River.

To assure water supplies to each of the stakeholder needs in Southern California, an array of governmental actors – summarized in Table 1 below- are involved in the governance of water (Blanco et al. 2012). A full description of governmental actors in California water governance can be found in the work of Blanco et al. (2012).

Table 1 above summarizes the many differentiated water agencies and their roles in the Southern California water management system. At a minimum, these many differentiate agencies and their roles demonstrate this characteristic of complex adaptive space.

3.3.2. *Emergent quality*

In addition to the existence of many differentiated agencies and their roles, the Southern California water space exhibits emergent qualities. With the many water agency authorities working at different levels and across water system functions as they seek to maintain their stakes within a macro-system in the process of absorbing system stress and shock, there is evidence of a capacity of learning and changing (adaptation) among agencies. Such evidence includes the (re)formation of alliances, partnerships and coalitions – as evidenced in the swarming of connections among water agencies – such as those developed among members of the Association of California Water Agencies (ACWA) – is indicative of the emergent quality of water governance in California. In addition, consistent and incremental development of policy initiatives that embrace regional solutions to water management is evident in the passage of Propositions 50

Table 1. Governmental water agencies in California.

Level of government	Governing agency	Role/goals	Projects

Federal	– Dept. of Interior Bureau of Reclamation
	  – Bureau of Reclamation
	  – EPA
	  – U.S. Army Corps of Engineers
		– Provides state oversight and regulation of water resources	– Water supply
			– Flood protection
			– Water Quality

State	– California Natural Resources Agency Department
	  – Department of Water Resources
	  – California EPA
	  – State Water Resources Board
	– California Health and Human Services Agency
		– Protects natural resources
		– Water Resources Planning
		– State Water Project
		– CA Water Supply
		– Allocating Water Rights
			– Water Rights
			– Operating State Water Project
			– Drinking Water
			– Environmental Management

Regional	– Metropolitan Water District – Water Basin Districts	– Transport Water from Colorado River to Southern California – Adjudicate water allocations	– Infrastructure Providing Water
Local	– Water Districts and Companies	– Authorized to design, construct, operate and maintain public recreational facilities	– Restoring the delta and creating clean, reliable water supply

Water Code Section 12849.

(2002), 84 (2006), and 1 (2014). Each proposition – passed by citizens of the state -enhances the emergent architecture necessary for water governance.

In addition to differentiated water agency interactions, numerous other strategies in the water governance system are operating at the same time – conservation by local agencies, state determined land furloughs, planting cycle changes, volunteer reductions in residential use, altered business orientations, the introduction of new technologies offer evidence of emerging shifts in water governance. Indeed, the fragmented nature of the water governance system means that new kinds of patterns emerge and can emerge.

3.3.3. No central control – multiple authorities

Additionally, the Southern California water space has no central controlling feature. The outline of multiple agencies (listed previously) indicates a rather elaborate functional differentiation of roles among water governance agencies – federal, state, regional and local. There are important joint efforts undertaken by the agencies (joint federal/state water projects) and evidence of significant interactions among agencies in the management of water resources. There is a hierarchy of responsibilities. For example, the State can seek to fund infrastructure or environmental projects; the state can declare water warnings or emergences; the state can furlough agricultural areas to assure water supplies to urban areas under conditions of scarcity. Yet, there is significant regional capacity control of water resource management by regional agencies. These agencies operate within the general parameters of watermasters and overall water supply in relation to member agencies to assure safe and secure supplies for all stakeholders.

Cities, private homeowners and industries have significant influence over their water usage and the amount of water resources utilized in the system. Indeed, individual reduction of water use will be a significant contributor to water sustainability and system resiliency in the coming years. The 2009 State Water Conservation Bill SBX7-7 services the interests in saving water using at the individual level by establishing standards that combine to replace inefficient indoor water plumbing fixtures with water efficient ones for new construction.

3.3.4. Many levels of interaction

Additional evidence that the water governance space is complex can be found in its many levels of interaction. Multiplicity of interconnections (meetings, legislative preparation) occurs for water agencies through the Association of California Water Agencies (ACWA). Formed in 1910, ACWA includes 430 public agency members who collectively are responsible for 90% of the water delivered to the urban and rural areas of California. The ACWA provides members with scientific information, facilitates interests within the association, contributes to setting water resource objectives in water management and is a source of interaction among members. According to the ACWA report of 2013, the association agencies are 'playing increasing vital roles in planning, building and maintaining the water projects and systems needed for their regions' (ACWA Facts, 2013). In 2005, the agency adopted policy principles that 'embrace environmental and economic stability as co-equal priorities for water management in California' (ACWA Facts, 2013). The association has a number of services that support many levels of interaction across water authorities, including: advocacy for state legislation, federal legislation, and member workshops. Local water agencies also hold numerous outreach educational seminars and workshops for cities and local leaders.

3.3.5. *Evidence of system learning – cultivating resiliency*

Finally, system learning is evidenced by the emergence of numerous stakeholder and agency actions and promulgation of policies and procedures addressing the shock of the drought. For example, this is particularly evident in local agencies. As just noted in the report on ACWA, the agency continues to develop information capacity of water agencies to meet the continuous challenges of water management though issuing reports, water management objectives and communication. The agency, in essence is seeking resiliency in system capacity though supporting collective interests of its members.

At the state level, similar concerns in establishing complexity-informed practices is evident in the pattern of propositions since 2000. Propositions passed in 2002, 2006 and 2014 each passed significant general obligation bonds that seek regional solutions to water management (Morrison 2014). According to Lester Snow, former head of the Department of Water Resources, these recent policy approaches reveal the 'all of the above' approach to water diversification of supplies (Morrison 2014). Below (Table 2) is a listing of the evolving commitment to water capacity in California, one that seek to develop resiliency in the system through improved infrastructure and regional management of resources.

In addition, current projects within the state are designed to increase resiliency of the system. For one example, due to the concern over the safe and reliable delivery of water to Southern California from the Sierra Nevada Mountains that travels through the Bay Delta area, the state is considering a significant plan ($23 Billion) – the Bay Delta Plan – to construct tunnels for water from the mountains to by-pass the delta. This plan would increase the reliability of imported water to Southern California. The project itself invades the interests of a multiplicity of stakeholders and sub-systems. The project necessarily provokes spatial complexity to the extent the project forces the integration of a multiplicity of differentiated interests. And as these interests collide and respond to one another, learning and comprehension is achieved, all of which favours progressive and adaptive outcomes, and ultimately advances spatial resiliency.

3.4. *Summary – Southern California water management is a complex adaptive space*

In summary, the Southern California water governance space exhibits the attributes of spatial complexity. As the analysis above demonstrates, the space consists of a network of many agents, possesses emergent qualities, exhibits decentralized controlling features, involved multi-dimensional interactions and exhibits spatial learning. In the examination of Southern California water governance, it is evident that the complex adaptive system articulated here has enormous geo-governance implications. The reach of Southern California water governance moves hundreds of miles to the east and the Colorado River and hundreds of miles north to the Sierra Nevada mountain range. The complex adaptive nature of water governance is necessarily intergovernmental, cross-jurisdictional and embraces the collective interests of varied stakeholders. The water governance system of Southern California significantly overlaps the water governance system of California. These are deeply administrative systems with overlapping and necessarily conjunctive roles. Table 3 offers a summary of the characteristics of water governance in relation to the complex adaptive system characterized in previous sections of the paper.

Table 2. Recent California propositions enhancing water governance capacity.

Year	Action	Comment	% Vote affirming
2002	Proposition 50 Water Quality, Supply and Safe Drinking Water Projects Act	$3.4 billion in general obligation bonds for water projects – CALFED Bay-Delta Program projects including urban and agricultural water use efficiency projects; grants and loans to reduce Colorado River water use; purchasing, protecting and restoring coastal wetlands near urban areas; competitive grants for water management and water quality improvement projects; development of river parkways; improved security for state, local and regional water systems; and grants for desalination and drinking water disinfecting projects	55
2006	Proposition 84 Safe Drinking Water, Water Quality and Supply, Flood Control, River and Coastal Protection Bond Act	$5.388 billion in general obligation bonds to fund safe drinking water, water quality and supply, flood control, waterway and natural resource protection, water pollution and contamination control, state and local park improvements, public access to natural resources, and water conservation efforts	54
2014	Proposition 1 Water Bond	$7.5 Billion enact the Water Quality, Supply, and Infrastructure Improvement Act of 2014 – for state water supply infrastructure projects, such as public water system improvements, surface and groundwater storage, drinking water protection, water recycling and advanced water treatment technology, water supply management and conveyance, wastewater treatment, drought relief, emergency water supplies, and ecosystem and watershed protection and restoration	67

California Natural Resources Agency (accessed 2015).

Table 3. Water governance as a complex adaptive system.

Complex adaptive system characteristics	Water Governance in Southern California, USA
Network of many agents Multiple interconnected parts	Users – urban, rural, businesses, corporations Interests – economic, ecological, environmental
System reflects an emergent quality Elements have capacity of learning and changing	Forming alliances, partnerships, coalitions, policies Local, regional, economic, ecological combinations
No central controlling feature Behaviour is not uniform (or linear); not a sum of the parts	Conservation, land furloughs, planting changes, residential use, altered business orientations
Many levels of interaction Multiplicity of inter-connections	Ecological influences economic, influences practices, influences commons
Evidence of System Learning New kinds of behaviour – emergence New behaviours influence the system	Incremental capacity building, resiliency

4. Case of the City of Claremont

4.1. *Background*

The City of Claremont is one of 188 cities in the Southern California region. While most of the region is served by publically held and managed water governance systems (such as city or regional water agencies), the city of Claremont was served by a for-profit entity since 1925. The company acquired water management responsibility in Claremont initially to fund water clean-up responsibilities viewed as beyond the financial capacity of the city at the time. Over time, the for-profit entity provided water to Claremont for decades without significant concern. However, in recent decades, it was perceived that water costs to individual homes were significantly higher that homes in adjacent cities served by publically held and managed water systems. These price concerns were raised by citizens with the company and later by the city with the Public Utilities Commission (PUC) that determined that the company was in its prerogative to establish the price due to its responsibilities for water system maintenance.

With the onset of system-wide drought in California and Southern California during 2010–2015, water management and pricing strategies became an even more significant concern. The City alleged that Claremont's water-governance-space was not sustainable because of paradoxical pricing practices that discouraged conservation. The company maintained that its anti-conservatory practices were a means to make sure the company could afford and maintain the infrastructure necessary to sustain the water-governance-space. In essence, Claremont asserted that the water prices were too high; that water costs were exaggerated; and, that the quality of water questionable. Thus, Claremont sought to negotiate a solution (integrate and associate voluntary solution). Failing that, the City – with the enormous support of the citizens – sought to use the power of law to force a reorganization of the space by asserting eminent domain, whereby control of water governance would be placed in the hands of city or regional public management, much like most of the surrounding cities. Litigation followed and opened the portal for access and eventual assessment through discovery – where experts, stakeholders, citizens, and even a judge assessed the evidentiary data for the purposes of determining whether the local Claremont space was absorbing the shock of the drought in the most efficient and effective manner (Mayor Pedroza's Statement, December 13, Mayor Sam Pedroza's Statement on Court Decision on the City's Acquisition of the Claremont Water System, December 2016). This comprehensive interaction ultimately advanced spatial learning and understanding resulting in a more robust water management space.

4.2. Complexity informed/friendly practice – the Claremont initiative

The Claremont case reveals that the entire system was placed under enormous stress (by a severe and sustaining draught) from the many differentiated and competing demands emanating from consumers, industry and ecological systems. The environment of scarcity within which these demands manifested further confounded the water system's stresses and, over time, ultimately forced stakeholders to engage in integrated and associative actions and behaviours in an effort to address the scarcity precipitated by the drought. In the spatial arena associated with the City of Claremont, these integrated and associated actions were evident. As noted in Claremont Mayor Sam Pedroza's Statement in on the Court Decision of the City's acquisition of the Claremont water system (Mayor Sam Pedroza Mayor Sam Pedroza's Statement on Court Decision on the City's Acquisition of the Claremont Water System, December 2016), these actions included:

(1) Individual citizen practices reducing water consumption,
(2) City action (required by the state) to reduce water consumption,

(3) Private water agency (GSWC) action to assure system maintenance through requiring a maintenance fee required of all properties regardless of water usage,

(4) Civic leaders expressing concern regarding private water company charges and resource allocation (including system wide maintenance and investor profits), and

(5) City action to acquire rights to the Private water agency infrastructure and management through eminent domain action (currently under court determination.

It was through such integrative and associative actions that potential resilient solutions emerged. Through a plethora of private and public conservation initiatives and measures, as well as through public and quasi-public regulatory responses, resilient properties of the system were evolving. While perceived to be the intentional design and result of agent-based decision-making, spatial resiliency is actually an emerging property of a complex adaptive system. And although such resiliency is difficult to intentionally manifest through reductionist strategies, it is nonetheless often cultivated and experienced by the spatial agents under stress (Dahlberg 2015, 547).

It is important to reiterate that the any perceived equilibrium experienced in complex space is only temporary because the space is in a constant evolutionary process of adaptation. Even simple systems (systems with little or no differentiation and integrative action or behaviour) are influenced by and even succumb to the complexities of the macro-environment within which the simple system is located. The Claremont case reveals how local stakeholder action processed and challenged the perceived spatial stability and control. The proprietary nature and boundaries of the for-profit water company introduces elements of simplicity to the complex-macro system in which it operates because of its ability to impede stakeholder integration with its propriety walls. And as this case study further illustrates, this guarded simplicity is only temporary because of the complex-macro-systems evolutionary persistence as evidenced ultimately by Claremont's decision to pursue access and control through eminent domain proceedings.

The City of Claremont case illustrates that the shock of the California draught organically energized actors in the water management system that exercised complexity-informed and -friendly practices cultivated by: (1) civic actors, (2) integrated contract negotiations, and (3) legal process. The integrated and associative behaviour of the many competing stakeholders acting within the complex system became frustrated the spatial status quo. This frustration was caused by the proprietary nature of the water company serving the system. The for-profit-water company maintenance of proprietary boundaries operated as an impediment to: (1) assessing the Claremont approach to water governance and management; (2) assessing or accommodating the emergence of new structures and functions; (3) accommodating or facilitating further differentiation, integration and feedback loops; (4) accommodating or facilitating self-organization as a spatial driver; and (5) accommodating time and path dependencies; all of which is congruent with aspiration to cultivate spatial resiliency.

While the City of Claremont was ultimately unsuccessful in persuading the trial court to re-assign to the City the assets owned by the for-profit, investor-owned, PUC-regulated water utility currently servicing the city, the integrative action manifested by the lawsuit nonetheless constituted a complexity-informed practice that ultimately contributed to the spatial resiliency. At the conclusion of a bench trial that spanned twenty-one days during which the court heard evidence from twenty-six witnesses and reviewed more than a hundred documentary exhibits, the trial Judge ruled to dismiss the City's eminent domain complaint because it failed to establish that its proposed ownership and infrastructure changes was: (1) in the public interest and of necessity; (2) would result in the greatest public good; and (3)was a more necessary public use than the use to which it was already appropriated (City of Claremont v. Golden State Water Company, Superior Court of the State of California for the County of Los Angeles Statement of Tentative Decision of Richard L. Fruin, Jr., November 10, 2016). While the city failed to alter the spatial status quo, it nonetheless influenced the spatial landscape in terms of re-framing and enhancing the spatial knowledge and understanding with respect to local water governance. In this regard, it is important to remember that resilience does not necessarily mean change, in fact a resilience space may necessitate a rejection of change. The importance is that the status of the space be grounded on current and robust information. Such information informs all stakeholders about possibilities in the management of the space. It is also worthy to note, the space is under continued assessment as the city contemplates its appeal (and perhaps even an initiates an actual appeal) of the trial court's decision. Such an appeal continues the integrated learning process within the complex space.

5. Summary – moving towards resilience and future challenges

The Claremont case illustrates stakeholder action attempting to challenge the status quo of the local water management and governance space – a space under severe stress and shock. In fact, Claremont proposed to disrupt the spatial-status-quo (and with such action put additional stress on the system). And while the Claremont initiatives were ultimately unsuccessful, its actions were at a minimum complexity-friendly (and possibly even complexity-informed) in that its actions refused to be constrained by status quo and sought to accommodate or facilitate the emergence of new structures and functions (i.e. new management control). Moreover, its actions accommodated and facilitated differentiation, integration and more feedback loops. More generally, the Claremont case demonstrates the inherent ability of a complex-space to self-monitor its adaptive capacity and perhaps most importantly, learn so as to modulate its adaptive capacities as it continues to respond to arising situations, events, opportunities and disruptions

Water management is tasked with implementing collaborative action for the purpose of maintaining water supplies and quality. Often, the water governance systems must address spatial shock – such as severe or sustained drought – and seek to restore (and even advance) pre-shock spatial conditions. It is frequently perceived that crisis management is grounded on intentional design and advanced by reductionist approaches. And yet, experience often illustrates that it is actually manifested within complex-adaptive spatial environments resistant to reductionism and intentionality. It is from this perspective that Claremont case demonstrates that crisis management, and ultimately the spatial environment within which it manifests, actually benefits from practices that nurture, promote and embrace spatial complexity. Complexity-informed or – friendly practices are wary of simplistic approaches. They value and embrace spatial complexity because such complexity begets spatial resiliency. To embrace such practices requires a reframing of administrative intentionality. Rather than understand or approach spatial scarcity from a reductionist perspective of control through simplification and abstraction, a complexity-informed or – friendly practice or approach requires more administrative reliance and trust on the emergent and adaptive outcomes of spatial-complexity.

In closing, this paper seeks to identify the emergence of resiliency in Southern California water management from the perspective of a complex adaptive space. The role of stakeholder involvement and action in the water governance system is critical in cultivating resilience. Complex spaces are incredibly unwieldy, and rather than resist spatial complexity through intentional reductionist approaches, public administration and management should not only embrace spatial complexity, but should also nurture and promote spatial complexity and thereby cultivate a sustaining and resilient environment.

Disclosure statement

No potential conflict of interest was reported by the authors.

ORCID

Jack W. Meek ⓘ http://orcid.org/0000-0003-2819-0515

References

Association of California Water Agencies. 2013. *Statewide Water Action Plan for California.* Sacramento, CA: Association of California Water Agencies. www.acwa.com.
Bar-Yam, Y. 2004. *Making Things Work: Solving Complex Problems in a Complex World.* NECSI: Knowledge Press.
Blanco, H., J. Newell, L. Stott, and M. Alberti. 2012. *Water Supply Scarcity in Southern California: Assessing Water District Level Strategies.* Los Angeles, CA: Center for Sustainable Cities, Price School of Public Policy, University of Southern California.
Bohensky, E., and T. Lynam. 2005. "Evaluating Responses in Complex Adaptive Systems: Insights on Water Management from the Southern African Millennium Ecosystem Assessment (SAfMA)." *Ecology and Society* 10 (1): 11. doi:10.5751/ES-01198-100111.

Boin, A., L. K. Comfort, and C. C. Demchack. 2010. "The Rise of Resilience." In *Designing Resilience, Preparing for Extreme Events*, edited by L. K. Comfort, A. Boin, and C. C. Demchak, 19–51. Pittsburgh, PA: University of Pittsburgh Press.

Boin, A., and M. Lodge. 2016. "Designing Resilient Institutions for Transboundary Crisis Management: Time for Public Administration." *Public Administration* 94 (2): 289–298. doi:10.1111/padm.12264.

Buijs, J.-M., N. Van Der Bol, G. R. Theisman, D. Brune, G. Teisman, A. Van Buuren, and L. Gerrits. 2009. "Metropolitan Regions as Self-Organizing Systems." In *Managing Complex Governance Systems:Dynamics, Self- Organization and Coevolution in Public Investments*, edited by Geert Teisman, Arwin van Buuren and Lasse Gerrits. New York: Routledge.

Christopher, K., L. Gerrits, M. L. Rhodes, and J. W. Meek. 2016. "Complexity Theory, Networks and Systems Analysis." In *Handbook on Network Governance*, edited by J. Torfing and C. Ansell. Cheltenham: Edwards Elgar Publishing.ISBN: 978 1 78254 849 2.

City of Claremont v. Golden State Water Company, Superior Court of the State of California for the County of Los Angeles Statement of Tentative Decision of Richard L. Fruin, Jr., November 10, 2016.

Comfort, L. K., O. Namkyung, G. Ertan, and S. Scheinert. 2010. "Designing Adaptive Systems for Disasters." In *Designing Resilience, Preparing for Extreme Events*, edited by L. K. Comfort, A. Boin, and C. C. Demchak, 105–143. Pittsburgh, PA: University of Pittsburgh Press.

Dahlberg, R. 2015. "Resilience and Complexity Conjoining the Discourses of Two Contested Concepts." *Culture Unbound* 7: 541–557. DOI:10.3384/cu.2000.1525.1572541.

Dent, M. C. 2012. "Catchment Management Agencies as Crucibles in Which to Develop Responsible Leaders in South Africa." *Water SA* 38 (2): 313–326. doi:10.4314/wsa.v38i2.17.

Edelenbos, J., I. van Meerkerk, and C. van Leeuwen. forthcoming. "Vitality of Complex Water Governance Systems: Condition and Evolution." *Journal of Environmental Policy & Planning*. doi:10.1080/1523908X.2014.936584.

Holland, J. 1995. *Hidden Order: How Adaptation Builds Complexity*. New York, NY: Addison-Wesley. ISBN: 0-201-40793-0

Hoffman, A. J., H. C. Riley, J. G. Toast, and M. Bazerman. 2002. "Cognitive and Institutional Barriers to New Forms of Cooperation on Environmental Protection: Insights Form Project XL and Habitat Conservation Plans." *American Behavioral Scientist*. doi:10.1177/0002764202045005006

Hollnagel, E., J. Paries, D. D. Woods, and J. Wreathall, eds. 2011. *Resilience Engineering in Practice. A Guidebook*. Farnham: Ashgate.

Innes, J., and D. E. Booher. 1999a. "Consensus Building and Complex Adaptive Systems: A Framework for Evaluating Collaborative Planning." *Journal of the American Planning Association* 65 (4): 412–423. doi:10.1080/01944369908976071.

Innes, J. E. and D. D. Booher. 1999b. "Metropolitan Development as a Complex System: A New Approach to Sustainability." *Economic Development Quarterly* 13 (2): 141–156. doi:10.1177/0891242499013000204.

Jiao, W., and F. Boons. 2017. "Policy Durability of Circular Economy in China: A Process Analysis of Policy Translation." *Resources, Conservation and Recycling*: 12–24. doi:10.1016/j.resconrec.2015.10.010.

Keast, R., and M. P. Mandell. 2013. "A Composite Theory of Leadership and Management: Process Catalyst and Strategic Leveraging – Theory of Deliberate Action in Collaborative Networks." In *Network Theory in the Public Sector: Building New Theoretical Networks*, edited by R. Keast, M. Mandell, and R. Agranoff, 33–50. New York: Routledge.

Marshall, K. 2014. "Creating and Maintaining Innovative Space—A Framework for Unraveling the Complexities of Entrepreneurial Systems." *Complexity, Governance & Networks* 23–40. doi:10.7564/14-CGN16.

Mayor Sam Pedroza's Statement on Court Decision on the City's Acquisition of the Claremont Water System, December 13, 2016. Accessed January 25, 2017 http://www.ci.claremont.ca.us/Home/Components/News/News/1489/18?backlist=%2F

McMillan, E. 2004. *Complexity, Organizations and Change*. New York: Routledge.

Morrison, P. 2014. "Water Wise." *Los Angeles Times* 12 (November): 11.

Murphy, J., M. L. Rhodes, J. W. Meek, and D. Denyer. 2016. "Managing the Entanglement: Complexity Leadership in Public Sector Systems." *Public Administration Review*. doi:10.1111/ puar.12698.

Teisman, G., and E. H. Klijn. 2008. "Complexity Theory and Public Management - An Introduction." *Public Management Review* 10 (3): 287-297. doi: 10.1080/14719030802002451.

Teisman, G. R., A. van Buuren, and L. Gerrits (eds.). 2009. *Managing Complex Governance Systems: Dynamics, Self -Organization and Coevolution in Public Investments*. London: Routledge.

van Buuren, A., and J. Edelenbos. 2006. "Innovations in the Dutch Polder: Communities of Practice and the Challenge of Coevolution." *Evolution: Complexity and Evolution* 8 (1): 42–49.

Index